A Social History of
the Nonconformist Ministry
in England and Wales
1800–1930

KENNETH D. BROWN

CLARENDON PRESS · OXFORD
1988

Oxford University Press, Walton Street, Oxford OX2 6DP
Oxford New York Toronto
Delhi Bombay Calcutta Madras Karachi
Petaling Jaya Singapore Hong Kong Tokyo
Nairobi Dar es Salaam Cape Town
Melbourne Auckland
and associated companies in
Beirut Berlin Ibadan Nicosia

Oxford is a trade mark of Oxford University Press

Published in the United States
by Oxford University Press, New York

© *Kenneth D. Brown 1988*

British Library Cataloguing in Publication Data
Brown, Kenneth D.
A social history of the Nonconformist ministry
in England and Wales 1800–1930.
1. Protestant churches—Great Britain—
Clergy—History
I. Title
262'.14   BX4838
ISBN 0-19-822763-9

Library of Congress Cataloging in Publication Data
Brown, Kenneth Douglas,
A social history of the nonconformist ministry in England and
Wales, 1800–1930/Kenneth D. Brown.
p.   cm.
Bibliography: p.
Includes index.
1. Protestant churches—England—Clergy—History—19th century.
2. Protestant churches—Wales—Clergy—History—19th century.
3. Protestant churches—England—Clergy—History—20th century.
4. Protestant churches—Wales—Clergy—History—20th century.
5. Dissenters, Religious—England—History—19th century.
6. Dissenters, Religious—England—History—20th century.
7. Dissenters, Religious—Wales—History—19th century.
8. Dissenters, Religious—Wales—History—20th century.   I. Title.
BR767.B76 1988   87-28247
284'.0942—dc19   CIP
ISBN 0-19-822763-9

Typeset by Graphicraft Typesetters Ltd, Hong Kong
Printed and bound in Great Britain by
Biddles Ltd, Guildford and King's Lynn

To my parents-in-law, Roy and Betty Beesley,
nonconformists both, though in rather different ways

ACKNOWLEDGEMENTS

As a newcomer to the field of nonconformist history I have benefited enormously from the advice and guidance so generously provided by Mr John Creasey (Dr Williams's Library, London); Revd W. R. Davies (Cliff College, Sheffield); Dr C. Field (University of Manchester); Dr R. T. Jones (Bala-Bangor College); Dr D. MacCulloch (Wesley College, Bristol); Dr H. McLeod (University of Birmingham); Dr S. Mayor (Westminster College, Cambridge); Revd H. Mowvley (Bristol Baptist College); Revd M. Nicholls (Spurgeon's College, London); Mr D. Riley (The Methodist Archives and Research Centre, John Rylands University Library of Manchester); Miss R. Roberts (National Library of Wales); Revd H. Rusling (Baptist Union); Dr S. Russell (Northern College, Manchester); Revd E. W. Trowell (Mansfield College, Oxford); Dr J. Walsh (Jesus College, Oxford); Revd B. White (Regent's Park College, Oxford). I am particularly grateful to Dr David Bebbington (University of Stirling), Dr Clyde Binfield (University of Sheffield), and to my colleague at Queen's, Belfast, Dr David Hempton, all of whom read the whole manuscript in draft and offered many helpful suggestions and correctives. They saved me from numerous errors of fact and interpretation but they must, of course, be exonerated for any failings that remain.

Parts of the arguments developed in Chapters 3 and 4 were advanced originally in *Victorian Studies*, *Journal of Ecclesiastical History*, and *Church History*.

Quotations from the New College Archives appear by permission of the Trustees of the Dr Williams's Library; those from the Cheshunt Archives with the permission of the Governors of the Cheshunt Foundation. Material from the Methodist Archive and Research Centre has been used with the kind permission of the Methodist Archives and History Committee.

Financial support was provided by the Social Science Research Council (now the Economic and Social Research Council), the Twenty-Seven Foundation, and the Research and Scholarships Committee of my own university.

K.D.B.

The Queen's University of Belfast

CONTENTS

LIST OF TABLES

Introduction

NINETEENTH-CENTURY British society was permeated by the Christian religion to an extent almost incomprehensible to the late twentieth-century mind. The great social institutions of Parliament, the law, the armed forces, the universities, and the schools were dominated by an Anglican Church whose elevated constitutional and social status was symbolized in a monarch at once head of both Church and State. At about 50 per cent of the population aged over ten years, church attendance in England and Wales in 1851 may have seemed alarmingly low to contemporaries. By subsequent standards it was enormous. Doubtless for some it was little more than a weekly formality, in the words of William Hale White, 'a certain routine performed which might one day save them from some disaster with which flames and brimstone had something to do'.[1] As a lapsed candidate for the Independent ministry, however, White was hardly a dispassionate judge and it is evident that for the majority religion was a serious business. It was woven intimately into the everyday experiences of life and thought, and in an age characterized by high death-rates it provided some rationale for the all too evident fact of human mortality. At the individual level the hold of religion on General Gordon was such that the British agent in Egypt, Evelyn Baring, despaired of ever getting him to obey orders. What could be expected, he complained in exasperation, of a soldier who 'habitually consults the prophet Isaiah when he is in a difficulty'?[2] Gordon, of course, was a peculiar and unique figure but his religious orientation was not all that unusual in the nineteenth century. From a very different position in the

---

[1] W. H. White (Mark Rutherford), *The Revolution in Tanner's Lane* (1927 edn.), 233–4.
[2] Quoted in G. Best, 'Evangelicalism and the Victorians', in A. Symondson (ed.), *The Victorian Crisis of Faith* (1970), 55.

social hierarchy Philip Snowden, the labour leader, recalled
a Lancashire childhood that had been spent in an atmosphere of constant and fervent theological debate between
his Wesleyan father and Baptist uncle.[3]

Naturally, the appeal of Christianity varied over time and
space as well as socially. Anglicanism had its aristocratic
adherents and Roman Catholicism its very poor but in the
main the churches were largely the preserve of the middle
classes. This was revealed plainly by the Religious Census of
1851 which indicated that most of those absent from church
on Census day belonged to the poorest working-class communities in the major cities. Later, less comprehensive sur-
veys showed little change. Oral evidence suggests that the
Church was more influential on working-class lives than
is indicated by official statistics, but only in Wales, where
nonconformity became the vehicle for a powerful, anti-
Anglican nationalism, was there anything approaching total
community involvement in church life.[4] There, the degree of
active membership and attendance was considerably higher
than the English average, especially among the poorer
classes. Significantly perhaps, it was in Wales that the last
major British mainland revival occurred, in 1904–5. Nor did
Wales share, at least not to the same extent, in the general
decline of popular religious life which was indicated in the
last decades of the nineteenth century by falling sales of
religious books, failing ministerial recruitment, and by stag-
nant or negative rates of church growth. Yet if religious
disputes attracted less public interest in England as the
nineteenth century progressed, susceptibilities could still
be stirred. The early years of King Edward's reign saw a
renewed campaign against ritualism, which had been a
potent source of sectarian conflict for much of the century.[5]
These same years saw also a determined nonconformist re-

[3] P. Snowden, *An Autobiography*, 2 vols. (1934), i. 20.

[4] For oral recollections see H. McLeod, 'New Perspectives on Victorian Class Religion: the Oral Evidence', *Oral History*, 4 (1986); E. Roberts, *A Woman's Place: An Oral
History of Working-Class Women, 1890–1940* (1984), 4–5.

[5] For the anti-ritualist campaign see G. I. T. Machin, 'The Last Victorian Anti-
Ritualist Campaign, 1895–1906', *Victorian Studies*, 25 (1982). For analyses of sectarianism see G. Best, 'Popular Protestantism in Victorian Britain', in R. Robson (ed.), *Ideas
and Institutions in Victorian Britain* (1967); and P. T. Phillips, *The Sectarian Spirit:
Sectarianism, Society and Politics in Victorian Cotton Towns* (Toronto, 1982).

sistance to the provisions of the 1902 Education Act, a stand
which produced almost 40,000 court actions against them.[6]

Yet what of the religiously indifferent, the five million or
so whose absence from church was exposed by the 1851
Census? Not all were absent through apathy. Legitimate
claims may have kept some away. But even those who chose
to ignore the Church and its message had to recognize its
controlling sanctions and norms. It was virtually impossible
to escape the influence of religion in a society whose very
customs and attitudes—for instance, towards Sunday obser-
vance, animal welfare, poverty, alcohol, and recreation—
were so largely shaped by it.[7] Certainly Christian belief
was often suffused with elements of folklore and popular
superstition, and religious practice frequently shaped by local culture, but there was much truth in the claim made
by one Congregational minister in 1849 that Christianity
had been one of the chief causes of social improvement
among the working classes; not in the sense that many had
been converted but in that 'great numbers are, more or
less (and now, far more than ever) under the *indirect* influence of the Christian religion'.[8] At the very least all but the
most doctrinaire unbeliever—and if the secularism bred by
Tom Paine and the *Age of Reason* remained quite strong in a
few centres like London there were probably few agnostics
and fewer conscious atheists in Victorian Britain—all but
these utilized the church for baptismal, marriage, and funeral rites.[9] Many who otherwise never entered a church or
chapel must have heard the street preaching of the aggressive, soul-seeking itinerant evangelists deployed by the nonconformists, particularly the Methodists and, later, the
Salvation Army. The middle years of Victoria's reign saw
also the great revival campaigns, designed primarily, it has

[6] For the campaign against the Education Act see J. E. B. Munson, 'A Study of
Nonconformity in Edwardian England as Revealed by the Passive Resistance Movement against the 1902 Education Act', Oxford D.Phil. thesis, 1973. For the impact of
the measure on one congregation see C. Binfield, *Pastors and People: The Biography of a
Baptist Church: Queen's Road, Coventry* (Coventry, 1984), 119–38.
[7] B. Harrison, 'Religion and Recreation in Nineteenth Century England', *Past and
Present*, 38 (1967).
[8] *Congregational Yearbook* (1849), 76. My italics.
[9] For unbelievers see S. Budd, *Varieties of Unbelief* (1977); E. Royle, *Victorian In-
fidels: the Origins of the British Secularist Movement, 1791–1866* (Manchester, 1974).

been argued, as instruments for the conversion of believers' children but which, in the hands of charismatic professional revivalists such as Moody and Sankey, had a much broader appeal.[10] Similarly, it has been shown that the shadow of sectarianism fell well beyond the church walls and over the wider community.[11]

Again, before the advent of widespread and systematic state intervention, both the form and the content of education were essentially Christian. The school curriculum, it has been argued, was a vehicle for the inculcation, as Christian virtues, of habits such as diligence, thrift, honesty, sobriety, and social pliability.[12] Structurally, the churches dominated the system. In 1861 the non-denominational British and Foreign School Society was responsible for 915 schools as against the 776 controlled by the Wesleyans, Congregationalists, and Baptists, and almost 20,000 National schools which were under the aegis of the Church of England.[13] For much of the nineteenth century, probably until the establishment of free, compulsory schooling, the Sunday schools were more influential in the instruction of the unchurched masses. As early as 1820 they were so numerous that one of their most recent historians has claimed that virtually every working-class child outside London must have attended one at some time or other.[14] True, there was an element of calculation in the way that attendances shot up in the weeks before the annual treat or the Christmas party but this does not invalidate the general argument that Sunday schools as well as day schools helped to create and sustain a religious atmosphere which few, if any, could escape entirely. The point is well made in Robert Tressell's satire, *The Ragged Trousered Philanthropists*. Describing the annual outing of Rushton and Co., Tressell writes of hymn-singing beginning in the coach carrying the employers. The workers, he con-

[10] J. Kent, *Holding the Fort: Studies in Victorian Revivalism* (1978).

[11] Phillips, p. 5.

[12] J. M. Goldstrom, *The Social Content of Education, 1808–1870* (Shannon, 1972).

[13] Ibid. 156.

[14] T. Laqueur, *Religion and Respectability: Sunday Schools and Working Class Culture* (New Haven, Conn., 1976), p. xi. The *Methodist Times*, 16 Apr. 1896, stressed that while there were 100,000 children currently attending Methodist day schools, their Sunday schools had a million members. Laqueur's interpretation has more recently been modified by P. B. Cliff, *The Sunday School Movement* (1986).

tinues, 'also sang the choruses. As they had all been brought up under "Christian" influences and educated in "Christian" schools, they all knew the words.'[15] Indeed, for much of the nineteenth century it seems likely that hymns provided the substance of much popular music, certainly until the advent of the music-hall.

Most important of all, however, was the position of the church in many communities as the natural focus for social and recreational activity as well as for spiritual needs. This was certainly so in rural areas and smaller towns for most of the century and probably remained so even when improvements in transport, communication, and living standards respectively improved the individual's mobility, expanded his intellectual horizons, and increased his disposable income. During the first half of the century the Church assumed a similarly central role in the situation of anomy created by rapid development in newly industrializing communities. By 1900, it is true, urban churches and chapels found it increasingly difficult to compete with the growing availability of specialized secular agencies.[16] Yet religious influence survived for a long time and inner city mission halls and settlements, both features of late Victorian church life, became communal centres for a variety of social and educational pursuits as well as providing facilities for religious services. At about the same time numerous para-church organizations began to appear, designed both to attract outsiders and to retain the interest of existing members and supporters. The Brotherhood (Pleasant Sunday Afternoon) movement, uniformed youth organizations, and sports teams, may all be seen in this light and if in the long run they were not successful in stemming the outward flow of church membership, they helped to preserve the central role of the church for many of the faithful. Social life, wrote one late Victorian, 'centred entirely round "our chapel". All their spare time was taken up with something or other connected with the chapel. Every evening was occupied.... All

---

[15] R. Tressell, *The Ragged Trousered Philanthropists* (Panther edn., 1965), 454–5.
[16] On this see S. Yeo, *Religious and Voluntary Organisations in Crisis* (1976); J. Cox, *The English Churches in a Secular Society: Lambeth, 1870–1930* (Oxford, 1982).

very smug and self centred to those outside, but, as I know, of real importance to those inside.'[17] Well into the 1920s the Primitive Methodist chapel in St Helens was described as being 'almost like a village'. Most of the people who belonged to it 'worked from the church and centred their lives round it. That started from childhood. The children always seemed to be practising for something ... we had a lot of midweek activity.'[18]

The dominant strain of the Christianity which thus enveloped even the indifferent during the nineteenth century was Evangelicalism. The moral tone of public and private life was greatly influenced by it, dashing the hopes of one contemporary that when Victoria, 'a gay, young, play-going Queen', ascended the throne, it would 'make a formidable counteraction to the progress of the Evangelicals, whose doctrines make all the noise now'.[19] Everywhere, Evangelicals sought to respond to exhortations to 'stir up every heart to more earnest and prayerful effort to rescue those who are placed by God in a less favourable position'.[20] As a result, hardly a single human need was left unconsidered. At one level this produced the great charitable works associated with individuals like Shaftesbury. At another, it led to the appearance on railway platforms of chained copies of the Bible for the perusal of waiting passengers. Theologically, the Evangelical shadow in the grim form of Sabbatarianism hung darkly over many a mid-Victorian. Ruskin reckoned that for him the 'horror of Sunday used even to cast its prescient gloom as far back in the week as Friday—and all the glory of Monday, with church seven days removed again, was not equivalent for it'.[21] Edward Kellett disagreed, be-

---

[17] R. Underwood, *Hidden Lights* (1937), 79. Beatrice Webb made similar comments of the 1880s: B. Webb, *My Apprenticeship* (Penguin edn., 1971), 166–80.
[18] C. Forman, *Industrial Town: Self Portrait of St. Helens in the 1920's* (1979), 175. See also C. Field, 'Sociological Profile of English Methodism', *Oral History*, 4 (1976); R. Moore, 'The Political Effects of Village Methodism', *Sociological Yearbook of Religion*, 6 (1973), 174.
[19] Quoted in I. Bradley, *The Call to Seriousness: The Evangelical Impact on the Victorians* (1976), 13.
[20] C. Wightman, *Haste to the Rescue* (1859), p. xi. Quoted in K. Heasman, *Evangelicals in Action* (1962), 25. For an example of Evangelical pressure at local level see J. Rule, 'Methodism, Popular Beliefs and Village Culture in Cornwall, 1800–1850', in R. D. Storch (ed.), *Popular Culture and Custom in Nineteenth Century England* (New York, 1982).
[21] Quoted in Bradley, p. 183.

lieving it inexcusable to dismiss the Evangelicals as stern killjoys and claiming that the exact opposite was true.[22] He was, however, writing from the standpoint of a believer and, moreover, of a later period by which time Evangelicalism had perhaps lost something not only of its earlier vitality and self-confidence but also something of its more puritanical overtones. It is true, too, that the cultural and political tones assumed by Evangelicalism varied from one denomination to another but there is no doubting its pervasiveness. There is more than a grain of truth in the observation that many Victorian autobiographies concern sensitive children brought up in Evangelical homes.[23]

The Church of England had its Evangelicals, but those who found them too emotional, too enthusiastic, or too demanding, could always turn instead to the comforts of ritualism or to the less metaphysical Broad Church. Unitarianism apart, nonconformity was more uniformly suffused with Evangelical sentiment and thus more closely identified with it. Methodism had been born out of the eighteenth-century Evangelical revival which had also breathed new life into the older forms of Baptist and Independent dissent. The Religious Census of 1851 revealed not only that church attendance was much lower than anyone had hitherto supposed but also that roughly half of those attending divine service on Census day did so in a nonconformist chapel. The Census also clearly delineated the geography of mid-century dissent; weak in the more affluent areas, since wealthy and ambitious individuals had no wish to be restricted by the civil and legal disabilities still attached to nonconformity; weak also in the poorest areas, especially urban ones, because low income earners were hardly likely to find much appeal in a church system whereby, notionally at least, each congregation was responsible for the maintenance of the chapel and the minister. Methodist strength lay mainly in those parts of the midlands, north-east, and west Yorkshire where the Church of England had most signally failed to

---

[22] E. Kellett, *As I Remember* (1936), 109–10. For similarly favourable recollections, though again from the standpoint of believers, see J. Ritson, *The World is Our Parish* (1939), 12: F. W. Macdonald, *As a Tale that is Told: Recollections of Many Years* (1919), 9.

[23] Quoted in J. Laver, *Museum Piece* (1963), 29.

keep in touch with the shifts in population consequent upon industrialization. The Congregationalists (successors of the Independents and the term used hereafter) were strong in a belt of counties running east from Devon to Sussex and Essex, while the Baptists were concentrated most heavily in the midlands and eastern counties such as Cambridge, Norfolk, and Essex.[24] It was from this territorial base that nonconformity gradually acquired its substantial position in contemporary society and there are few who would quibble with David Thompson's assertion that it was 'one of the most formative influences on Victorian Britain'.[25]

It was, however, an influence acquired only in the face of considerable hostility and prejudice. Physical violence was not uncommon in the first half of the nineteenth century, with the Primitive Methodists now inheriting the assaults which had been directed against the Wesleyans in an earlier period. Their itinerant preachers were thrown into ponds, stoned, attacked by dogs, and frequently arrested for causing breaches of the peace. Even the use of women preachers did not always evoke a less brutish response. The last recorded attack on a Primitive Methodist occurred in 1843, by which time the connexion, established in 1811, was well on its way to acquiring all the institutional trappings of a full-blown denomination.[26] But violence against nonconformists still persisted. Later in the century the Salvation Army's open-air meetings were regularly disrupted by the so-called 'skeleton armies'. At about the same time 'Owd Mo' recorded that the Wesleyans' Joyful News Mission team ran into similarly rowdy receptions, for example at Evesham in 1887. 'If hell had been opened and all the legions let out, it could not have been worse', he wrote. 'For nearly two hours hooting and hissing was the order. I could stand all that till they came to

---

[24] J. D. Gay, *The Geography of Religion in England* (1971), *passim*.

[25] D. Thompson, *Nonconformity in the Nineteenth Century* (1972), p. vi.

[26] There are numerous examples cited in G. Herod, *Historical and Biographical Sketches Forming a Compendium of the History of the Primitive Methodist Connexion to 1823* (1857); H. B. Kendall, *The Origins and History of the Primitive Methodist Church*, 2 vols. (1905); W. M. Patterson, *Northern Primitive Methodism* (1909); H. Woodcock, *Piety Among the Peasantry: Being Sketches of Primitive Methodism on the Yorkshire Wolds* (1889). A number of cases of obstruction were brought against Primitive street preachers in the 1870s. Not all of them were dismissed.

put their hand on Drummer; but of course I stood up for the horse.'[27]

By this later period it is possible that such physical opposition had less to do with innate hostility to nonconformity and rather more to do with amusement opportunities afforded by the presence of open-air evangelists. This was not generally true earlier in the century. Much of the violence was connived at, if not positively encouraged, by Anglican clergymen and justices. Furthermore, there is plenty of evidence of intellectual prejudice which in less refined minds could easily degenerate into violence. Charles Kingsley was contemptuous of local Baptist pastors, dismissing them as 'muck enthroned on their respective dung hills, screeching on their scrannel pipes of ragged straw'.[28] When W. F. Freeman told his Anglican father that he had been converted at a Methodist service in 1876 he was told that it was presumptuous to talk of sins being forgiven and that it was foolish to join the ranters instead of a respectable church. 'We have had doubts about your sanity', concluded his parent, 'and now these doubts are confirmed.'[29] Equally unfriendly sentiments inform many of the fictional portrayals of Victorian nonconformists. Like those of businessmen, they are frequently nothing more than grotesque caricatures, 'ignorant, drab, provincial and depressing'.[30] Such attitudes never disappeared entirely and could be quickly brought into the open by nonconformist intransigence over issues such as education, but on the whole with the passage of time anti-nonconformist prejudice diminished. In part,

[27] 'Owd Mo', *From Coalpit to Joyful News Mission: Fragments of an Autobiography* (n.d.), 29.
[28] Quoted in P. Hammond, *The Parson and the Victorian Parish* (1977), 181. It was not unknown either for parish charities to be applied only to Anglicans, or for leases to include clauses barring the use of buildings for religious purposes.
[29] W. F. Freeman, *Age Challenges Youth* (1949), 13. For similar reactions see C. Slim, *My Contemporaries of the Nineteenth Century: Brief Memorials of More Than 400 Ministers* (n.d.), 231.
[30] M. Maison, *Search Your Soul, Eustace* (1961), 183. On nonconformists in nineteenth-century literature see V. Cunningham, *Everywhere Spoken Against: Dissent in the Victorian Novel* (Oxford, 1975); M. J. Townsend, 'An Examination of the Nature and Role of the Nonconformist Ministry and Congregation in some English Novels, 1845–1890', Leicester M.Phil. thesis, 1975. For businessmen see D. Coleman, *What has Happened to Economic History? An Inaugural Lecture* (Cambridge, 1972), 11: 'Look for the businessman in English fiction and either you will not find him at all or he will vary from the sinister to the absurd.'

this was due to the fact that by the last decades of the nineteenth century the Christian faith as a whole was on the defensive, both intellectually and socially. But it was also due to the growing influence and acceptability of nonconformity and its adherents. By now it was regarded as much less of a threat to the status quo, a situation which was both recognized and encouraged by the progressive removal of the nonconformists' social and legal disabilities.

As befits its importance in nineteenth-century society, British nonconformity has attracted a lot of attention from scholars. The earliest writings tended to concentrate on such themes as doctrinal or denominational development, while the analysis of nonconformist influence in society at large, for example in national or local government, trade unionism, and education, is still producing useful work.[31] More recently, a new generation of social historians has sought to shift attention away from nonconformity and on to the nonconformist, busying itself with investigations of social composition, plotting church growth rates, or unravelling the complexities of the ordinary believer's religious life.[32] Yet this leap from the institution to the pew has almost totally bypassed the pulpit, for the ministerial personnel of nonconformity have been largely ignored. This is a puzzling omission because whatever ideological, sociological, or even economic explanations historians subsequently put forward to explain the influence of nonconformity in Victorian Britain, contemporaries themselves had no doubts that the main vehicle of that influence was provided by the front men, the professional ministers. The minister, wrote Thomas Hunter in 1874, is 'by virtue of his office . . . a representative man; and it will be found that by the culture and faithfulness of ministers, more than any other cause, has Nonconformity been perpetuated. Where religious prosperity abounds,

---

[31] Recent excellent examples are S. Koss, *Nonconformity in Modern British Politics* (1974); D. Bebbington, *The Nonconformist Conscience: Chapel and Politics, 1870–1914* (1982); and D. Hempton, *Methodism and Politics in British Society, 1750–1850* (1984).
[32] For example, C. Binfield, *So Down to Prayers: Studies in English Nonconformity, 1780–1920* (1977); R. Currie, A. Gilbert, and L. Horsley, *Churches and Churchgoers: Patterns of Church Growth in the British Isles since 1700* (Oxford, 1977); A. D. Gilbert, *Religion and Society in Industrial England, 1740–1914* (1976); J. Obelkevich, *Religion and Rural Society: South Lindsey, 1825–1875* (Oxford, 1976).

where a Church is powerful, numerous and respected, the source of this may be traced not indirectly to the minister.'[33] Nor was Hunter alone in this opinion. At about the same time a witness told the Royal Commission on Trade Unions that in South Wales the nonconformist ministers had 'more influence ... than any man living'.[34] The Welsh ministers were exceptional in the power which they exercised because in the Principality nonconformity was intimately tied up with nationalism, but it is also apparent that in many of the newly emerging industrial communities of early nineteenth-century England ministers were frequently welcomed as almost the only figures of any standing or learning. In areas like these they were regarded as natural social leaders, and the rather vague definition of their job specification (beyond certain obvious religious activities) gave them ample opportunity to create a presence in the community out of all proportion to their actual numbers.

Certainly history has paid due homage to the most celebrated of the nonconformist divines, the majority of whom have found their biographers. But behind the denominational giants, Charles Spurgeon the Baptist, Dale and Horne the Congregationalists, and Wesleyans such as Hugh Price Hughes, lay an army of unknown men who carried the main burden of the ministry and administration. In 1851 the various Methodist connexions had 1,935 full-time ministers in post. The list of active and retired Baptist ministers for 1871 contained 1,648 names, while the Congregational churches

---

[33] *Inquirer*, 12 Dec. 1874. Most modern work on the role of ministers has been confined to the Anglican clergy. Thus, D. L. Edwards, *Leaders of the Church of England, 1828–1944* (Oxford, 1971); A. J. Drewett, 'The Social Status of the Ordained Minister in the Nineteenth and Twentieth Centuries', *Modern Churchman*, 9 (1966); R. Towler and P. Coxon, *The Fate of the Anglican Clergy* (1979); B. Heeney, *A Different Kind of Gentleman: Parish Clergy as Professional Men in Early and Mid-Victorian England* (Hamden, Conn., 1976); A. J. Russell, *The Clerical Profession* (1980); A. G. L. Haig, *The Victorian Clergy: An Ancient Profession under Strain* (1984). R. S. Blakey, *The Man in the Manse* (Edinburgh, 1978), is a rather impressionistic study of Church of Scotland ministers in the twentieth century. The only published historical study of nonconformist ministers is J. C. Bowmer, *Pastor and People: A Study of Church and Ministry in Wesleyan Methodism from the Death of John Wesley to the Death of Jabez Bunting* (1975). There is also much useful material in C. D. Field, 'Methodism in Metropolitan London', Oxford D.Phil. thesis, 1974. I am very grateful for Dr Field's generosity in allowing me to draw so freely on his work.

[34] Quoted in E. T. Davies, *Religion in the Industrial Revolution in South Wales* (Cardiff, 1965), 65.

employed about 1,400 ministers in 1847. By 1900 ministerial strength had greatly increased within these three denominations which among them represented the most powerful Protestant forces outside the Established Church, claiming the allegiance of about 95 per cent of all nonconformists. At this later date there was a total of 8,756. Of these 1,963 were Baptists, 3,086 were Congregationalists, while the Wesleyan, Primitive, New, United Free, and Bible Christian connexions of the Methodists shared 3,707 between them.[35] For these impersonal statistics the Revd J. Gaskell, a United Methodist who died in 1914, may stand symbol:

He never walked in Connexional high places, but plodded patiently on in lowly and somewhat sequestered paths. Not widely known, but where well-known, beloved. He was one of the many who, in undemonstrative yet faithful fulfilment of duty wherever they may be called to labour, contribute largely to our Connexional stability and progress. The service of such is highly prized by the Great Head of the Church.[36]

Prized by the Lord he may have been, but for the majority of such ministers their names emerged only briefly from obscurity when they died and their earthly memorials are few; a short obituary in a denominational publication; a weathered tombstone in some now neglected graveyard; or a fading photograph in a musty chapel vestry. Of these once highly influential individuals history has made very little and they remain largely anonymous. Even though prosopography has a long pedigree and has been particularly useful when applied to the history of religious groups, historians have preferred to generalize on the basis of the experience of a few prominent individuals, an approach which reveals nothing about the ministerial group as a whole.[37] What, for example, of the ministers' social and geographical origins, their education and training, their religious experiences, their family lives, career patterns, and involvements in the wider world of public life? Such questions have barely been raised, let alone answered. In part, this may be because

---

[35] Figures from Currie, Gilbert, and Horsley, pp. 203–10.
[36] *United Methodist*, 9 July 1914.
[37] For the applications of prosopography see L. Stone, *The Past and the Present* (1981), 30–69.

other questions have, perhaps rightly, assumed priority. It may reflect the nonconformists' understanding of the minister's role which was, in the Old Dissent at least, very much a matter of leadership in mutuality. Or it may be that the historians have simply followed the sociologists of religion who, in Britain at any rate, have tended to ignore the role of the religious functionary.[38]

More likely, however, this neglect has arisen because of the difficulties involved in acquiring adequate historical evidence. There is certainly no shortage of ministerial biography and autobiography, its very abundance testifying to the perceived importance of the ministry in Victorian society. But the former tends to be hagiographical, the latter subjective and selective. Neither includes as a matter of course the sort of detail so useful to the social historian, mainly because the majority of such works either fought over old theological battles or were presented as instruments of propaganda for desirable Christian virtues.[39] They also tend to be marked by a stylization and predictability which must raise doubts as to their overall veracity and reliability. Many of them, for example, portrayed life as a journey, a feature which Wesley certainly encouraged among his preachers. He recommended that they read widely, but he especially commended the lives of Haliburton, de Renty, Lopez, and Brainerd. These, he believed, were all highly instructive examples from which his men could learn. They learned perhaps more faithfully than he expected, for nineteenth-century Methodist biography was frequently presented in the form of the spiritual pilgrimage which characterized these works.[40] So, too, were the lives of men in other denominations, and if the immediate literary inspiration was Bunyan and *Pilgrim's Progress* the ultimate origin of this approach was, of course, the book of Exodus. Most accounts

---

[38] Though see B. R. Wilson, *Religion in Secular Society* (1966) and R. Ransom, A. Bryman, and B. Hinings, *Clergy, Ministers and Priests* (1977).
[39] C. Kendall, *The Christian Minister in Earnest* (1854), 10: 'Few books are more suited to the young than such as contain well written memoirs of the good and the great, and especially so when the characters described have been deeply pious.'
[40] I. Rivers, 'Strangers and Pilgrims: Sources and Patterns in Methodist Narrative', in J. C. Hilson, M. M. B. Jones, and J. R. Watson (eds.), *Augustan Worlds* (Leicester, 1978).

began in a wilderness of youthful sin, although its snares often appear rather anodyne to the modern eye. Parkinson Milson's, for example, consisted mainly of 'kite-flying, marbles, rabbit trapping, fishing, and field and wood sports'.[41] A compelling conversion experience usually followed, although some of the Congregational ones were rather quieter and less emotional. This generally led on to the ministerial call and a life of service. It is indicative of the stylization of these accounts that similar anecdotes appeared in so many of them. Judging by the frequency with which ministers were saved from plotting felons or godless opponents by the timely appearance of fierce dogs, the hounds of heaven appear to have been freely available to them, especially the early Primitive Methodists in whose accounts this emphasis on the supernatural is perhaps the most apparent.

It was on the death-bed that the tendency to uniformity was most marked and also most overtly propagandist. George McCree's biographer was quite candid about this, inviting his readers to pause and pray before reading the chapter on McCree's death, so that 'this record of his ebbing life may be blessed to his or her own soul'.[42] In almost every case the dying one had to fight off last minute satanic attempts to suborn his soul, before the onset of peace and a gloriously victorious death. Every last word was faithfully recorded, clear substantiation of Professor Best's contention that narrators frequently tried to shape events to fit the normative model.[43] John Angell James certainly felt impelled to explain exactly why Richard Keynes' departure did not conform to the expected pattern:

Grace works no miracles for the most distinguished of God's servants, in counteracting the effects of disease on the cerebral functions. ... I have thus enlarged upon the subject because I believe

---

[41] G. Shaw, *Life of Rev Parkinson Milson* (1893), 10. For a comment on the stylization of conversion experience accounts see S. G. Dimond, *The Psychology of the Methodist Revival* (1926), 162.

[42] *George William McCree: His Life and Work. By His Elder Son* (1893), 190. W. O'Neill, *Notes and Incidents of Home Missionary Life and Work* (1870), 181, explained that he had included a whole chapter on death-bed scenes because they were 'always solemn, sometimes glorious, frequently very useful, and never uninstructive'.

[43] Best, 'Evangelicalism', p. 55. D. Canadine, 'War and Death, Grief and Mourning in Modern Britain', in J. Whaley (ed.), *Mirrors of Mortality* (1981), suggests this interpretation of the Victorian death-bed is romanticized and unsubtle.

the secrets of his dying chamber have transpired, and had by some been misinterpreted into mental despondency and spiritual gloom. ... Medical science will attest that, even where there is no delirium, some diseases tend to excitement and exhilaration, while others produce gloom and despondency.[44]

Another writer was similarly constrained to explain away his subject's death-bed silence. Had his faculties remained unimpaired, he wrote, then 'he would doubtless have said many things at last that would have contributed to the comfort of his family, and the edification of the church ...'.[45] Such an emphasis on death and its ritualized, triumphalist presentation is not surprising in an age of high death-rates and it is significant that the death-bed scenes started to disappear as mortality rates turned down most clearly in the 1870s. At the same time growing theological uncertainties about the reality of an afterlife may have worked in the same direction. Certainly the earlier emphasis on death drew much of its inspiration from the belief that it was a doorway, leading from the rigours of earthly life to the benefits of an everlasting heavenly paradise. One denominational historian even claimed that for those who took religion seriously, life itself was one long (or short) preparation for death.[46] This may appear an exaggeration but it is well supported in contemporary sources. Long before she actually died Mary Bingham wrote in her diary that she felt 'such a blessed preparedness for death. ... Now let me die, my Jesus, if it be thy will. Take me, receive my spirit.'[47] In similar vein, a well-known Bible Christian hymn contained a sombre warning for its singers:

> Death has been here, and borne away
> A sister from our side ...
> We cannot tell who next may fall
> Before Thy chastening rod;
> One must be first: but let us all
> Prepare to meet our God.[48]

---

[44] *Evangelical Magazine*, 32 (1854), 4.

[45] Kendall, *Christian Minister*, 98.

[46] T. Shaw, *The Bible Christians, 1815–1907* (1965), 107. Cf. J. A. Turner (ed.), *The Life of a Chimney Boy. Written by Himself* (1901), 73–4.

[47] J. Bustard, *Memoir of Mary Helen Bingham and of Her Brother Mr John Bingham* (1832), 75.

[48] Shaw, p. 97.

The main drawback to using life stories as a source, however, is that they do not constitute a sample which properly reflects the typical individual in the profession. Biographies are normally written only about the well known or unusually interesting, while to write one's own life history is an untypical act.[49] When Thomas Hunter contacted some four thousand Free Church ministers in 1878, asking them to furnish him with personal information so that he could build up a corporate picture of the pastorate, he received only seventy-four replies and most of them were under no illusions as to their significance within their own denominations. One asked that his reply be placed 'among the similar stratification of your folio Mss to be consulted possibly, but more likely not, by the antiquaries of future centuries'.[50]

What is required for a full and statistically sound investigation of the ministry is an adequate sample of the whole group. This present study rests, in the main, on two such samples. The career line sample which forms the basis of Chapter 4 is derived from the experience of men who entered the ministry at every tenth year between 1831 and 1911. The main sample on which the core of the work rests was constituted initially from ministers who died in each of the periods 1851–5, 1871–5, 1891–5, 1911–15, 1931–5, 1951–5, and 1971–5, giving a total of some 2,554 individuals in all. These were then regrouped according to that decade between 1790 and 1929 in which they entered the ministry. These procedures were followed with respect to each of the five denominations—Baptist, Congregational, Wesleyan, Primitive, and United Methodist—who among them embraced about 95 per cent of nonconformists in most areas. Although the United Methodists did not come into existence until 1907 as an amalgam of Bible Christians, New Connexion, and United Free Methodists, they have been treated as a single entity throughout the period covered by this book. So, too, have the New Connexion and Particular

---

[49] For a useful discussion of historical biography as a source see J. Burnett, *Useful Toil* (1974), 9–18.

[50] E. Higginson to T. Hunter, 27 Aug. 1878, 'Autobiographical Notices' (by Thomas Hunter), Dr Williams's Library (hereafter DWL), MS 37/64.

Baptists who merged in 1891. Denominations such as Presbyterianism, whose main geographical strength lay outside
England and Wales, or whose membership was almost ex-
clusive to small limited areas, such as the Welsh Calvinistic
Methodists, have been excluded. Unitarians have been
ignored as well. Despite the adherence of a number of distinguished public figures they were outside the prevailing
Evangelical orthodoxy and always had well under four hundred ministers in the nineteenth century.

It should be noted that all the ministers considered are
male. The Wesleyans virtually banned women preachers in
1803 unless they could produce evidence of an extraordinary
calling. Baptists and Congregationalists did not admit
female ministers until relatively late and even then it was
sometimes a controversial issue. The smaller Methodist
groups were more liberal in their attitude but the number of
women preachers diminished after mid-century and was
always very small. The last female itinerant among the
Primitives was Elizabeth Bultitude who began work in 1832
and was superannuated thirty years later. The use of women
was more marked and persisted rather longer among the
Bible Christians, although strictly speaking they were not
ministers at all since they were not officially ordained.
Furthermore, their numbers were always liable to reduction
since the church authorities encouraged male ministers to
pick their wives from among them. Between 1819 and 1861
about seventy-one female itinerants are listed in the Bible
Christian Conference *Minutes*. By 1860 only five were still
active and twelve years later this had fallen to one. There
was still one on trial, however, as late as 1901.[51]

The obituaries which form the initial basis of the main
sample naturally display many of the same drawbacks as
the fuller published sources and were often used quite

---

[51] R. Pyke, *The Early Bible Christians* (1941), 29–30. See also W. F. Swift, 'The
Women Itinerant Preachers of Early Methodism', *Proceedings of the Wesley Historical
Society*, 29 (1953–4). He is wrong, however, in stating that the last woman was taken
on in 1861. The Bible Christian Conference, *Minutes* (1901), 10, refer to Lettie Edwards
as 'female preacher at home'. O. Chadwick, *Victorian Miniature* (1960), 179–80, refers
to the death of Caroline Boileau, a travelling female Methodist preacher, in 1877. It is
not clear, however, to which connexion she was attached. See also D. Valenze, *Prophe-
tic Sons and Daughters* (Princeton, 1985).

consciously to underwrite the view which chapel members had of themselves. The early ones concentrate very much on their subjects' piety, the later ones on their fund-raising abilities or administrative skills, a shift which reveals much about the nature of nineteenth-century nonconformity. In either case social detail is included incidentally. The obituaries tend to be moralizing, their obvious intent, as one obituarist admitted, being 'not to confer benefit upon the dead' but rather to 'enforce lessons of great practical utility on the attention of the living'.[52] The stylized death-bed scenes are again faithfully reproduced. But some of the earlier ones do display a refreshing candour, even though as the century wore on this was increasingly glossed over by a veneer of respectability that would permit no ill-speaking of the dead. One correspondent of the *Primitive Methodist Leader* was moved to comment drily about the obituaries which appeared in the *Aldersgate Magazine*: 'A special providence seems to have watched over their selection of wives ... according to the magazine ... they were all noble women and model wives.'[53] Even so, the obituary lists do provide the basis of a more genuinely representative sample of the ministerial group than any other source. Although there were occasional omissions, most men merited some mention in the appropriate denominational yearbook when they died. This information, occasionally quite detailed but usually little more than a name, a few dates, and an appreciation, has been supplemented with material culled from newspapers, other denominational publications, private correspondence, institutional archives and, where they exist, biographies and autobiographies. It has of necessity been a laborious and often tedious process of reconstruction and one in which there are still gaps, some of them probably now unfillable. But if it succeeds it will provide us with a more accurate picture of ministerial life and secure for nineteenth-century Free Church ministers a sort of life after death, though not perhaps of the sort which most of them so keenly anticipated.

[52] G. Pocher, 'The Rev. Andrew Lynn', *Methodist New Connexion Magazine* (July 1873), 385.
[53] *Primitive Methodist Leader*, 7 Dec. 1911.

1

Origins

IN July 1809 the Bishop of Durham wrote to Viscount Sidmouth expressing his concern at the way in which the Toleration Act was, in his opinion, currently being abused. Although the measure permitted the conduct of religious services and duties in duly appointed places by suitably qualified and mature individuals it was, he asserted, being evaded by 'modern sectaries'. Methodists, he went on, 'assemble in barns, in rooms of private houses, or in other buildings of the most improper kind, to hear the wild effusions of a mechanic or a ploughboy, perhaps not more than 15 years of age, destitute of the first rudiments of learning, sacred or profane'.[1] Two years later Sidmouth introduced a parliamentary bill to tighten up the administration of the Toleration Act. Somewhat disingenuously perhaps, he argued that it was all for the dissenters' own good, but it is evident that he had accepted the bishop's case more or less wholesale, for the nub of his argument was that 'very improper persons had intruded themselves into the ministry such as blacksmiths, chimney sweepers, pig drivers, pedlars, cobblers etc.'.[2]

His contemptuous view of the nature of the Methodist ministry was one which in the early nineteenth century was widely held of the Old Dissenting ministry too. At about the same time as Sidmouth was introducing his proposals, one Anglican vicar's daughter, who was herself to marry a Baptist pastor, wrote of dissenting ministers that 'none but the very ignorant were found amongst them'.[3] While historians

[1] G. Pellew, *The Life and Correspondence of the Right Honourable Henry Addington, First Viscount Sidmouth*, 3 vols. (1847), iii. 41.
[2] Quoted in D. E. Evans, *As Mad as a Hatter* (1982), 111.
[3] J. Statham, *Memoir of Louisa Maria Staham* (1842), 2.

may not have been prey to the latent prejudices behind such judgements they have not generally made much progress in defining any more accurately the ministry's social parameters. Indeed, it is only relatively recently that the social composition of nonconformity itself has attracted much systematic attention. Some study has been undertaken of missionary personnel but as far as the ministry is concerned it remains largely an unknown quantity.[4] It seems simply to have been assumed that it reflected the social hierarchy of dissent, Congregationalists drawn from the higher echelons of society, the Wesleyans and Free Methodists a little lower, then the Baptists, with the Primitive Methodists and Bible Christians, who recruited from furthest down in the social scale, bringing up the rear. This chapter begins, therefore, with an attempt to outline the social origins of the Free Church ministry.

Social structure is usually approached through the medium of occupational analysis. The classification employed in Tables 1.1 to 1.5 is that used in the 1951 Census, amended in the light of the 1921 Census along lines suggested by Professor Armstrong.[5] Armstrong's essay also contains a perceptive discussion of the difficulties inherent in occupational analysis which need not be rehearsed here, save to add that when a man had more than one job prior to his entry to the ministry, the most proximate one was taken as the best indicator of his social status. In those many cases where information about occupations was lacking, it sometimes proved possible to classify a particular individual according to his father's occupation. Where the jobs of both a father

[4] For the social analysis of nonconformity in general see A. D. Gilbert, *Religion and Society in Industrial England, 1740–1914* (1976), 59–68. For missionaries see C. P. Williams, 'Not Quite Gentlemen: an Examination of "Middling Class" Protestant Missionaries from Britain, c1850–1900', *Journal of Ecclesiastical History*, 31 (1980); S. Potter, 'The Making of Missionaries in the Nineteenth Century: Conversion and Convention', *Sociological Yearbook of Religion in Britain*, 8 (1974); F. S. Piggin, 'The Social Background, Motivation and Training of British Protestant Missionaries to India, 1789–1858', London Ph.D. thesis, 1974.

[5] A. Armstrong, 'The Use of Information about Occupations', in E. A. Wrigley (ed.), *Nineteenth Century Society: Essays in the Use of Quantitative Methods for the Study of Social Data* (Cambridge, 1972), 191–310. There is a useful discussion of this classification system in S. Royle, 'Social Stratification from Early Census returns: A New Approach', *Area*, 9 (1977).

TABLE 1.1. Occupational and Social Structure: Congregational Ministry

Cohort	1810–39		1820–49		1830–59		1840–69		1850–79		1860–89		1870–99		1880–1909		1890–1919		1900–29	
	S	F	S	F	S	F	S	F	S	F	S	F	S	F	S	F	S	F	S	F
n*	50		69		84		102		115		116		107		102		98		76	
CLASS I																				
Architect														1		1		1		1
Accountant														1		1		1		1
Army Officer		1		1		1						1								
Barrister		1		1		1														
Doctor		2																		
Journalist						1		1		1		1		1		1		1		1
Lawyer		2		2																
Minister		13		14		17		15		17		16	1	20	1	22	1	20		13
Naval Officer												1		1		1		1		
Surveyor						1		1		1				1		1		1		
Vicar										1										
Percentage	Not Valid		Not Valid		Not Valid		15.6		16.5		15.5		22.4		25.4		24.4		Invalid	
CLASS II																				
Artist						1		1		1										
Bookseller		1		1		1		1												
Builder		1		3		4		4		1		1								
Corn Dealer		1		1						1		1								
Customs Officer		1						1						1		1				1
Factor				1		1				1		1		1						
Farmer		7		9		5		5		5		5		6		4		5		3
Manager				1				1		2		2		1						2
Manufacturer		2		1		1		1		1		1		1		1				
Merchant		3		3		4		3		2		1		1		1				3
Teacher		7		13		14		15		14		16		18		17		12		6
Percentage	Not Valid		Not Valid		Not Valid		27.4		20.8		23.2		25.2		20.5		17.3		Invalid	

TABLE 1.1. Occupational and Social Structure: Congregational Ministry

Cohort	1810–39		1820–49		1830–59		1840–69		1850–79		1860–89		1870–99		1880–1909		1890–1919		1900–29	
	F		S	F	S	F	S	F	S	F	S	F	S	F	S	F	S	F	S	F
CLASS III																				
White-collar																				
Chemist											1					1	1	1	1	1
Civil Servant										1	1				1					
Clerk	2		4		5		7		12		12		11		10		10		10	
Designer														1	1					
Draper	3	4	5		7		5		4		2	1	1							
Grocer									1		1		1							
Harbour Master							1			1										
Iron Monger	1								1	1	1				1		1			
Postmaster																		1		
Shop Assistant									1		1		2		2		2		2	2
Traveller											1						1		1	1
Artisan																				
Bookbinder	1																			
Blacksmith					1		1		1		1									
Brass Finisher										1	1		1		1					
Carpenter	2		2		3		2		2		1									
Coach Builder	1			1				1	1		1									
Copper Smith											1			1						
Cotton Doubler											1			1	1					
Cutler				1	1			1												
Engineer			1		1		2		4		4		6		3		4		3	
Fisherman			1				1		1											
Iron Worker							1		1		1		1							
Instrument Maker							1		1		1									
Jeweller						1	1		1		1									
Mason	1						1		1		1				1		1		1	
Mechanic																				
Miller							1		1		1									
Miner							4		7		8	1	7	2	6	2	8	1	6	
Potter	1		1																	

Occupation	Not Valid		Valid						Invalid
Printer						1		2	2
Railwayman			1		1				1
Sailor				1		1			1
Shipwright		3	1			1			
Shoemaker		3	2			1			
Slater		1			1		1		
Soldier		1			1				
Spinner		1	1		1				
Tailor		1	1			1			
Tinplate Worker				1	2	2	1	1	1
Toolmaker					1				
Upholsterer	1	1	1		2			1	
Weaver	1	2	3	2			2		
Woodturner				1	1		1		
Percentage	Not	Valid	34.3	40.0	37.9	35.5	30.3	31.6	Invalid
CLASS IV/V									
Brewer			1	1		1		1	
Carrier							1		
Coalman				1	1	1		1	
Factory Hand	1		3	2	3	2	1	1	
Farm Labourer		1	1	3		4	3	5	2
Gardener	1								
Quarryman				1		1			
Warehouseman						1		1	1
Percentage	Not	Valid	6.8	7.8	5.1	2.8	5.8	6.1	Invalid
OTHER									
Colporteur							1	1	2
Inventor	1	1	1	1					
Missionary	1	1	1	1	1	1	1	2	1
Salvation Army									1
Scripture Reader					1				
Student			1	1	1	1			
n	2	4	11	13	19	15	16	17	13
Percentage	Not	Valid	15.7	14.8	18.1	14.0	17.6	20.4	Invalid

*n = number of individuals used in calculating percentage in each social class.

F = father

S = son

and his son were known, in Tables 1.1 to 1.5 only the former was used in calculating the percentage drawn from each social class. The percentages given in these tables are not, therefore, based on the total number of individuals listed in each class, but on figures adjusted to eliminate double counting. Despite widening the net in this way there is still insufficient evidence to permit of any statistically valid statements being made about any of the Methodist connexions. Rather more information was found for the Baptists and Congregationalists, although definitive conclusions can still be drawn only for certain periods. Two minor adjustments to Armstrong's original scheme have been incorporated in the following tables. Classes IV and V, both of which in any case contained a relatively small number of jobs in the Registrar-General's original classification, have been amalgamated. This is mainly because at that level many of the jobs done by ministers or their fathers were described too vaguely to accommodate the fine shading required by the Census definitions. Secondly, class III has been subdivided into artisans and white-collar/shop worker occupations in order to test some hypotheses about the ministry's social origins.

In 1848 the Secretary of the Congregational Union, Algernon Wells, observed that the denomination and everything about it, 'preaching, buildings, ministers, notions and practices—all have on them the air and impress of English middle class life'.[6] Leaving aside the knotty problem of what exactly Wells meant by middle class, there is no doubt that many Victorians in the mid-nineteenth century believed that Congregationalism had a special mission to the middle classes rather like that thought to have been exercised by Primitive Methodists towards the working classes. Certainly, as Wells suspected, such a middle-class bias was evident in the Congregational ministry, Table 1.1 showing that after 1840 social class III was consistently the largest single provider of ministerial recruits. Too few jobs are known for statistically valid percentages to be calculated for the period prior to 1840 but the raw figures do indicate a broadly

---

[6] *Congregational Yearbook* (1848), 88.

TABLE 1.2. Social Structure of Hoxton–Highbury Students, 1790–1851*

Social Class	Hoxton	Highbury	Total	Percentage
I	2	5	7	3.0
II	2	35	38	16.3
III				
White-collar	25	74	}136	58.6
Artisan	16	21		
IV/V	1	4	5	2.1
Students	16	30	46	19.8

* Based on the students' own previous occupations.

similar pattern, and some further indication of this tendency
is provided in Table 1.2, which analyses the occupations of
about 224 of the 500 or so students who entered Hoxton
Academy and its successor, Highbury College, between 1790
and 1851. Once again, the dominance of men drawn from
social class III is apparent; indeed, at almost 60 per cent it is
overwhelming and about twice the level noted in Table 1.1.
The disparity is explained, however, by the fact that Table
1.1 is based on a sample of all ministers, including the 38
per cent who, according to the *Congregational Yearbook* for
1846, had no formal institutional training at all. In the main,
those who went to Hoxton or Highbury must have come
from the highest social groups within Congregationalism
since they were best able to afford the necessary costs incur-
red by attending the largest and most prestigious of the
Independents' training institutions. Furthermore, it is clear
from other information contained in the students' letters of
application that the college exerted a particularly strong
pull on those living in London and its adjacent counties. It is
only to be expected, therefore, that the student body should
reflect the occupational and social structure of the country's
commercial and political capital.[7]

R. T. Jones has suggested that towards the end of the
century the Congregational ministry became less the preserve of the middle classes, but it is an impression only,

[7] For a fuller examination of these points see my article, 'The Congregational
Ministry in the First Half of the Nineteenth Century: a Preliminary Survey', *Journal of
the United Reformed Church History Society*, 3 (1983).

TABLE 1.3.   Social Structure of Cheshunt College Students, 1900–10 (n = 45)

Social Class	Number of Students
I	1
II	10 (including 7 teachers)
III	
White-collar	13
Artisan	5
IV/V	—
Students	8
'None'	4
Unknown	4

Source: Derived from Cheshunt College, Admissions Register, 1900–10. Cheshunt College Archives, C6/5 Westminster College, Cambridge.

lacking any real statistical authority.[8] His contention is certainly not borne out by Table 1.1 in the sense that there was any significant increase in the proportion of ministers coming from classes IV/V. With one odd exception, the contribution of these lowest segments of society remained fairly constant at around 6 per cent for the entire period between 1840 and 1900. Clearly, considerations of expense and poor academic preparation prevented the denomination's poorest members from entering the ministry, 80 per cent of which was undergoing formal training by 1900.[9] Nor can Jones's claim be substantiated by any shift in the balance between the artisan and white-collar elements. This, too, remained steady, with the artisanate always providing more than 50 per cent and less than 60 per cent of class III. If anything, Table 1.1 shows some late century move towards a white-collar preponderance, especially if teachers are included from class II, and this reflected changes occurring in the occupational structure of late nineteenth-century society as employments in clerical and commercial occupations expanded rapidly. Analysis of the 45 students who entered Cheshunt College between 1900 and 1910 reveals a similar weighting in favour of the white-collar element (see Table

[8] R. T. Jones, *Congregationalism in England, 1662–1962* (1962), 323. The comment is based on the occupations of only thirteen men, all of whom died between 1919 and 1925.
[9] Calculated from details of ministers in *Congregational Yearbook* (1900).

TABLE 1.4. Social Structure of Lancashire Independent College Students, 1880–1910 (by percentage) (n = 174)

Years of admission	1880–9	1890–9	1900–10
Number admitted	77	60	37
Social Class			
I	1.2	1.6	2.7
II	19.4	15.0	10.8
III	48.0	53.3	62.0
IV/V	1.2	1.6	—
Student	18.1	21.6	21.6
Unknown	11.6	6.6	2.7
Ratio of White-Collar to	64	64	78
Artisan	36	36	22

Source: Lancashire Independent College, Register of Students, A–Z, Northern College, Manchester.

1.3). Of the 41 whose previous occupations are known, 20 were white-collar workers as against only 5 artisans. The same pattern emerges in Table 1.4, which classifies the occupations of students entering the Lancashire Independent College between 1880 and 1910. The ratio between white-collar and artisan workers moved from about 2 to 1 among students entering the college between 1880 and 1899, to almost 4 to 1 among those entering in the following decade.

The only trend which appears to lend much support at all to Jones's hypothesis is the reduction in the number of ministerial recruits coming from class II, although even then the pattern is somewhat erratic and affected mainly by fluctuations in the number of farmers—a group whose social classification presents peculiar difficulties as the term 'farmer' could mean anything from a substantial landholder to someone barely distinguishable from a farm labourer.[10] Erratic or not, both Tables 1.1 and 1.4 reveal this same trend, with a reduction of about half in the proportion of class II students going to the Lancashire Independent College over the thirty-year period prior to the First World War. It is possible that this decline reflected the movement of upwardly mobile Congregationalists, who were transferring to the Church of England in significant numbers at this time. The social

[10] This point is fully discussed in Professor Armstrong's essay, n. 5 above.

prestige of Anglicanism remained high and its appeal as
the faith of the nation was probably increasing in an age of
imperialism. It is also possible that more class II applicants
were entering college or the ministry direct from full-time
study. They thus appear in the tables as 'students' rather
than in class II. On the other hand, there seems no obvious
reason why the rising real incomes which made this increasingly possible after 1870 should have benefited those
from class II rather than class III, and it seems just as
plausible to suggest that the rising numbers of 'students' in
Table 1.1 reflected the reduction in class III entrants apparent after 1880. Analysis of missionary recruitment shows a
similar late century dominance of middle-class, particularly
white-collar, entrants, while Table 1.4 points to a marked
increase in class III admissions to Lancashire College. Furthermore, the late nineteenth century saw growing concern
among the Congregational authorities about the deteriorating quality of student intake, more evidence perhaps that
class II men were coming forward in fewer numbers, prefer-
ring instead to take advantage of growing employment
opportunities provided by the expanding public sector, local
government development, and changes in recruitment practices for government offices.[11]

Finally, the expansion in the proportion of men drawn
from class I hardly seems to support the notion that ministerial recruitment was spreading down the social scale in the
late nineteenth century, although there is a relatively simple
explanation for this apparently puzzling phenomenon. It
can be explained by the inclusion of ministers in class I of
the Registrar-General's classification of jobs. If ministerial
fathers are discounted then the numbers originating in class
I become very much smaller, running in Table 1.1 between
1.3 per cent (1840–69) to 4.0 per cent for the 1900–29 entry
cohort. Over the whole period the average is about 2.8 per
cent. Similarly at Lancashire College where the social stratification can be based on the known occupations of the students

---

[11] For a fuller discussion of these points see my article, 'Ministerial Recruitment
and Training: An Aspect of the Crisis of Victorian Nonconformity', *Victorian Studies*, 30
(1987). Similar problems were affecting the Anglican Church at this time, too. See A. P.
M. Coxon, 'Patterns of Occupational Recruitment: the Anglican Ministry', *Sociology* 1
(1967).

themselves: of 174 men who entered the college between 1880 and 1910 only 3, or 1.7 per cent, had previously held jobs classified as social class I. Based on student occupations alone, only 3.0 per cent of the Hoxton and Highbury men were from class I in the period 1790 to 1851. Yet almost a quarter of them (22.5 per cent) had ministerial fathers. Again, at Cheshunt in the Edwardian era only 3.4 per cent of the students for whom information about previous occupations has been found were drawn from the top social group, although 40.0 per cent were sons of the manse. This explains why the Congregational ministry, as analysed in Table 1.1, contains an unexpectedly high proportion of class I men. Yet this also points up another aspect of the origins of the ministry which was to be of some considerable importance in explaining its post-war problems. By the last third of the nineteenth century about one in five of all new recruits to the ministry were coming from ministerial homes.

This same feature of a high proportion of class I men is also evident among the Baptists (Table 1.5). Here, however, it is worth noting that if ministerial fathers are discounted there still remain 3.6, 6.7, and 4.8 per cent respectively in the cohorts entering the Baptist pastorate between 1860 and 1909, figures too high to be explained away, for example, by obituarists consciously trying to upgrade the rather fustian social image borne by their denomination. There is no reason to quarrel with Dr Armstrong's verdict that in the period prior to 1850 the majority of Baptist ministers were 'very obscure men'.[12] In Mark Rutherford's fictional village of Cowfold in the 1840s the Anglican, Independent, and Wesleyan ministers all had nothing to do with the Baptist pastor. This was not, wrote Rutherford, due to any doctrinal differences but simply because the Baptist was 'a poor man, and poor persons sat under him ... his ministrations were confined to about fifty sullen, half-stupid, wholly ignorant people'.[13] Yet it is known from Dr Champion's study of the Stennett family that the Baptist ministry in the eighteenth

[12] A. Armstrong, *The Church of England, the Methodists and Society, 1700–1850* (1973), 175.
[13] W. H. White (Mark Rutherford), *The Revolution in Tanner's Lane* (1927 edn.), 197.

TABLE 1.5. Occupational and Social Structure: Baptist Ministry

Cohort	1810–39 S	1810–39 F	1820–49 S	1820–49 F	1830–59 S	1830–59 F	1840–69 S	1840–69 F	1850–79 S	1850–79 F	1860–89 S	1860–89 F	1870–99 S	1870–99 F	1880–1909 S	1880–1909 F	1890–1919 S	1890–1919 F	1900–29 S	1900–29 F
n		49		66		73		85		92		111		112		104		83		62
CLASS I																				
Accountant																				
Architect							1		1		1		1		1		1		1	
Auctioneer													1		1					
Dentist			1		1		1		1						1		1			
Journalist			1		1		1													
Land Agent															1		1			
Minister		10		12		11	1	10	1	6	1	8	1	11	1	15	1	14	1	11
Naval Architect											1		1							
Naval Officer									1		1		1							
Publisher									1		1		1		1					
Solicitor			1		1												1			
Stockbroker					1		1												1	
Percentage	Not	Valid	Not	Valid	Not	Valid				11.9		10.8		16.0		20.1		Invalid		
CLASS II																				
Artist	1		1																	
Builder										1		1	1	1	1	2	2	2		1
Farmer		7	1	7		7	2	8	3	8	2	7	1	4		3				
Manager		1		1						1		1		1						
Manufacturer					1		1		1		1		1		1					
Merchant				1	1		1		1		1			2		2		2		
Mill Owner								1		1		1								
Teacher		7		7		9	11	3	11	4	11	5	7	2	8	1	6		6	
Percentage	Not	Valid	Not	Valid	Not	Valid				27.1		21.6		13.3		12.5		Invalid		

CLASS III

White-collar

Occupation											
Chemist	1		1	1	2	1	1	13	12		7	6
Clerk	1	3	4	5	7	10	7	3	2		2	1
Draper	2	3	3	4	3	4	3	3	2		1	
Grocer		1	1		1	2	1	3			1	
Lab Demonstrator											1	
Optician												1
Photographer											1	1
Postmaster		1	1			1						
Salesman				1								
Shopworker					1			1			1	1
Traveller			1	1	1	1	1	1	2	1	2	1

Artisan

Occupation											
Blacksmith		1	1									1
Boat Builder				2	2	1		2				1
Boot Maker	1		1		1						1	
Brazier	1	1	1		1							
Cabinet Maker		1	1	2	2	2			1		2	
Carpenter	1	1	1									
Chainmaker		1	1	1								
Coach Builder				1								
Dyer	1	1	2	2	1	2						
Engineer		1	1	1	2	2	1	3	3		3	2
Gasman						1		1	1			
Iron Maker	2	2		2	2	1						
Mantua Maker	1	1										
Metal Moulder												1
Miller		1	1	1	1						1	
Miner	1		3	4	7	10	7	8	6		2	
Plasterer					1	1		1	1		1	3
Printer	3	3		1	2	1	2	1			1	1
Railwayman	1	3		1	1	1	1				1	1

TABLE 1.5. Occupational and Social Structure: Baptist Ministry

Cohort	1810–39 F	1810–39 S	1820–49 F	1820–49 S	1830–59 F	1830–59 S	1840–69 F	1840–69 S	1850–79 F	1850–79 S	1860–89 F	1860–89 S	1870–99 F	1870–99 S	1880–1909 F	1880–1909 S	1890–1919 F	1890–1919 S	1900–29 F	1900–29 S
Saddler																1				
Sailor				1			1	1	3	1	2	1	2	1		1	1	1	1	1
Shipwright										1		1								
Silversmith										1		1								
Soldier												1				1				
Spinner	1		1		1					1				1						
Tailor			1		1					1		2		1						
Tinplate Worker										2		1								
Watchmaker	1					2		2				1				1				
Weaver					1			1				1								
Woodturner							1			1				1		1				
Percentage	Not Valid		Valid		Valid		Valid			41.3		37.8		38.5		30.7	Invalid			
CLASS IV/V																				
Farm Labourer	5		4		3	1		2		1		2	1	1		2	1	3		2
Millhand	1		2		3			1		1		1		1		2		1		
Warehouseman								1		1		1								
Percentage	Not Valid		Valid		Valid		Valid			2.1		3.6		4.8		7.7	Invalid			
OTHER																				
Colporteur																1		1		
Evangelist														1				1		1
Missionary	1		2				2				3			3		1				
Salvation Army																1		1		1
Student		11		13		11		11		13		25		29		30		21		14
Percentage	Not Valid		Valid		Valid		Valid			17.3		26.1		29.5		28.8	Invalid			

century contained a core of men drawn from the highest
social groups, and Table 1.5 suggests that this continued to
be a feature of the denomination's ministry throughout the
nineteenth century as well.[14]

It also appears that as the century progressed so the Baptist intake from classes IV/V increased. In common with
other denominations, the proportion of Baptist ministers
who received formal training rose steadily after mid-century.
Figures calculated from information in the *Baptist Handbook*
show that in 1871 only 58 per cent of all Baptist ministers
had been trained at an academy or college. By 1911 some
84.5 per cent of all the ministers in the denomination had
received formal training. Within that total, however,
one institution came to account for an ever increasing
share. The Pastor's or Metropolitan College, which ultimately assumed the name of its founder, Spurgeon, trained
rather more than a tenth of Baptist ministers listed in the
Handbook for 1871, and over a fifth of those in the 1891
edition. By 1911 24 per cent of Baptist ministers had come
from Spurgeon's College. By this last date its nearest rival
was Regent's Park, responsible for a mere 6 per cent. The
relevance of these statistics to the present discussion about
the rising Baptist recruitment from classes IV/V is that right
from its inauguration Spurgeon's College had made a point
of trying to cater for those men who felt called to the ministry but who lacked the educational background or monetary
resources necessary for admission to the other Baptist colleges. 'What was wanted', Spurgeon believed, 'was an institution where these rough-and-ready men could be drilled
in the simple rudiments of education, and so fitted for the
work of preaching and the discharge of plain pastoral duties.
... I shall not, in order to increase our prestige, refuse poor
men, or zealous young Christians whose early education has
been neglected.'[15] No fees were levied on the students,
Spurgeon himself raising a substantial share of the voluntary contributions which sustained the college. As a result,
it seems highly likely, although no documentary proof is

---

[14] L. G. Champion, 'The Social Status of Some Eighteenth Century Baptist Ministers', *Baptist Quarterly*, 25 (1973–4).
[15] A. Dallimore, *Spurgeon* (Chicago, 1984), 102.

extant, that Spurgeon's did take in men from lower classes
than might otherwise have found their way into Baptist
pastorates. Over two-thirds of the obituaries of Spurgeon's
men contained in Table 1.5, for instance, contain no reference to any former occupation, suggesting perhaps that
they were of a low standing, not thought worthy of record.
The only Methodist institution in any way comparable to
Spurgeon's was Cliff College which similarly played down
formal education, emphasizing among its admission requirements virtues such as personal holiness, experiential knowledge of the Bible, and preaching ability. It was, however,
very small, did not open until 1882, and trained men only as
evangelists, not ministers.[16] J. B. Paton's Congregational Institute at Nottingham, like Spurgeon's, intended to provide
access to the ministry for men lacking in formal education,
those of 'poorer educational qualifications, men for the most
part of humbler origin, but touched with live coal from off
the altar'.[17] Even so, it produced a much smaller proportion
of the total denominational ministry, about 7.2 per cent in
1900.[18]

Table 1.5 also shows, though much more obviously and
consistently, the same diminution in recruitment from class
II as was apparent among the Congregationalists, and similar reasons probably apply. The number of Baptist farmers
entering the ministry declined while a growing number of
men entered directly from education rather than after some
secular work experience. It is possible that the reduction in
class II entrants reflected a drift into Anglicanism on the
part of upwardly mobile Baptist families. Although there
were some Baptists like Colonel Griffin, President of the
Union in 1892, who placed a high priority on the uniqueness
of Baptist doctrine, especially the place of believer's baptism
by immersion, for the majority it was general evangelical
teaching that was important—and this did not provide an
obstacle against movement into Anglicanism. Certainly, as
Dr Bebbington has shown, the social appeal of the Anglican

[16] See A. Cresswell, *The Story of Cliff* (Sheffield, 1965).
[17] J. L. Paton, *John Brown Paton. A Biography* (1914), 83.
[18] Calculated from information in *Congregational Yearbook* (1900).

establishment was not much reduced by the progressive removal of the nonconformists' social and legal disabilities.[19]

Again in line with Congregationalist experience, there is strong evidence that the Baptist ministry was undergoing the same process of white-collaring. If, as has been suggested, small craftsmen came to dominate the Baptist ministry after the middle of the eighteenth century, this was a sector which declined with the continuous advance of technology in the next century.[20] The 1860–89 cohort of new Baptist ministers is almost evenly divided between white-collar (including teachers) workers and artisans. By the period 1870–99 the balance was shifting in favour of the white-collar sector, reaching a ratio of three to two in the next entry cohort, 1880–1909.

There is insufficient evidence to allow of anything more than speculation about the social origin of the Methodists' ministers in the years before 1929. Although the sample size is too small to be of any statistical significance, Table 1.6 suggests that, as with the Baptists and Congregationalists, white-collar workers became increasingly important as a source of ministerial manpower for the United Methodists. Free Methodists have traditionally been accorded a high place in the Methodist hierarchy, ranking second only to the Wesleyans. In view of this it is interesting to note that class I seems to have provided hardly any men at all. The Bible Christian element, which for the purpose of this study has been included with the United Methodists for the whole of the period under examination, is reflected in the number of farmers and other rural occupations recorded. Bible Christianity always remained the church of Hodge, the countryman.

The Primitives are generally thought to have been more successful than other branches of nonconformity in reaching the lower social orders. It is thus not surprising that many of their early preachers were, in the words of an early Methodist historian, reared in 'homes of poverty and obscurity', a

---

[19] See D. Bebbington, 'Baptist M.P.'s in the Nineteenth Century', *Baptist Quarterly*, 29 (1981). For Griffin's comments see *Christian World*, 30 Apr. 1891.

[20] T. M. Bassett, *The Welsh Baptists* (Swansea, 1977), 94.

TABLE 1.6. Occupational and Social Structure: United Methodist Ministry

Cohort	1810–39		1820–49		1830–59		1840–69		1850–79		1860–89		1870–99		1880–1909		1890–1919		1900–29	
	F	S	F	S	F	S	F	S	F	S	F	S	F	S	F	S	F	S	F	S
n	15		23		35		47		50		49		44		44		37		32	
CLASS I																				
Minister	1		3		3		5		9		9		9	1	6	1	5	1	3			
Solicitor			1										1		1		1			
Percentage					Not				Valid											
CLASS II																				
Bookseller							1		1		1									
Builder			1		1										1	1	1			
Farmer	3		3		3	3	3	3	3		1	2	2	3	1	2	1			
Manager											1									
Manufacturer	1				1		1		1		1		1							1
Teacher	2	2	2	2	3	1	3	1	5	1	6	1	7		8		8		7	
Trader	2		1		1		1				1									
Traveller	1		1		1		1													
Percentage					Not				Valid											
CLASS III																				
White-collar																				
Cashier																				
Chemist	1		1		1															
Civil Servant															1		2	2	2	1
Clerk	1		1		2		5		5		7		4		4				1	
Coastguard					1															
Draper											1			1	1					
Grocer	1		1				1		1		1									
Ironmonger							1		1		1									
Loc Gov Officer					1															
Pottery Seller					1		1				1									
Secretary			1		1		2		1		1									1

	1	2	3	4	5	6	7	8	9
Artisan									
Blacksmith					1	1			1
Bricklayer	1					1		1	1
Butler	1	1							
Cabinet Maker	2	2							
Cutler	2	2			2	1		2	
Domestic Servant	1		1	1	1	1	1		
Engineer			1	1	1			2	
Farrier	1								
Fisherman						1	1		
Forester								1	
Hosier			1	1		1			1
Iron Worker	1	1		1	1		1	1	1
Joiner	1	1	3		2	2	1		2
Miner	1	1	1	1	1	1	1	1	
Printer				1					
Saddler					1				
Sailor	1								
Shoemaker	1	1	1	1	3	3		1	1
Stocking Maker	1	1	1	1	1				
Tailor	1		3	3	3	2	1		
Watchmaker	1	2	1	2	1	1	1		
Percentage	N	o	t		V	a	l	i	d
CLASS IV/V									
Carter	1					1			
Farm Labourer	1	1	1	1	1		1		1
Labourer	1	1	1	1	1	1			
Mill Hand				1	1				
Quarryman	1		1	1					
Percentage	N	o	t		V	a	l	i	d
OTHER									
Lay Agent					1			1	1
Student	2	3	5	6	10	12	12	10	9
Unspecified } Apprentice }	2		2		2				
Percentage	N	o	t		V	a	l	i	d

sentiment reiterated in a more recent, local study which
concludes that ministry among the Primitives offered 'a
working class lad a professional future'.[21] Both suggestions
might seem excessively romanticized but Table 1.7 does
appear to lend some numerical weight to such claims, the
emphasis within class III being much more heavily on the
artisans than the white-collar group. As might be expected
in a connexion which relied heavily on the midland and
north-east coalfields for its support, miners appear to figure
quite prominently among ministerial recruits.

As for the Wesleyans, Table 1.8 again appears to bear out
the impression that this was the élite of Methodism.
Together, classes I and II were more significant sources of
ministers than was the case for either the United or Primitive Methodists. For most of the century very few were
recruited from classes IV/V, while the white-collar element
always dominated class III. This latter trend can be confirmed from an independent source, an analysis of ministerial candidates based on the Minutes of District Synods for
1906 and 1907. Out of 94 candidates, 58 were white-collar
workers, including 29 clerks, and 14 teachers and students.
Only 16 were described as working class, mainly artisans.[22]
As with the other Methodist connexions, a substantial proportion of Wesleyans appear to have come from ministerial
homes.

All this points to three general conclusions about the social sources of the nineteenth-century Free Church ministry.
There was first of all a steady reduction in the proportion of
men drawn from social classes I and II, though the former
was never high if ministerial fathers are not counted.
Secondly, a growing percentage of men in all denominations
tended to be sons of the manse. The inclination of sons to
follow fathers' occupations was common at many levels of
Victorian society, but it was a pattern of particular significance in the case of the nonconformist ministry, and one

---

[21] The comments respectively of J. Ritson, *The Romance of Primitive Methodism*
(1909), 191, and G. M. Morris, 'Primitive Methodism in Nottinghamshire', Nottingham
Ph.D. thesis, 1967, p. 58.
[22] R. B. Walker, 'The Growth of Wesleyan Methodism in Victorian England and
Wales', *Journal of Ecclesiastical History*, 24 (1973), 282.

whose implications will be explored in later chapters.[23]
Finally, within social class III it was increasingly the white-
collar workers, clerks and shop assistants who, along with
the teachers from class II, tended to form the mainstay of
ministerial recruitment, although among Baptists and Primitive Methodists classes IV/V were more highly represented. Dr Binfield's suggestion that by the late nineteenth
century the ministry was drawn more and more from families 'poised uncomfortably between the middle and lower
classes' seems well founded.[24]

To some extent, of course, the social origins of the ministry mirrored the geographical distribution and strength of
nonconformity. Reference has already been made, for example, to the late nineteenth-century prevalence of miners
among the Primitive Methodists, whose strongest areas lay
astride the coalfields of the north-east and midlands. Miners
also appeared quite prominently among the Baptists, reflect-
ing that denomination's strong following in Wales. Now it is
possible to establish reasonably accurate figures for the distribution of the major denominations county by county, certainly for the period after 1851. Before that date only the
more accurate and comprehensive Methodist statistics are
amenable to such a disaggregation. There is no intrinsic
reason, however, why there should be any close match, certainly not at the level of the individual, between a minister's
geographical origins and the county strengths of each denomination. Individual decisions to enter the ministry were
the product of many different considerations, few of which
had anything to do with geography. For one thing, some of
the Methodist connexions did not place a very high premium
on the idea of a professional ministry anyway, an attitude
which may have deterred many. Conversely, it is just conceivable that the existence of a conveniently situated college
or academy might have encouraged some young Baptist or
Congregational men to avail themselves of the opportunity

---

[23] For example, see M. J. Peterson, *The Medical Profession in Mid-Victorian London*
(1978), 4; C. B. Otley, 'Social Origins of British Army Officers', *Sociological Review*, 18
(1970); R. K. Kelsall, 'Self Recruitment in Four Professions', in D. V. Glass (ed.), *Social
Mobility in Britain* (1953); S. Rothblatt, *The Revolution of the Dons* (1968), 89.
[24] C. Binfield, *So Down to Prayers: Studies in English Nonconformity, 1780–1920*
(1977), 241.

TABLE 1.7. Occupational and Social Structure: Primitive Methodist Ministry

Cohort	1810–39		1820–49		1830–59		1840–69		1850–79		1860–89		1870–99		1880–1909		1890–1919		1900–29	
	S	F	S	F	S	F	S	F	S	F	S	F	S	F	S	F	S	F	S	F
n	19		26		31		43		49		48		39		50		51		53	
CLASS I																				
Army Officer														1		1		1		
Journalist																1		1		
Minister				1		1		5		6		7		7		10		13		12
Percentage	N		o		t				V		a		l		i		d		
CLASS II																				
Bailiff										1		1								
Bookseller				1	1			1												
Builder								1		1		1		1						
Farmer		1		2		4		4	1	5	1	4	1	3		3		3		4
Manager												1		1		1				
Railway Inspector														1		1				
Sculptor																		1		
Teacher		1				1		1	3	1	5		1	6	6		1	5	3	
Trader		1			1															
Percentage	N		o		t				V		a		l		i		d		
CLASS III																				
White-collar																				
Chemist		1																		
Clerk		1		2	2	1	2		2		2	1	3	1	5	1	4	1	6	1
Draper						1										1				
Grocer				1	1										2					
Ironmonger		1				1														
Salesman																		1		
Shop Assistant		2		2		1				1		1		1						
Artisan																				
Blacksmith	1	1	1	1	1													1		1
Chain Maker																		1		1
Checkweighman														1				1		1

Clothworker						1	1					1				
Coach Builder						1	1						
Docker			1			1							1
Electrician	1		1		1	1	1	1			1	
Engineer	1	1	1		1	1	1	1			1	
Forester			1	1	1						
Forgeworker			1		1	1					
Glassblower					1	1					
Iron Worker	1	1	1	1	1	1	1	1	1	1	1
Joiner	1	2	6	7	7	5	8	6	2
Miner	1	1	1	2	2	1	3	1	1	1	1	4
Nailmaker			1		1		1	1		1
Pattern Maker											1
Sailor			1	1							1
Shipwright	1										
Shoemaker	4	3	2								
Signalman											
Soldier	1	1	1	1							
Spinner			2	1	2	1					
Percentage	N	o	t	V	a	l	i	d

CLASSES IV/V
Factory Hand	5	1	4	4	4	2	2	2	2
Farm Labourer	4	5	3	2	1	1	1	1	1	1	2	1
Gardener			1		1	1	1		1	1
Quarryman											
Warehouseman							1		1
Percentage	N	o	t	V	a	l	i	d

OTHER
Missionary	1	1						1		2
Student		1	2	3	3	2	4	3	6	11
Unspecified			3	3	3					
Apprentice	2	1								
Percentage	N	o	t	V	a	l	i	d

TABLE 1.8. Occupational and Social Structure: Wesleyan Ministry

Cohort	1810–39		1820–49		1830–59		1840–69		1850–79		1860–89		1870–99		1880–1909		1890–1919		1900–29	
		Ḟ	S	F	S	F	S	F	S	F	S	F	S	F	S	F	S	F	S	F
n		17		33		38		44		42		59		78		80		83		68
CLASS I																				
Accountant																				
Architect																			1	
Army Officer				1	1		2		3		3		2		1				1	
Dentist														1		1				
Employer							1										1			
Journalist			1				1		1		1							1		1
Lawyer							1		2		3		3							
Minister		10		17		19		14		9		11		19		19		18		11
Solicitor										1			1		1			1	1	
Percentage				N		o		t		V		a		l		i		d		
CLASS II																				
Farmer	1			1			1		1		1		1					4		
Manager				1					1		1	2	1	2	1	5	1		1	
Manufacturer						1		1				1		1		1	1			
Merchant								1		1		1	1	1	1	1	1	2		
Teacher		3		6		7	1	1	1	5	2	8	2	12	1	10	1	11		7
Percentage				N		o		t		V		a		l		i		d		
CLASS III																				
White-collar																				
Chemist				1		1	1	1		1		2		1	1			1		1
Clerk		3		4		4		2		2		3		3	4			9		9
Civil Servant								1		2		1			1			1		2
Draper				1		3		3		1				2		1		1		2
Florist								3		3						1		1		1

					Not	Valid		
Fruiterer								1	1
Grocer								1	2
Shop Assistant			1		2			2	2
Traveller					1				
Artisan									
Baker								1	1
Blacksmith									2
Compositor					1		1	1	1
Electrician					1		1	1	1
Engineer							1	1	1
Ironfounder							1	1	1
Joiner			1		1		1	1	1
Miner									1
Printer				1					
Soldier				1				1	1
Steelworker					1		1	1	1
Stonemason								1	1
Weaver				1	1		1		
Percentage	N	o	t		V	a	l	i	d
CLASSES IV/V									
Caretaker							1		1
Farm Labourer								1	1
Messenger								1	1
Mill Hand							3	2	1
Quarryman				1	2			1	1
Warehouseman		1		1					
Percentage	N	o	t		V	a	l	i	d
OTHER									
Lay Agent								1	
Missionary							2		
Student	2	3	5	9	11	16	21	20	20	17
Percentage									

of acquiring a ministerial education. More generally, in so
far as the ministry was deemed to be a vocation resting on a
divine call from God, then such calls were, quite clearly,
independent of geography. Similarly, one influential, charismatic preacher such as Dale or Spurgeon could perhaps
inspire any number of youths to follow him into the ministry. Equally, it is likely that a religious revival or some other
perceived move of the Holy Spirit, however interpreted by
secular historians, could send a stream of ministerial recruits forward from a specific region or congregation,
irrespective of local denominational strength. It is also
possible that, in some cases at least, a decision to enter the
ministry was governed by the lack of any alternative job
opportunities, although some very elaborate statistical calculations produced nothing more than the vaguest hint of
this.[25] On the whole, therefore, it seemed more promising to
pursue the matter of ministers' geographical origins along
different lines.

Table 1.9 classifies birth places by country, Table 1.10 by
type, whether urban, market town, or rural. It is immediately apparent that Wales made a disproportionately large
contribution to the Wesleyan ministry. It produced rather
more than a tenth of the connexion's ministers over a period
when Welsh Wesleyan membership represented only about a
sixth of the total.[26] Similarly, about a fifth of those who
entered the Baptist ministry between 1810 and 1860 were
Welsh, although too much should not be made of this. T. M.
Bassett has estimated that in 1851 22.1 per cent of all Baptist

[25] The purpose of these calculations was to isolate those counties which consistently
over- or under-produced ministers between 1851 and 1914, when denominational
membership figures were reasonably reliable. This was done by establishing the density of denominational membership in each county at twenty-year intervals. The result
was divided by a similarly calculated ministerial density figure. Little could be de-
duced from the resulting index, however, save that there was some slight tendency
towards the end of the century for rural counties to over-produce ministers. The only
other consistent feature which emerged was the failure of Monmouth, a county heavily
populated by Baptists, to contribute a due proportion of ministers to the denomination. It is possible that this was due to the availability of ample work opportunities in
the adjacent and expanding economy of South Wales.
[26] The calculations of percentages of Welsh and Scottish memberships in this and
the succeeding paragraph are based on figures given in R. Currie, A. Gilbert, and
L. Horsley, *Churches and Churchgoers: Patterns of Church Growth in the British Isles
since 1700* (Oxford, 1977), 142–9.

TABLE 1.9. Geographical Origins of Nonconformist Ministers by Country (%)

	Dates of Entry									
	1810–39	1820–49	1830–59	1840–69	1850–79	1860–89	1870–99	1880–1909	1890–1919	1900–29
Wesleyan n			100	120	135	157	158	156	157	131
England			77.0	76.7	80.0	80.1	79.7	76.9	78.3	80.9
Wales			10.0	10.8	11.1	10.8	11.3	13.4	13.3	12.9
Scotland			3.0	4.1	3.7	3.8	2.5	1.9	1.2	1.5
Ireland			2.0	0.8			0.6	0.6	0.6	
Other/Unknown			8.0	7.6	5.2	5.3	6.9	7.2	6.6	4.8
Primitive n			101	113	128	111	106	118	136	118
England			96.0	91.1	89.8	88.2	88.6	88.1	90.4	91.5
Wales					0.7	1.8	5.6	7.6	5.8	5.0
Scotland				2.6	3.1	3.6	0.9		0.7	0.8
Ireland				0.8	0.7	0.9				
Other/Unknown			4.0	5.5	5.7	5.5	4.9	4.3	3.1	2.7
United n				108	155	164	158	131	98	
England				92.5	94.1	94.5	95.5	94.6	94.8	
Wales				1.8	1.2	2.4	1.2	2.2	2.0	
Scotland					1.2	1.2	0.6	0.7		
Ireland										
Other/Unknown				2.7	3.5	1.9	2.7	2.5	3.2	
Baptist n		116	126	150	165	203	215	216	186	140
England		68.1	65.8	64.0	60.0	57.6	53.0	51.8	53.7	60.0
Wales		18.1	18.2	21.3	23.6	29.0	31.1	34.2	31.7	30.7
Scotland		6.8	5.5	3.3	4.2	5.4	10.2	10.6	9.6	5.0
Ireland				0.6	1.8	1.9	1.8	0.9	1.0	0.7
Other/Unknown		7.0	10.5	10.8	10.4	6.1	3.9	2.5	4.0	3.6
Congregational n	107	131	136	161	192	205	203	197	176	150
England	72.8	69.4	63.9	58.3	55.7	55.6	55.1	55.8	55.1	62.0
Wales	14.9	16.0	18.3	22.9	25.5	27.8	31.0	34.0	36.9	32.0
Scotland	6.5	8.3	8.8	8.0	8.3	8.2	7.8	6.0	4.5	2.6
Ireland	2.8	3.8	3.6	3.1	1.5	2.4	1.4	2.0	1.1	0.6
Other/Unknown	3.0	2.5	5.4	7.7	9.0	6.2	4.7	2.2	2.4	2.8

membership was Welsh, a figure virtually identical with the proportion of new ministers originating in Wales between 1840 and 1869—21.3 per cent. Only in the years 1860 to 1889 did Wales produce more Baptist ministers than its share of denominational membership indicated. About 30 per cent of the new men in that period were Welsh, although the Principality accounted for only 23.5 per cent of the denomination's overall population. Here perhaps we may detect the influence of the 1859–60 revival, which was particularly strong in Wales. On the other hand, the later and better known revival of 1904–5, which was confined to Wales, does not seem to have drawn much new blood into the ministry. Bassett puts the share of Welsh membership at 30.4 per cent in 1911, compared with 31.7 per cent of new Welsh ministers in the period 1890–1919.[27] Wales's contribution to the Congregational ministry was pretty well in line with its share of total denominational membership for most of the century. Some 26.6 per cent of membership was Welsh in 1851, as against 22.9 per cent of men entering the ministry between 1840 and 1869. Although the balance had shifted slightly by 1911, the figures were still quite close. Between 1890 and 1919 36.9 per cent of new ministers came from Wales which in 1911 accounted for 34.1 per cent of the total denominational membership.

It was in fact Scotland which provided the most disproportionate input into the ministry of the Old Dissent. There was an influx of Scots into Baptist pulpits in the third quarter of the nineteenth century, a time when Scottish Baptists made up only some 4 or 5 per cent of the total. This was the combined outcome of the establishment of full-time ministerial training in 1869 by the Baptist Union of Scotland and the emergence in Scotland of the English pattern of a congregation being pastored by a single, trained minister instead of the traditional plurality of elders. Even more striking was the persistent Scottish presence in Congregational pulpits. Traditionally, many of the abler students at the various Congregational academies and colleges had gone on to take degrees at the Scottish universities, especially Glas-

---

[27] Bassett, p. 232.

gow, Edinburgh, and St Andrews. The Scottish link was further strengthened in mid-century by ferments within contemporary Presbyterianism. Many Scots who could not make the eligible grade in Scottish parishes sought situations in the English Congregational ministry, since in Scotland there were now few suitable alternatives outside the Presbyterian Establishment. Thus for most of the period between 1830 and 1879 about 8 per cent of the men serving in the English and Welsh ministry were Scottish. This trend also shows up in the various college records. Notwithstanding the problems of travel rather more than a tenth of those admitted to Hoxton and Highbury before 1851 were from Scotland, while Lancashire Independent College and its predecessor, Blackburn Academy, also had a 10 per cent Scottish intake between 1810 and 1879.[28]

Given the economic structure of Britain in the first half of the nineteenth century, it is not surprising that Table 1.10 should indicate a rural origin for the majority of ministers at that time. If market towns are included as being places where the predominant rhythm and ethos of life were agrarian rather than urban, then about 70 per cent of Baptists and Congregational ministers had rural roots in the years prior to 1879. With the exception of the Primitives, the Methodists were rather less countrified. The main significance of Table 1.10, however, lies in what it reveals about the pattern of ministerial recruitment in the later nineteenth century. By 1901 78 per cent of the population of England and Wales was officially classified as urban.[29] Yet in the years between 1890 and 1919 it was, with the exception of the Primitives, overwhelmingly from rural areas that the ministers came. Even if, for the sake of argument, market towns are counted as urban rather than rural entities by 1900, there was still a disproportionately small urban contribution. At a time when four-fifths of the population lived in urban regions, less than two-thirds of the ministerial personnel in most denominations (slightly over half in the case of

[28] Calculated from information relating to student applications in Lancashire Independent College (hereafter LIC), Register of Students, A–Z, Northern College, Manchester. For the Hoxton and Highbury figures see Brown, 'The Congregational Ministry', 6.
[29] P. J. Waller, *Town, City and Nation: England, 1850–1914* (1983), 8.

TABLE 1.10. Geographical Origins of Nonconformist Ministers by Type (%)

					Dates of Entry					
	1810–39	1820–49	1830–59	1840–69	1850–79	1860–89	1870–99	1880–1909	1890–1919	1900–29
Wesleyan n			100	120	135	157	158	156	157	131
Rural			34.0	34.1	42.2	38.9	41.7	37.8	33.7	31.2
Market Town			31.0	31.6	26.7	26.1	22.8	24.3	27.4	29.0
Urban			27.0	26.7	25.9	30.6	31.0	32.0	33.8	35.1
Unknown/Abroad			8.0	7.6	5.2	4.4	4.5	6.2	5.1	4.7
Primitive n			101	113	128	111	106	118	136	118
Rural			64.3	59.2	47.6	43.2	39.6	38.1	36.0	33.0
Market Town			23.7	23.9	25.8	27.9	23.6	15.2	11.8	15.3
Urban			8.9	13.2	21.8	24.3	32.1	43.2	50.0	50.0
Unknown/Abroad			3.1	4.3	4.8	4.6	4.7	3.5	2.2	2.0
United n				108	155	164	158	131	98	
Rural				34.2	36.8	36.6	36.7	32.1	32.6	
Market Town				25.0	27.7	23.8	22.2	19.8	23.5	
Urban				37.9	32.3	38.3	38.6	45.8	40.8	
Unknown/Abroad				2.9	3.2	1.3	2.5	2.3	3.1	
Baptist n		116	126	150	165	203	215	216	186	140
Rural		39.7	33.3	36.6	36.9	40.8	39.0	38.8	35.4	29.2
Market Town		31.9	31.7	27.3	23.6	24.1	23.7	22.7	23.1	22.8
Urban		21.6	24.6	25.3	29.7	29.6	33.9	35.6	38.7	44.2
Unknown/Abroad		6.8	10.4	10.8	9.8	5.5	3.4	2.9	2.8	3.8
Congregational n	117	131	136	161	192	205	203	197	176	150
Rural	48.5	51.1	45.5	49.0	43.7	43.9	39.9	41.6	40.8	36.0
Market Town	26.2	25.9	30.1	23.0	22.4	21.5	25.6	24.9	26.1	24.0
Urban	22.4	21.3	24.6	21.1	25.0	28.8	30.0	31.5	31.3	37.3
Unknown/Abroad	2.9	1.7	4.5	6.9	8.9	5.8	4.5	2.0	1.8	2.7

the Congregationalists) had been born in urban areas. Dr Waller has rightly observed that there is a danger of exaggerating the divergence of town and country in the Victorian period. There was, he suggests, a continuum of ideas, people, material, and experience which linked the two rather more intimately than some contemporary romanticizing commentators have allowed.[30] Furthermore, it is to be borne in mind that in 1900 about one in nine of all urban dwellers lived in small towns (those with populations of under 10,000). Even so, it is legitimate to ask how far the nonconformists' declining growth rates after 1880 were due to the fact that their ministers were increasingly divorced by experience from the everyday environment of the majority of the population. Ministers perhaps could hold and fortify the various ecclesiastical establishments to which they belonged but they could no longer expand them. Certainly there is considerable evidence, to which we shall return in later chapters, of concern in the late nineteenth century that ministerial *training* was not relevant to the needs of people living in an urban, industrialized society.[31] Perhaps, too, ministers themselves were unsuitable to meet this challenge?

We turn finally to ministers' spiritual origins. Information about individual conversion ages does survive but it is patchy and permits only of generalization about nonconformity as a whole. The limited availability of evidence is partly a matter of historical accident, but mainly a reflection of changes which occurred in nonconformist vocabulary and theology during the later Victorian years. For much of the nineteenth century Free Churchmen were familiar with both the idea and experience of salvation and conversion. A few such conversions were rather quiet and vague occurrences. Thus Thomas Guttery never knew 'what it was to be quite unconscious of the presence of God and the realities of religion'.[32] Thomas Waterhouse's conversion was similar:

---

[30] Waller, pp. 185–8.
[31] See especially Chapter 3, below.
[32] J. G. Bowran, *The Life of Arthur Thomas Guttery DD* (1922), 14.

'not sudden, but gradual, not boisterous, but pacific'.[33] But the majority of conversions which occurred in the first half of the century were quite precisely located in time and space, and usually involved a considerable degree of emotional upheaval. Thus one man, converted in 1843, later wrote that 'the blessed assurance of His pardoning love made me leap for joy, and everything around me seemed bright and beautiful'.[34] Billy Bray recorded that for him 'everything looked new ... the people, the fields, the cattle, the trees. I was like a man in a new world. I spent a greater part of my time praising the Lord.'[35] On the day of his conversion Peter Featherstone's 'heart leaped within me for joy. As I walked home a full mile along the solitary lane on a January evening, "all nature" seemed to rejoice with my forgiven soul.'[36] S. G. Dimond may have been referring to eighteenth-century Wesleyans when he first drew attention to the stylization of such conversion stories but it is clear that, stylized or not, emotional and cathartic conversions remained the norm in all denominations well into the next century.[37]

Table 1.11 shows that after 1860 conversion ages were not so frequently recorded in obituaries, indicative of changed perceptions on the part of both the writers and their subjects. In general the second half of the century saw a shift towards a more materialistic understanding of life. In their respective fields Marx, Wagner, and Darwin all asserted the primacy of matter rather than feeling or moral sentiment and the impact of this on nonconformist theology was reinforced by the development of biblical criticism.[38] As a result, much less emphasis came to be placed on the doctrines of hell, judgement, and damnation, all often seen as vital elements in the promotion of personal repentance and conversion. By 1900 many ministers were left preaching little more than an amorphous gospel of good works and ethics. Increasingly, action rather than feeling or belief became the

---

[33] *Methodist New Connexion Magazine* (Jan. 1854), 2.
[34] D. Barr, *Climbing the Ladder* (1910), 28.
[35] F. W. Bourne, *The King's Son; or a Memoir of Billy Bray* (1937 edn.), 15.
[36] P. Featherstone, *Reminiscences of a Long Life* (1905), 5.
[37] S. G. Dimond, *The Psychology of the Methodist Revival* (1926), 162.
[38] J. Barzun, *Darwin, Marx, Wagner: Critique of a Heritage* (1958).

Table 1.11. Conversions among Nonconformist Ministers

Years of Entry to Ministry	Percentage of Main Sample With Known Conversion Age	Total Number of Conversions recorded in Each Denomination				
		Wesleyan	Primitive	United	Baptist	Congregational
1810–19	40.9					
1820–9	47.8					
1830–9	45.7	47	89	64	61	47
1840–9	38.6					
1850–9	41.4					
1860–9	34.9					
1870–9	24.7					
1880–9	18.1	20	83	74	79	17
1890–9	13.5					
1900–9	5.0					

hallmark of nonconformity and this transition from faith to
works was seen, for example, in the growing cult of temperance. The changed perception was captured by J. B. Brooks
in his account of Sunday school life in Lancashire. At the
annual mission of the New Connexion Methodists he was
asked if he believed in Jesus. His affirmative reply was
enough to cause his name to be included in the list of those
saved even though he felt no different. Later, he noted, 'as I
came to think for myself, my faith, I saw, rested simply in
the way of life that Jesus taught and lived, backed by its
embodiment in the lives and witness of my teachers ... and
several of our young ministers'.[39]
  Some further indication of the change, albeit only impressionistic, is provided by a comparison of early and late
nineteenth-century letters of application to the theological
colleges. Compare, for instance, the passion for souls and
conversion expressed in Mr Woodward's letter to Highbury
in the 1830s with the lack-lustre and limp approach adopted
to Lancashire College by R. R. Whittington in 1906. Woodward's underlying motivation was quite clear. He was 'desirous of telling the good news of salvation to my fellow
sinners'.[40] Whittington, on the other hand, felt that it was in
the sphere of the ministry that he could 'best proclaim the
way to experience the highest joy obtainable in life ...
looking to Him as our pattern and observing His principles
as our mode of life'.[41] At about the same time another Lancashire applicant, P. H. Goodwin, thought that his main
function as a minister would be 'teaching the people about
God and helping them to lead better lives'.[42] Christ, the
expiator to be experienced, had vanished, to be replaced by
Christ, the exemplar of good works to be emulated. It would
be misleading, of course, to imply that this transformation
was either sudden or total. Nor was it uniform. There remained many, especially among the Baptists and Primitive
and United Methodists, who were suspicious of the new
theological currents and who continued to stress the need

[39] J. B. Brooks, *Lancashire Bred: An Autobiography* (1950), 86–8.
[40] B. Woodward to Highbury College, c.1837/8, New College Archives, 308/18/li,
Dr Williams's Library (cited hereafter as DWL. NCA.).
[41] LIC, Register of Students, T–Z, Northern College, Manchester.
[42] Ibid. E–G.

for personal salvation. As Table 1.11 shows, it was among Wesleyans and Congregationalists that declining adherence to the concept was apparently most marked. The *Methodist Recorder* drew attention to the subject in 1903, noting that at the recent Wesleyan conference less than half of the new ministerial candidates had attested to any definite conversion experience. The majority had referred instead to processes of gradual enlightenment or conviction.[43] By 1914 the Primitives were equally alarmed, lamenting in the words of one delegate at the annual conference that the connexion had lost its 'redeeming passion'.[44]

This gradual diminution in the number of conversions recorded was not caused only by these changes in theological outlook, however. Its roots lay also in slowing growth rates. With the passage of time the nonconformists tended to expand less and less into new social catchment areas. Growth was increasingly a matter of natural increase from within the indigenous nonconformist community. Revivalism was aimed less at the outside world and more at the believers' own children. Faith Osgerby, sent by her mother to the local Primitive Sunday school, dreaded the annual evangelistic campaign 'because then I knew I should have to be "saved" again'.[45] In the hands of teams of professional revivalists conversion tended to become more formal and mechanistic. Certainly this was true of George Acorn whose experience bore little resemblance to the passionate struggles so common in the early nineteenth century. 'One Sunday night', Acorn wrote, his friend Simpson, 'told me in a most matter-of-fact tone that he was about to be converted. I was greatly surprised. In my innocence I imagined one only became converted after much wrestling with strange passions and sins. . . . Yet here was Simpson talking as if being converted was like going for a walk!' And so it turned out. That night the two friends went to chapel. After the sermon they were pushed together into a small side room by a counsellor who was 'not zealous in his attempts to win converts', told to pray, and then, although he felt nothing, Acorn was 'assured with Simpson that I was "saved"', after

[43] *Methodist Recorder*, 6 Aug. 1903.
[44] Primitive Methodist Conference, *Minutes* (1913), 6.
[45] J. Burnett, *Destiny Obscure* (1982), 94.

1. Origins

TABLE 1.12. Nonconformist Ministers: Conversion Ages (%)

Source	1 Main Sample	2 Bonner	3 Freeman	4 Field
n	581	212	178	178
Date	1810–1909	Not given	Not given	1841–1900
Age at Conversion				
Under 10 ⎱		1.4	1.6 ⎱	
10 – 12 ⎰	12.3	10.8	8.0 ⎰	15.1
13 – 15	27.7	29.2	23.5	30.4
16 – 18	40.4	44.3	33.1	42.7
19 – 21	13.9	11.7	16.9	7.8 (19 – 20)
22 – 4	3.4	1.8	4.4	3.9 (21 +)
25 +	2.4		12.1	

which their names were written down in a small pocket book and they were dismissed.[46]

Table 1.12 contains an analysis of ministerial conversion ages based on this study's main sample and also includes the findings of some other similar investigations. Column 2 is calculated from some enquiries into ministers' conversion ages undertaken by Carey Bonner for his Ridley Lectures in 1911. They were published in the same year as *The Christ, The Church, and the Child.* Some of Bonner's raw data was provided by W. F. Freeman, who a few years earlier had surveyed the conversion ages of a large number of Methodists, including women. He published his own results much later in *Age Challenges Youth.*[47] Column 4 is an analysis of Wesleyan ministers' conversion ages for the period 1841 to 1900 prepared by Clive Field as part of his 1974 Oxford doctoral dissertation.[48] Given that the four sources are not directly comparable, covering different groups and spanning different time periods, there is a good measure of agreement between them, except perhaps at the margins. They indicate quite clearly that ministers tended to get converted at the same ages as everyone else. Around 70 per cent of them were converted between the ages of 13 and 18, with 16 to 18 being

[46] G. Acorn, *One of the Multitude* (1911), 158–60.
[47] W. F. Freeman, *Age Challenges Youth* (1949), 39.
[48] C. D. Field, 'Methodism in Metropolitan London', Oxford D.Phil. thesis, 1974, p. 232.

the most important single period. This accords well with the
findings of G. W. Allport that the peak age for conversion
was between 14 and 17 years, and also with E. D. Starbuck's
study of American ministerial students which suggests 14 to
18 years as the crucial age.[49] A similar pattern showed up in
a more limited analysis of Congregational ministers whose
deaths occurred between 1868 and 1875. Of the 340 individuals in that study whose conversion ages were known, the
years between 16 and 20 saw most conversions (44.7 per
cent), with only 15.2 per cent being converted after the age
of 20.[50] In their spiritual origins, therefore, ministers were
apparently no different from ordinary believers, although it
is impossible to say anything about the intensity or nature of
their conversion experiences. More obviously, what most set
them apart was the direction in which the urge to Christian
service took them.

[49] G. W. Allport, *The Individual and His Religion* (1951), quoted in S. Budd, *Varieties
of Unbelief* (1977), 105. E. D. Starbuck, *The Psychology of Religion* (1899), 28.
[50] Calculated from figures given in J. Mirams, 'Averages of Ministerial Life and
Services', *Congregational Yearbook* (1877), 526–7.

2

Training, 1800–c.1860

EARLY in the summer of 1799 the young Robert Newton
saddled his horse, filled his pack with the equipment
deemed necessary for an itinerant Wesleyan preacher—
books, Bible, clean linen, and shaving tackle—and left home.
Undeterred by a chance encounter with a local physician
who tried to persuade him that a man of his talents would
be better suited to a more elevated occupation, he rode off
towards his first circuit at Pocklington and a distinguished
career in the Wesleyan ministry. In the tradition of all of
Wesley's early preachers, who were seen primarily as
evangelists rather than teachers or pastors, his formal preparation had been minimal, little more than a year's lay
preaching. Yet once the break with Anglicanism had been
accepted as irreparable, voices were raised in Methodism
urging a more structured approach towards ministerial
training as a way of improving the connexion's image and
status. Prominent among them was Adam Clarke's. 'We
want', he wrote, 'God knows! We want some kind of seminary for educating workmen for the vineyard of our God,
as need not be ashamed. We need to get such a place
established.'[1] The time had already come, he went on, 'when
an *illiterate piety* can do no more for the interest and *per-
manency* of the work of God, than *lettered irreligion* did
formerly.'[2]

But the early nineteenth century was a time of very rapid

[1] Quoted in W. B. Brash, *The Story of Our Colleges, 1835–1935: A Centenary History of Ministerial Training in the Methodist Church* (1935), 26.
[2] Quoted in D. A. Johnson, 'The Methodist Quest for an Educated Ministry', *Church History*, 51 (1982), 306.

expansion for the Wesleyans. It was widely argued that men could not be spared for full-time training, especially as the expansion was set against a background of wartime inflation and then post-war distress, both of which placed considerable strain on the connexion's financial resources. Furthermore, these were also years in which a number of secessions occurred from the parent Methodist body. As most of them involved differences about the proper balance of power that ought to prevail between the ministry and lay elements, the Wesleyans' leaders were reluctant to do anything which might appear to widen further the gap between the two. In the event, therefore, all that was done was to strengthen the oversight exercised over recruitment by circuit chairmen and district meetings. After 1802 district meetings were required to examine ministerial candidates rather than simply to approve them. The examinations could be quite rigorous. Benjamin Hellier's, for example, began at 5 a.m., lasted for an hour and a half, and covered details of his conversion, his current religious experience, his call to the ministry, and his understanding of basic doctrines such as the Trinity, the nature and work of Christ, and the resurrection. Successful candidates were then discussed by the annual conference and, if accepted, were sent into circuit work on a four-year trial or placed on a reserve list for subsequent deployment as the president of Conference decided.

Gradually, however, the proponents of a seminary gained ground. The continued outworking of the Evangelical revival ensured that there was no lack of candidates but it also increased the need for men with pastoral and teaching skills in order to consolidate the ground won by the evangelists. It is clear, too, that, despite the changes introduced in 1802, not all those sent into circuit work were men of desirable Methodist quality. At the Conference of 1824:

Four preachers were expelled—Mr John Bryan of the Epworth Circuit for having criminal connections with his housekeeper (he being a widower). He is now married to her. He prospered in the Connection as a celebrated Revivalist, but he was a vain, self sufficient man who despised all his Brethren.... Jonas Jagger was expelled for intemperance and impudent conduct towards some female or females—and Theobald of Halifax for S—d—y. He is fled, but whither perhaps nobody knows—and Joshua Bryan, he is one of the incurables ...[3]

The presence in their ministerial ranks of men such as these was clearly an embarrassment to the Wesleyans and in 1827 Conference increased the powers of the district chairman still further. Now his oversight was to include not only strictly religious matters but also moral character, debt, and other possible secular encumbrances to the effective discharge of the ministry. It was argued by some that such moral defects might be more readily identified under a more rigorous and highly controlled system of training.

But the strongest argument of all for formalizing ministerial preparation was born out of the growing realization that the general expansion of educational provision in the first four decades of the nineteenth century was producing more knowledgeable congregations who might well be dissatisfied with men of mediocre academic attainment. The people, Joseph Sutcliffe suggested to Jabez Bunting, would 'either look up to the sanctuary or they will wander elsewhere ...'.[4] Certainly in this respect the Wesleyans compared very unfavourably with both the Anglican clergy and also the ministry of the Old Dissent, as Joseph Entwisle realized: 'Unless the improvement of young preachers keep pace with the general improvement of Society—our ministry will not be supported ... the Clergy and our brethren the Dissenters will take our glory from us.'[5] Table 2.1 shows that almost 80 per cent of the Congregationalists and just under 50 per cent of the Baptists who entered the ministry between 1820 and 1849 had been educated at an academy, a college, or even a university. Thus the logic of development was irresistible, although the Wesleyans' decision to establish a Theological Institution—in the building formerly occupied by the Independent Academy at Hoxton—did not go uncontested. Some still insisted that ministers could only be called of God, not

---

[3] C. Radcliffe to J. Shipman, 24 Nov. 1824, Methodist Archives, PLP 86–4–7, Rylands Library, University of Manchester (cited hereafter as MAM. PLP.).

[4] J. Sutcliffe to J. Bunting, 17 July 1834. Quoted in W. R. Ward, *Early Victorian Methodism: The Correspondence of Jabez Bunting, 1830–1858* (Oxford, 1976), 82.

[5] J. Entwisle to J. Bunting, 23 June 1831. Quoted in ibid. 14.

educated or trained by men. Samuel Warren resigned in a fit of pique when Bunting was nominated first president of the Theological Institution, a post to which, it was said, Warren himself aspired. Suspicions were expressed that the training would be used to enforce a uniformity of ministry and practice within Wesleyanism and it is true that some of the scheme's supporters urged in its favour that it would tend to diminish ministerial heterodoxy. Other fears were more prosaic. One critic suggested that incarceration in an all male college would cause students to become 'effeminate and fastidious'.[6] There was an echo of this in the Didsbury House Governor's report for 1844 when he said:

Though their seclusion from the secular engagements of life may be supposed to exempt them from some of the most formidable difficulties and temptations to which Christians are ordinarily exposed, yet there are others, incident to their age, to the association of a large number of young persons, to their peculiar studies, and even to the Ministerial Office itself—which require the utmost wisdom and vigilance on the part of those who are entrusted with their pastoral oversight.[7]

The depth of the need created by rapid Wesleyan expansion in the first decades of the century was quickly revealed. Within six years of its opening, sixty students were enrolled at Hoxton and an overflow building, Abney House, had to be acquired. The first branch proper opened at Didsbury in 1842 and was followed a year later by a second branch at Richmond. Both did well enough to convince all but the most sceptical, and their products were soon in some demand as there was a distinct kudos attached to having a college man in a circuit. In 1869 a third branch opened at Headingley and Table 2.1 indicates that by 1840–69 over half the men entering the Wesleyan ministry had been to the Theological Institution. The rest continued to enter circuit work direct through the old system, except that there were now examinations, both written and oral, plus a trial

---

[6] Quoted in R. Lowery, 'The Wesleyan Theological Institution. Hoxton: a Further Study', *Proceedings of the Wesley Historical Society*, 39 (1973), 129.
[7] Didsbury Management Committee Executive Minutes, 10 May 1844, Didsbury College Archives, A1/2/1, Wesley College, Bristol.

TABLE 2.1. Percentage of Ministers Formally Trained. Main Sample

		1810–29	1820–49	1830–59	1840–69	1850–79	1860–89	1870–99	1880–1909	1890–1919	1900–29
							Dates of Entry				
Wesleyan	n			101	120	135	158	158	156	156	131
	College			44.5	54.1	60.0	71.5	83.5	87.1	83.9	81.6
	College and University			0.9		0.7	1.2	3.1	6.4	9.6	11.4
Primitive	n				114	129	111	106	118	136	119
	College				9.6	22.4	38.7	56.6	74.5	82.3	84.8
	College and University					0.7	1.8	3.7	2.5	2.2	5.8
United	n				108	150	159	153	131	98	—
	College				5.5	20.0	35.8	48.3	53.4	53.0	
	College and University				2.7	4.0	3.7	4.5	4.5	6.1	
Baptist	n		120	121	145	162	202	215	216	186	140
	College		46.0	46.3	51.9	63.6	70.7	65.1	60.6	60.7	66.4
	College and University		1.7	2.3	2.6	3.6	5.9	10.6	12.5	15.0	16.4
Congregational	n	107	131	136	161	193	206	203	196	175	151
	College	63.7	70.0	62.4	60.8	61.1	58.6	59.0	55.0	56.5	53.3
	College and University	6.5	9.9	11.0	11.8	11.3	14.5	18.2	19.8	20.0	21.3

sermon, interposed between the district meeting and the annual conference assessment.

Initially, the Institution was designed to provide a basic education for those whose academic background was deemed inadequate for the work of the ministry and candidates were selected from the President's List of those new preachers not immediately allocated to a circuit. Quite soon, however, the decision was taken that, in principle, all men should attend the Institution. All students had to serve a preliminary year as a lay preacher and the wise ones took advantage of this to improve their learning. Joseph Bush, for example, combined his lay preaching stint with private study under a local minister, reading the great staples of early nineteenth-century theological education, Butler's *Analogy* and Paley's *Evidences*. Examinations by district and quarterly meetings followed. Then came the July examination, in Bush's case, an oral ordeal taken simultaneously with a dozen other young men and conducted by the president. A trial sermon was also required, preached before a congregation which included specially appointed ministerial listeners.

Once admitted, students remained for one or two years, depending on the connexional need for men and their own need for training. Apart from Wesley's own sermons the curriculum included English literature, logic, philosophy, theology, Latin, and Greek, a taxing diet for men whose scholarly attainments were generally low. David Waller, for example, stayed only three terms at Richmond in 1856 before he went into circuit work, the victim of ill health and an inability to cope with classical grammar. Perhaps not surprisingly, the standard was low. Peter Duncan expressed some concern on this score to Bunting in 1856: 'The late examination of students at Didsbury has been the means of awakening some anxious and painful feelings in my mind. Their knowledge of the Holy Scriptures we found so lamentably defective, as that we were forced to notice it in the Report.'[8] Yet Bunting and his colleagues resisted pressure to issue a circular letter urging the imposition of higher

---

[8] P. Duncan to J. Bunting, 14 July 1856. Quoted in Ward, p. 418.

standards for potential ministerial recruits. It would, Bunting felt, deter too many men from offering themselves and herein lay the dilemma facing all ministerial educators in the nineteenth century.[9] How could the Church's need for ministers, the demand that they be intellectually adequate, and also that they be clearly called and gifted of God, be reconciled? Peter Mackenzie scored no marks at all on his literary papers in the preliminary examinations for the Theological Institution, yet he was admitted because the committee was convinced of his call and ability.

Among the other Methodist groups little was done to provide formal training before the 1860s, as Table 2.1 suggests. Association and Reform Wesleyans (forerunners of the United Methodist Free Churches), and Bible Christians were too small and too poor to support institutional schemes. The New Connexion considered the matter in 1839 but did nothing on the grounds that 'the engagements of the Connexion will not at present enable it'.[10] As with the Wesleyans, there was some fear that spiritual fervour would be unduly diluted by education and there was also concern that training ministers would set them apart from the ordinary chapel member, thus re-creating the trend to ministerial dominance which had led them out of Wesleyanism in the first place. Finance was also a difficulty. When an appeal was made in 1847 for £20,000 to support, among other ventures, a ministerial training college, only about a third of the money was raised. A New Connexion college did not materialize until 1864 and even then its opening was made possible only by a generous donation from a wealthy Sheffield steel maker, Thomas Firth. In the mean time, such ministerial training as was available took the form of working with a succession of experienced and learned individuals, Thomas Allin, William Cooke, and James Stacey, although only a small number of New Connexion ministers were able to benefit from this scheme. The Primitives also remained largely untrained until the Sunderland Institute began its work in the 1860s. After its emergence in 1811–12 the con-

[9] J. Bunting to J. Crowther, 23 Feb. 1848. Quoted in Ward, p. 364.
[10] Methodist New Connexion, *Minutes* (1839), 46.

nexion had grown very quickly and Hugh Bourne, the founder, had tried to emulate Wesley, encouraging his preachers
to self-education by means of his own works and the connexional magazine. But unsuitable men found their way into
the ministry and in 1854 the general committee was in-
structed to draw up rules for testing candidates' efficiency.
Oral exams were instituted in 1855 and became written tests
on prescribed texts in the early part of the next decade.
There was considerable opposition to anything more formal,
a sentiment encouraged perhaps by the survival among the
Primitives of free gospelism and certainly by the belief that
the connection had a special mission to the lower orders and
did not, therefore, require a highly trained ministry.

Neither the Baptists nor the Congregationalists had any
formal mechanisms of ministerial recruitment. It was always open to any individual to rent premises, gather a congregation, and call himself 'pastor' in the hope of establishing a 'cause'. Such 'causes' might then develop into true
churches, bodies of individuals bound together in covenant
relationships which were expressed in church membership
and, ultimately, by association with other groups of like
order and belief. Such origins were particularly common
among the Baptists. John Grace, a shopkeeper, built and
opened a Baptist chapel at Eastbourne in 1823. Visiting
preachers shared the ministry until ultimately Grace started
another congregation and served it as full-time pastor.[11]
John Warburton, a Strict Baptist, began his ministerial
career in a similar way. He supplemented his weaver's income with the 4s. he received each week for preaching at a
local chapel near his home on the outskirts of Manchester.[12]
Congregational causes were also initiated in this way, but
with their higher social pretensions and more generally opu-
lent backgrounds most aspiring Congregational ministers
did try to acquire some education before taking on a pastorate. Some served what amounted to an apprenticeship as a
co-pastor, although such situations tended to be available

---

[11] J. Grace, *Recollections of John Grace* (1893), 28 ff.
[12] J. Warburton, *Mercies of a Covenant God* (Manchester, 1838), 81. George Dawson,
the famous propagator of the social gospel, established his own cause in Birmingham
in this way in 1847.

only in the larger city chapels with the financial resources necessary to pay two men. In any case, such churches usually preferred to take on men who had been formally trained. More commonly, therefore, would-be Congregational ministers undertook some preliminary study with an experienced man as a prelude to entering one or other of the numerous dissenting academies. John Stoughton, for instance, studied classics and theology with a Baptist minister before going to Highbury College in 1827.

Highbury was probably the largest and most prestigious of the many institutions which had grown up to provide higher educational opportunities for the dissenters in the aftermath of the Act of Uniformity of 1662. They were a natural attraction to nonconformists denied access to the English universities, and in the course of time many came to concentrate specifically on ministerial training. Indeed, the oldest of all, Bristol Baptist College, traced its history back to 1679. Some, such as Homerton, were opened in order to safeguard the traditions of Evangelical dissent against the trend towards Unitarianism which set in during the eighteenth century. Others were the product of the zeal sparked off by the Evangelical revival. The Congregational Fund Board, for instance, helped to establish the Western Academy at Ottery St Mary in 1752. The academy which settled at Hoxton in 1791 had been in operation at a different site since 1778. The General Baptists established what became Midland College in 1797. It was largely because of this long tradition of education that both Congregationalists and Baptists had quite high proportions of trained men in their ranks from the very start of the nineteenth century (see Table 2.1). Certainly, many of those without training felt themselves to be inferior. 'I feel my great deficiencies', wrote the Baptist, Thomas Lewis. 'O, what an advantage is learning as the handmaid of religion! I cannot esteem it too highly. I bewail the lack.'[13]

As with the Wesleyans, the Evangelical revival stimulated both the demand for trained men and the supply of applicants. The early nineteenth century witnessed, therefore,

---

[13] J. Burrell, *Memoir of Rev Thomas Lewis* (1853), 24.

pressure for an expansion and improvement of institutional training facilities within both denominations. Although some negative voices were raised, the tide was running strongly against the conservatives and the majority view was expressed by the Baptist, Joseph Kinghorn. He dismissed the critics, accusing them of raising nothing more than a 'foolish outcry'.[14] All but the most dogmatic opposition crumbled when the establishment of the Wesleyan Theological Institution undermined the resistance of those who pointed to the success of untrained Wesleyanism.

Three arguments gave particular force to the case for expansion. The most commonly expressed was the belief, shared also by the Wesleyans, that nonconformists would be left behind by the spread of general educational provision. Thus John Ryland said at Stepney in 1812 that 'an illiterate, though pious ministry must be exposed to needless contempt'.[15] Another Baptist, Isaac Mann, warned his hearers in 1829 on the same lines, arguing that if they did not keep up with trends in general education then their congregations would turn away to what he termed 'a more enlightened ministry'.[16] Professor Godwin was still making this point when he preached at the jubilee services of Rawdon College in 1854. Spiritual qualifications must remain the prime requirement for the ministry, he emphasized, but in the enlightened age in which they lived, they alone were 'not sufficient ... qualifications of an intellectual character are needed, the power both of acquiring and imparting knowledge'.[17] Similar arguments were used in Congregational circles. In the 1820s the trustees of Airedale College pointed out that if nothing was done to improve and extend training then the time would come when 'in many of our congregations, the Minister shall be a man of less ability and attainments than a large proportion of his people'.[18] 'We are losing ground', wrote another worried Congregationalist in

---

[14] Quoted in J. O. Barrett, *Rawdon College: A Short History* (1954), 7.
[15] Quoted in N. S. Moon, *Education for Ministry: Bristol Baptist College, 1679–1979* (Bristol, 1979), 28.
[16] Quoted in D. M. Himbury, 'Training Baptist Ministers', *Baptist Quarterly*, 21 (1966), 343.
[17] Quoted in Barrett, p. 48.
[18] Airedale Independent College, *Report* (1826), 8.

1831, 'compared with the progress of the Evangel. Clergy and Methodists'.[19] A few years later the Congregational Union appointed a committee to consider how the actual quality of candidates might be improved.

Secondly, there is no doubt that among the Congregationalists a trained ministry was thought to provide some safeguard for their social pretensions, serving both to distance them from the Methodists as well as preserving some sort of standing relative to that of the Established Church. This was a line of thought uppermost in John Harris's mind when he spoke at the opening of the Lancashire Independent College in 1843. In the past, he conceded, God had 'greatly blessed the preaching of some uneducated ministers', but, he went on, 'He did not bless *on account* of their ignorance, but *in spite* of it'.[20] Only by acquiring a more highly educated ministry, he concluded, would the denomination preserve its position and standing.

Robert Hall, the Baptist, adduced a third argument. He suggested that an educated ministry was the only reliable buttress for sound religion. It is possible that Methodism was included by implication in his definition of unsound religion, as were some of the extremer versions of eschatological and charismatic religion as found among the Southcottians and Irvingites. It is more likely, however, that he had foremost in his mind the atheistic irreligion popularly associated with Tom Paine and the French Revolution, a fear which found ready echoes among Congregationalists as well:

It might be deemed superfluous to insist on the importance of Academical Institutions in an age of general inquiry and information.... Not only does the state of increased mental cultivation which, in various grades, characterises our population, require corresponding degrees of superior scholarship in those who are to be their religious instructors, but the adversaries of the gospel must be adequately met on their own ground, and manfully fought with their own weapons, in so far as these may legitimately be employed ...[21]

---

[19] J. Bowden to T. Wilson, 12 May 1831, DWL. NCA. 302/9. The importance of competitive considerations in shaping denominational development is brought out in W. R. Ward, *Religion and Society in England, 1790–1850* (1972), *passim*.

[20] J. Harris, *The Importance of An Educated Ministry: A Discourse Preached Preparatory to the Opening of the Lancashire Independent College* (1843), 29.

[21] Highbury College, *Report* (1835), 6–7.

For these reasons, then, the training facilities of the Old Dissent expanded considerably in the first half of the nineteenth century. The Baptists opened Horton at Bradford (which later became Rawdon College), and Stepney, which later became Regent's Park. Later, the Baptists of North Wales opened a house at Llangollen to provide for their region what southern Baptists had been providing at Abergavenny since 1807. Vint's famous academy at Idle became Airedale College, while across the Pennines the Blackburn Academy opened in 1816 and became Lancashire Independent College a quarter of a century later. Elsewhere merger and amalgamation were the order of the day in the search for greater efficiency and coverage. New College opened in 1851, a merger of the older institutions, Highbury, Homerton, and Coward. As a result of this activity the Baptists increased the proportion of trained men in their ranks to about 67 per cent of those entering the ministry between 1850 and 1879, as against 45 per cent of those entering between 1830 and 1859. The Congregationalists, however, failed to keep up with the demands created by rising population and increased chapel building. Even though the Congregational Union summoned a special conference of the colleges to discuss the problem they still had about the same proportion of trained men entering between 1850 and 1879 as they had had between 1830 and 1859. It is worth noting in this context that between 1847 and 1871 the total number of Congregational ministers rose from about 1,400 to 2,503, and that the number of chapels and places of worship increased from 3,244 in 1851 to 4,113 in 1874.[22]

The processes of admission to the dissenting colleges varied in detail and machinery but the requirements and principles were broadly the same between different institutions and denominations. Wesleyans, as we have seen, were filtered through a series of tests administered at different levels until college entry was finally approved by Conference. In the case of the Older Dissenting traditions candidates usually had to be recommended by their own churches,

---

[22] See H. S. Skeats, 'Statistics Relating to the Support of Religious Institutions in England and Wales', *Journal of the Statistical Society*, 39 (1876), 333. The estimates of the number of ministers are calculated for 1847 from the *Congregational Yearbook* (1848), 208.

provide written proof of their Christian experience and work, and, sometimes, an indication of their financial resources. College committees and staffs interviewed the most promising, giving a written or oral exam on the classics, mathematics, English language and literature, and the Bible. It could be something of an ordeal and E. W. Tongue later likened the whole process to being in a dentist's anteroom with the actual interview reminiscent of the Spanish Inquisition. Worst of all was the sermon which candidates were required to preach before the committee. Tongue's was, he recalled, interrupted and eviscerated at will by all the committee members in turn, a practice G. W. Conder subsequently damned, and not without reason, as barbarous.[23] No comprehensive statistics remain as to what proportion of students survived this ordeal and in any case it is evident that the number of applicants, their quality and thus the acceptance rate, must have varied with the prestige and location of the individual institution. Between 1791 and 1825 Hoxton admitted 127 men and rejected 53, while over the next quarter-century its successor, Highbury, generally regarded as the premier Congregational college, took in 181 and turned down 51.[24] The overall ratio of acceptances to rejections over the whole sixty-year period appears to have been about three to one.

Candidates were required to meet certain minimum levels of health and intellect. Occasionally, age was also a consideration. Cheshunt would admit no one over twenty-eight and some members of the Hoxton committee wanted to reject Mr Lamb in 1820, deeming him too old at twenty-four, though the real reason appears to have been a fear that Lamb would go the way of his father, who had made a rather spectacular shipwreck of his faith. A Mr Macdonald was turned down on medical grounds: 'A little general inquiry into his symptoms made yesterday is quite confirmed by a fuller and closer investigation today.'[25] Mr Slatterie did

---

[23] E. W. Tongue, 'Recollections and Reflections'. LIC, Register of Students, T–Z, Northern College, Manchester. Conder's comment is in G. W. Conder (ed.), *Memoir and Remains of the Late Rev J. Glyde* (1858), 19.

[24] These figures are calculated from applications to Hoxton and Highbury surviving in DWL. NCA. 218–418.

[25] (Illegible) to Hoxton Committee, 19 Feb. 1819, ibid. 323/13.

not gain admission at his first attempt because it was felt, wisely as events turned out, that he had not been converted long enough (see p. 74, below). Henry Bunn was thought to be too dim, while Mr Reid received a rather unpromising reference from his tutor at Rowell, the preparatory institution which educated men for college entry: 'There is something in his manner in company which is considerably against him; a queerness which exposes him to ridicule, and which at times would lead one to think that he is hardly perfectly sane.'[26] The positive attributes for which committees looked were sound evangelical religious sentiment and experience, coupled with preaching ability. For this latter reason stammerers were ruthlessly excluded while many of the Welsh applicants to Hoxton and to Bristol Baptist College (which became a great attraction to Baptists from South Wales after the closure of Trosnant Academy) were turned down because their command of the English language was weak. Thus Mr Lewis was rejected by the Highbury committee in 1827 because he had 'so bad an articulation ... it is very difficult to carry on conversation with him'. He was, the committee concluded, 'very unfit for the business of his class'.[27] A few years later Mr Saville's application foundered on his trial sermon, 'very defective as a specimen of his ability, he did not appear in the judgement of the Committee to possess the requisite qualifications'.[28]

Given that piety and preaching were the most highly sought-after requirements in ministerial candidates it is perhaps not surprising that mistakes were made, even among the Wesleyans where admission was centrally monitored. Table 2.2 sets out some surviving evidence relating to drop-out rates among college men. Long-term analysis is possible only in the cases of Bristol Baptist and Lancashire Independent, although there is also some surviving material relating to some of the other Congregational colleges for shorter periods. The figures for Didsbury, the first branch of the Wesleyan Theological Institution, are 'guestimates', calculated as the percentage of students who, according to

[26] W. Scott to Hoxton Committee, n.d., ibid. 226/2/2.

[27] Hoxton College, Reports on Interviews with Candidates, 14 Dec. 1827, ibid. 56/3.

[28] Note by the Hoxton Committee on Mr Saville's Trial Sermon, ibid. 306/13/5.

TABLE 2.2. Student Drop-Out Rates (%)

	Didsbury			Bristol Baptist				Lancashire Independent		
	1842–69	1870–99	1900–10	1810–39	1840–69	1870–99	1900–19	1810–39	1840–69	1870–99
Number	444	626	268	178	176	153	80	66	216	236
Cause of leaving										
Death				4.4	1.7	0.6		1.5	1.8	2.9
Illness				3.9	5.1	4.5		4.5	5.0	2.9
Education				1.6	0.5			3.0	6.0	0.4
Transfer				0.5	0.5	0.6				
Doctrinal				0.5	1.7	0.6		1.5		
Moral					0.5		1.2	3.0	0.9	0.4
Expelled				1.1		3.2	5.0	1.5	0.4	2.1
Other				3.9	6.8			1.5	5.0	7.6
Total Loss	23.6	20.9	22.0	15.9	16.8	9.5	6.2	16.5	19.1	16.3

Source: Didsbury figures calculated from W. B. Brash and C. J. Wright, *Didsbury College Centenary, 1842–1942* (1942); Bristol from the index of students kept at Baptist College, Bristol; Lancashire from LIC, Register of Students, A–Z.

the official college history, entered the college in the stated periods but who subsequently failed to appear in the various editions of William Hill's *Alphabetical Arrangement of All the Wesleyan Methodist Preachers* (1819–1932). This can provide only a crude approximation, since some of those not listed in Hill may well have completed the course and then, for some reason, not have proceeded into the Methodist ministry. Even if some allowance is made for this, the drop-out rate seems inordinately high, about a quarter of the 1842–69 cohort of students failing to reach the ministry. This seems consistent with the complaints noted earlier about the poor quality of the students. Bristol Baptist lost rather less, about one in six over the half century to 1869. Lancashire's loss rate was about the same as Bristol's initially but then rose as student intake increased with its metamorphosis into Lancashire College. Turning next to the shorter term material analysed in Table 2.3, Hoxton and Highbury appear to have been quite effective at spotting weak applicants, although it is possible that the institution's position as the largest and most prestigious Independent college in the first half of the century attracted an abler range of students. It would be unwise to make too much of the Homerton figures since they cover such a short period but Cheshunt's record appears to be consistently disastrous. Even if the losses caused by death and sickness are discounted—committees could hardly be *that* percipient—the college still lost about a fifth of those students who attended between 1847 and 1885. Hackney and New College also had quite high drop-out rates, respectively 11.1 and 13.3 per cent, discounting death and illness.

Of course, not all of those Baptists and Congregationalists who dropped out of their college courses were subsequently lost to the ministry. As Tables 2.2 and 2.3 indicate, some small proportion of the losses represented transfers to other institutions. Again, courses tended to be long. At Stepney and Bristol it was four years, and a similar period was common at the Independent colleges. At Airedale the best qualified students could get through in three years, but weaker ones took five years. Lancashire men did five or six years. At the Baptist's Horton College the four-year course

TABLE 2.3. Student Drop-Out Rates (%): Congregational Colleges

	Hoxton 1791–1825	Highbury 1826–51	Homerton 1830–8	Cheshunt 1847–85	Hackney 1803–1922	New 1851–1900
Number	127	181	31	300	624	580
Cause of leaving						
Death	1.5	2.2	9.6	1.0	1.1	1.6
Illness	0.7		6.4	5.0	3.8	4.8
Education				2.0	5.4	4.6
Transfer				5.0		
Doctrinal				4.0	1.4	
Moral						
Expelled	1.5	1.1		1.6		4.4
Resigned				4.6		4.3
Other	2.3	4.4	6.4	2.3	4.3	
Total Loss	6.0	7.7	22.4	25.5	16.0	19.7

Sources: Hoxton and Highbury figures are calculated from DWL. NCA. 218–357; Homerton from Homerton College, Register of Students, 1831–48, DWL. NCA. 119; Cheshunt from Cheshunt College, Admissions Register, 1847–85, Cheshunt College Archives, C6/2; Hackney from Hackney College, Register of Students, DWL. NCA. 79/3; New College from ibid., 15 3/1.

was extended to five when the college linked with London University in the 1840s and Cheshunt tried to make a similar extension for the same reason in 1869. These long courses were prescribed against a background of continuous nonconformist expansion and chapel building. College trained men were at something of a premium among status-conscious congregations who had the added incentive of striving to show that their particular churches were in no whit inferior to those of the Anglican Establishment which could call upon the products of the ancient universities to man its pulpits. In such a seller's market it is hardly surprising that students were sometimes tempted by an attractive offer of settlement before their studies were finished.

This was not a problem for the Methodist connexions, all of whom made their ministerial appointments annually through a central authority. But among the Old Dissent this outward flow was encouraged by the practice of sending senior students out to preach at weekends. True, the recipient congregations were not always impressed. On the contrary, some complained bitterly about the poor quality. Mr Marsh informed Principal Pye Smith of Homerton on one occasion that while his congregation had been 'much obliged for your kindness' in sending a student preacher, 'the brethren are of opinion that he is too young to occupy our pulpit a second time'.[29] But if a good impression was made and a sufficiently appealing offer of settlement resulted, students sometimes responded positively and withdrew from their college courses prematurely. Edward Miall, who completed only half of his five years at Wymondley, received a very disgruntled note from the trustees when he left. Stepney students had to sign an undertaking that they would not accept invitations to settle before they had finished at college. But since most students were self-financed, the colleges had few sanctions to impose, save perhaps that of an appeal to an individual's sense of honour. When four men left Hoxton prematurely in 1821 all that the trustees could do was to issue a rather limp appeal to the effect that they felt bound 'to state their earnest desire that every student

[29] J. Marsh to J. Pye Smith, 8 Mar. 1849, DWL. NCA. 286/45.

may complete his academical course; and their regret that by sacrificing any portion of it, the permanent advantage of a congregation should be subordinated to its temporary convenience'.[30] In fact, the appeal was counterproductive. An attempt to compel students to provide such an undertaking the following year provoked a number of resignations. Among them was G. S. Woods who felt that such a procedure was incompatible with the principles of Congregationalism. It was, he protested, 'a direct attack on the essential right of churches to elect their own officers ... a procedure manifestly leading to the establishment of a dissenting hierarchy'.[31]

Except in the event of death or sickness, college records do not always specify the precise cause of a particular individual's removal but it is clear that college life sometimes exposed moral flaws, even if they were often disguised in college minute books beneath bland terms such as 'withdrawn' or the harsher 'expelled'. In 1821 the Hoxton committee changed its mind and admitted William Slatterie, the applicant rejected earlier on the grounds of his too recent conversion (see p. 69, above). A few months later, Slatterie was expelled in disgrace, having teamed up with a pair of Welsh students to steal money and a gold watch from other college residents. Others fell foul of the high expectations which college authorities had of their personal conduct. Blackburn threw out a student in 1836 because he had 'fallen into levities and been guilty of indiscretion'.[32] Didsbury sacked nine students in 1855 because they had attended a Manchester theatre in order to see a performance by the celebrated American actor, Edwin Booth. Some students found the demands of corporate life in an intensely Evangelical religious setting too taxing. The rules at Wymondley, for example, required all students to be present at family prayer, morning and evening, a fine being imposed on all absentees. Lecture attendance was compulsory. No gambling was allowed and the resident tutor was charged with

[30] Hoxton Academy, *Report* (1821), pp. vi–vii.
[31] G. S. Woods to Hoxton Committee, 8 Jan. 1822, DWL. NCA. 292/24.
[32] Blackburn Independent Academy, LIC, Register of Students, C–D, Northern College, Manchester.

preventing any 'unreasonable expense of time on recreation'.[33] Students were fined if they rose from bed any later than 6 a.m. in the summer and 7 a.m. in the winter. In colleges that were invariably small—Highbury was one of the largest and it had only forty students in the 1830s—personal differences could easily degenerate into intense animosities. At Homerton in 1831 Pye Smith had to deal with a complaint from the body of students against two of their number who, it was alleged, had displayed undue bad temper, flouted college rules, smoked, borrowed money, and ridiculed all forms of experiential religion. The fact that such men were at college at all perhaps illustrates just how frustrating the ban on university attendance by nonconformists could in practice be.

Nor is it surprising that among Baptists and Congregationalists, both denominations based on notions of individual congregational sovereignty, disciplinary problems of a more overtly 'political' nature should sometimes have surfaced, the more so perhaps in a period when popular radical politics was increasingly concerning itself with ideas of democracy and advocating more popular forms of government. The Homerton trustees ejected half a dozen students who had ganged up to oppose the house rules laid down by Pye Smith in the 1820s. Similar insubordination led to the dismissal of two Hoxton men in 1823, and some years later a number of students resigned from Cheshunt, partly because the trustees would not permit them to meet as a body without the consent of the theological tutor. Individual students, on the other hand, sometimes managed to flout the rules quite flagrantly. If he had any conscience at all James Stallybrass must have wondered to his dying day how he got away with his conduct at Homerton where Pye Smith was not noted for a particularly soft approach. Yet Stallybrass somehow survived, even with the appalling record revealed in Smith's private register of students. Between March and June 1846 he missed thirteen of Smith's weekly classes. In January 1847 another spate of absences occurred, his excuse being that he 'forgot'. By November further dereliction so

---

[33] Wymondley College, Academical Register, DWL. NCA. CT 11.

annoyed Smith that he sent for Stallybrass, who—typically
—failed to appear. In February 1848 he missed yet another
set of classes, ostensibly because he was ill, although Smith
dismissed this as yet another example of his 'sad propensity
to frame excuses'. The spring of 1848 heralded another series
of Smith's lectures and another series of Stallybrass's colds.
By January 1849 he was, if his explanations for repeated
absences can be believed, chronically ill, though his frequent
excursions to nearby towns, all meticulously recorded in
Smith's notes, might suggest otherwise. In November Smith
remonstrated with him 'most severely' but his attendance
continued to be perfunctory until he left for good in the
summer of 1850. It says something for the status which
college products enjoyed in Congregational circles that Stallybrass was able to find a church, his abysmal record notwithstanding. Not surprisingly, he remained in the ministry
for only a couple of years before turning his mind—at last—
to learning and becoming 'a well known educationalist'.[34]

Another quite common cause of student withdrawal was
change of religious belief or conviction, although the
teaching methods and principles, like those in other early
Victorian educational establishments, were certainly not designed to encourage much independent thought and enquiry.
In all subjects, but especially in theology and Scripture
study, all that was required was the rote learning of facts
deemed to be irrefutable. One Blackburn student recalled
that 'we were trained to love and reverence ascertained
truth. Whatever was clearly taught in the inspired Scriptures was regarded as certain, final, authoritative'.[35] The
classics tutor at Cheshunt apologized to the trustees in 1834
because his report was so like those of previous years but, he
explained, his lectures remained the same from year to year
because more was achieved by 'plodding regularity' than by
'attractive varieties of ever changing invention'.[36] The resi-

[34] The comment is Charles Surman's note on Stallybrass's card in the Surman
'Index of Congregational Ministers' housed at Dr Williams's Library. For the details of
Stallybrass's misdemeanours see the Lecture Attendance Register of John Pye Smith,
DWL. NCA. 116/1.

[35] W. Stowell, *Memoirs of the Life and Labours of W. Stowell* (1859), 31.

[36] Report of the Studies in the Classical Department, 30 Apr. 1834, Cheshunt College
Archives, C6/6, Westminster College, Cambridge.

dent tutor agreed: 'The experience of years has only confirmed the judgement which the Resident Tutor had long
before formed—that the regular drilling in those facts of
learning which comprize a good general Education is that
which, under God, tells most in the real and efficient improvement of the students.'[37] Similarly, at Didsbury Thomas
Jackson wrote his lectures out in full, read them to the
students, and then expected their contents to be regurgitated
in the examinations. Except for those with poor memories or
slothful application such an approach was hardly likely to
lead to much difficulty as long as Scriptural inspiration and
authority were widely accepted. In any case, college authorities tended to keep a diligent eye on heterodox tendencies.
The Brecon Committee, for example, called Mr Thomas
Lewis to account in 1844, questioned him closely about his
views, and finally judged him 'correct in his views of Christian Theology'. The committee resolved, however, to exercise
'increased watchfulness . . . in order to prevent the existence
of unsound doctrine in the College'.[38]

Thus most students who left college in the first half of the
nineteenth century over what might be termed doctrinal
issues did so on account of disputes about matters such as
church government, modes of baptism, or the nature of the
Trinity. Baptists were generally held together, however, by
their common subscription to the doctrine of believer's baptism. Wesley's works, an important element in the Theological Institution's curriculum, perhaps performed a similar
function among the Wesleyans although there is evidence of
connexional concern in the 1840s about the drift of former
college men into the Church of England. At the conference of
1844 it was reported that 'the young men were closely ex-
amined, respecting their views of the Establishment—a few
who have been in the Institution, have left us and gone to
the church'.[39] It was in the Congregational colleges that the
scope for doctrinal dispute was widest, probably because as
a denomination the Congregationalists were very suspicious

---

[37] Report of the Resident Tutor, 29 Apr. 1835, ibid.
[38] Brecon Memorial College, Minute Book 1838–67, Minute of 31 Dec. 1844, National
Library of Wales.
[39] T. Garbutt to T. Newton, 8 Aug. 1844, MAM. PLP. 43–16–4.

of set doctrinal creeds and statements. Indeed, the Hackney prospectus of 1791 declared that students would be 'encouraged in forming their sentiments on all controversial subjects without subscription or any other restriction or imposition'.[40] For this reason, the Congregational colleges were to prove most susceptible to the intellectual storms that swept over theological thought in the second half of the century. The first disturbances appeared at New College in 1851. Three students, including William Hale White who later indicted nonconformity behind the pseudonym of Mark Rutherford, were expelled for questioning Scriptural authority and inspiration. White was particularly scathing about the theological tutor's approach. He had 'a course of lectures, delivered year after year to successive generations of his pupils upon ... [biblical] authenticity and inspiration. ... The President's task was all the easier because he knew nothing of German literature ...'.[41]

Finally, some of the student losses were due to intellectual inadequacies and while college records do sometimes specify 'education' as the cause it is likely that some such cases also appear in Tables 2.2 and 2.3 under the 'other' category. Given that the main criteria of entry were piety and preaching ability it was almost inevitable that the breadth and depth of the college courses would prove too formidable, even when students were required mainly to memorize rather than think. Although there were some slight variations between colleges and denominations the general coverage was the same, and not much different from that tackled in the Wesleyan Theological Institution—homiletics, Latin, Greek, biblical history and language, maths, philosophy, logic, English, sometimes a little science and history, and theology, which usually included such matters as Scriptural authority and Christian evidences. The Highbury course in the 1820s may stand as reasonably representative. Dr Henderson, recalled John Stoughton, 'drilled us in the languages of the Old Testament, initiated some small study in Syriac,

[40] 'The New College, Hackney', Haliday Pamphlet Collection, vol. 585, no. 3, Royal Irish Academy.
[41] Mark Rutherford (W. H. White), *The Autobiography of Mark Rutherford, Dissenting Minister* (1881), 13–14.

and delivered elaborate lectures on the evidences and doctrines of Christianity.... He regularly required the careful
preparation of comments on the original Scriptures ...'.[42]
With Dr Halley, he added, they read Greek tragedies and
received lectures on history and antiquities.

As the achievements of both Halley and Stoughton indicate, the colleges did contain individuals, both staff and
students, of undoubted academic and intellectual ability.
But casualties were inevitable, given the underlying philosophy of teaching and the evidence that the overall level of
student ability was not high. William Hale White reckoned
that his contemporaries at New College in the late 1840s
were 'mostly young men of no education ... and their spiritual life was not very deep. In many of them it did not even
exist.'[43] Nor can this be dismissed simply as sour grapes.
Newman Hall agreed, at least about the intellectual level.
Most of his fellows at Highbury in the 1830s had, he suggested, 'scarcely any other qualifications than piety and a
natural fitness for preaching'.[44] It should be remembered
that both White and Hall were writing about the premier
Congregational college. Similarly low standards prevailed
among the Baptists. Entrants to the South Wales college at
Abergavenny were so poor that in 1825 the college committee resolved to admit only those who came with some sort of
adequate testimonial to their educational potential and
achievement. Now it might be argued that Abergavenny's
catchment area, South Wales in the 1820s, was bound to
produce students of mediocre educational backgrounds, but
Bristol, the denomination's oldest institution, had similar
problems. Joseph Kinghorn commented rather tartly of his
fellows at the very end of the eighteenth century, 'it does not
appear to me that there is much genius among them ...'.[45]
There is not much evidence either that things had improved
half a century later.

[42] J. Stoughton, *Recollections of a Long Life* (1894), 17.
[43] Rutherford, *Autobiography*, 17.
[44] N. Hall, *An Autobiography* (1898), 38.
[45] M. H. Wilkin, *J. Kinghorn of Norwich: A Memoir* (Norwich, 1855), 71.

3

Training, c.1860–1914

THE 1870s represented something of a turning-point in the ministry of the Free Churches. The wider opportunities afforded to nonconformists at Oxford and Cambridge, the 1870 Education Act, the establishment of elected school boards, the growth of interest in technical education, the spread of public libraries, and the growing emphasis in later Victorian Britain on public examinations and formal educational qualifications, all generated pressure within non-conformity to improve ministerial quality. 'Ministerial education', Dr Davies told the Baptist Union's autumn assembly in 1867, 'whether in England or Wales, must keep pace with the education of the time. If the attention of the educated is to be secured, and if our cultivated young people are to be retained in the ranks of Nonconformity, the pastor must command their confidence and respect.'[1] As Davies went on to point out, the changing climate of scientific and theological thought was working in the same direction. With a well-prepared ministry, he said, 'there need be no alarm at the progress of science. The church, under such leadership, would be able to hold its own against all antagonists.... There would be no need to fear rationalism on the one hand, or ritualism on the other.'[2] Furthermore, the mid-century building boom had greatly increased the number of pulpits to be manned. H. S. Skeats calculated that between 1851 and 1874 the number of Methodist chapels and preaching places in England and Wales went up by over two and a half thousand. During the same period the Congregationalists

---

[1] B. Davies, 'Ministerial Education in Wales. A Paper Read before the Baptist Union of Great Britain and Ireland at Cardiff, October 1867', in *Cardiff Memorial: Five Papers Read at the Autumnal Session of the Baptist Union of Great Britain and Ireland* (1868), 6.
[2] Ibid. 15.

and the Baptists established 869 and 495 new causes respectively.[3]

The responses to these pressures varied. There was some small institutional expansion among both the Baptists and the Congregationalists. The Baptist Pastor's College became Spurgeon's College, after its founder, and expanded its intake enormously. In 1864 J. B. Paton set up the Nottingham Congregational Institute. Yet the Old Dissenters already had a high proportion of formally trained men entering their ministries. It was among the Methodists that the scope for improvement was largest and the institutional response most apparent. The Wesleyans expanded the capacity of the Theological Institution by opening a fourth branch at Handsworth in Birmingham in 1881, while the non-Wesleyan connexions all endeavoured to regularize the rather *ad hoc* arrangements which had hitherto prevailed. The New Connexion opened Ranmoor College in 1864. Shortly afterwards the United Methodist Free Churches opened an institution at Victoria Park in Manchester. Even the Bible Christians, poorest and smallest of the Methodist connexions, took steps, although not until the 1890s, to provide a year's ministerial training in their school at Shebbear. In 1901 a New Century Fund appeal was launched for £25,000. One of its objectives was to purchase a house in Cardiff which was to provide a further year of training for those who had completed the course at Shebbear. In the event, however, it was never opened. The Bible Christian merger in 1907 with the New Connexion and Free Methodists enabled their men to avail themselves of existing facilities at Ranmoor and Victoria Park. The establishment of a more comprehensive secular education system compelled some redefinition of attitudes among the Primitives too, although it is doubtful if a majority of them would have gone so far as the editor of the connexional newspaper, who had clearly succumbed very fully to the educators' blandishments:

The rustic dwellers in our villages, as well as the inhabitants of the large towns and cities, are better able to appreciate the truths of

---

[3] H. S. Skeats, 'Statistics Relative to the Support of Religious Institutions in England and Wales', *Journal of the Statistical Society*, 39 (1876), 333.

the gospel when they are presented decently and in order, and accompanied with the gifts and graces of a cultivated mind, than when they are flung pell mell from the voluble mouths of ignorant and totally unlettered men.[4]

The editorial went on to appeal for funds for the training institute which had been at work in Sunderland since the late 1860s. Changed perceptions by themselves were not enough, however. Only the generous intervention of William Hartley, the jam manufacturer, enabled sufficient funds to be raised and Hartley College opened in Manchester in 1881.

The results of this quite extensive development of ministerial training among the various Methodist connexions are seen in Table 2.1. Over 90 per cent of those entering the Wesleyan ministry between 1880 and 1909 had been educated at college or college and university. The rather lower figure for the Primitives, 77 per cent, reflected both their later start and the fact that they often had an insufficient supply of men for the available vacancies and many were sent directly into circuit work. In 1891, for example, Hartley turned out only fourteen men, although forty were required. The relatively late start by the New Connexion and the United Methodist Free Churches coupled with the low contribution of the Bible Christians, served to keep down the proportion of college trained men within their ranks to 58 per cent. Generally, however, as Table 2.1 indicates, the proportion of trained men entering the ministries of the two largest Methodist connexions between 1880 and 1909 compared very favourably with the proportion going into Baptist and Congregational pulpits, 73 and 75 per cent respectively. This should not be allowed to obscure the fact, however, that continued restraints of finance ensured that Methodist courses remained comparatively short. Until 1892 the course at Hartley was only one year although it was brought up to three in 1906. Ranmoor's two years was similarly topped up in 1910. By the end of the century about a half of Wesleyan students were getting a third year at college.

It is also clear that the overall level of academic

---

[4] *Primitive Methodist*, 23 Mar. 1871.

TABLE 3.1. Nonconformist Ministers: Higher Education Qualifications (%) (including Honorary Degrees)

	1810–39	1820–49	1830–59	1840–69	1850–79	1860–89	1870–99	1880–99	1890–1909	1900–1929
DEGREES										
Wes.		7.6	5.9	4.1	2.2	3.1	9.4	13.4	16.0	14.5
Prim.				1.7	2.3	3.6	2.8	1.6	2.9	6.7
United				1.8	2.6	3.7	4.5	3.8	5.1	10.3
Bapt.		7.6	7.8	6.6	4.2	5.9	10.6	17.1	21.5	26.4
Cong.	7.4	12.2	13.2	15.5	13.9	16.5	20.6	25.0	29.7	31.3
ATS/FTS										
Wes.										
Prim.										
United										
Bapt.					0.6	0.4	4.6	6.0	6.9	2.8
Cong.						0.9	6.8	10.2	10.2	4.0

attainment among the Methodists was generally inferior to
that of the older nonconformists. Most of the connexions
were shot through with a certain amount of anti-intellectual
prejudice. None of them had been involved in the discussions
which had led in 1879 to the establishment of the Senatus
Academicus, a medium designed to provide a common curriculum and examination system for nonconformist theological students. Thus, as Table 3.1 shows, no Methodist possessed an ATS diploma or fellowship. It is also apparent that
little importance was attached by Methodists to the pursuit
of university qualifications, certainly not when compared
with the Baptists and Congregationalists. Indeed, J. E. Rat-
tenbury reckoned that as a denomination the Wesleyans
positively 'discouraged pursuit of university degrees'.[5] Not
until 1912 did the Wesleyans decide to go ahead with the
idea of establishing a ministerial hostel in Cambridge,
although it was delayed by the war.

By contrast, the Baptists and Congregationalists had
sought to foster links with the universities long before the
ban on entry to Oxford and Cambridge was removed. Highbury, Stepney, and Airedale all linked up with London University in the 1840s, as did Horton in the next decade. The
opening of the provincial universities afforded similar
opportunities, Bristol Baptist establishing contact with the
local university in 1879, for example. It was also the Baptists
and Congregationalists who gave most enthusiastic support
to the Senatus Academicus. In part, this enthusiasm was
the natural inclination of denominations which had well-
established traditions of formal education for their ministers. Bristol had long encouraged its men to proceed to the
Scottish universities, as had the larger Congregational institutions. There had also been a considerable influx of
university-trained Scots into the ranks of Congregationalism
in the 1840s, following the disruptions in the Scottish
Church in those years. But the real expansion of higher
education, as seen in Table 3.1, occurred quite clearly with
the generations entering the ministry after 1870. The grow-

[5] Quoted in W. B. Brash and C. J. Wright, *Didsbury College Centenary, 1842–1942*
(1942), 101.

ing accessibility of Oxford and Cambridge to nonconformists encouraged them to consider the establishment of their own institutions in the ancient university towns. The Congregationalists opened Mansfield College at Oxford and Cheshunt moved to Cambridge in 1905. The Baptists were slower, not moving to Oxford until 1930. Even so, of the generation which entered the ministry between 1880 and 1909 almost a quarter of Baptists and over a third of Congregationalists held degrees or ATS diplomas. Despite the fears that were sometimes expressed in the denominational press that some ministers were availing themselves of the opportunity to acquire bogus American or European degrees, these were all qualifications obtained from British institutions.[6]

Yet despite the extensions of training facilities and the general increase in the acquisition of formal qualifications which occurred between 1870 and 1914, the evidence suggests strongly that all was not well with nonconformist ministerial education. By the end of the century it appears to have been in a state of crisis. Money was a chronic and ubiquitous problem. Didsbury and Richmond had been financed from the Wesleyan Centenary Fund and Handsworth from the Thanksgiving Fund, but the Theological Institution had never attracted much tangible support from the circuits. It was in the hope of stimulating such support that in 1860 the Wesleyan authorities decided that an address should be given on behalf of the Institution at the commencement of each annual session. Yet only a few years after it opened Handsworth was a candidate for closure on financial grounds. The 1881 Conference resolved that two annual collections should be taken in every circuit in order to raise money for ministerial education, but these did not produce very much for in 1903 a special appeal for funds was sanctioned. Even though this became an annual appeal the recurrence of inflation after 1900 exerted an adverse effect on the colleges' finances and the resulting difficulties dominated discussion at the Representative Session of the

---

[6] The *Christian World* was sued in 1903 for suggesting that Charles Garrett had purchased his DD degree from a bogus American institution for £18. This traffic in fake degrees is explored in R. Belcher, *Degrees and Degrees: or, Traffic in Theological, Medical and Other 'Diplomas' Exposed* (1872).

1908 Conference. The Primitives were similarly handi-
capped. Their main source of income—student fees of £30
a year—did not amount to very much when the first intake
of ten students assembled in 1881 at a college which could
accommodate thirty. An appeal in 1887 for every circuit
member to contribute to a levy of a halfpenny per head received only three favourable replies and it is doubtful if the
college could have survived, still less expanded both its
accommodation and course length, without the continued
generosity of Hartley.

Neither the Baptists nor Congregationalists had exercised
any central bureaucratic control over ministerial recruitment and training, even after the establishment of national
denominational unions. There was nothing to prevent any
group from opening a college or training institution. Nor,
indeed, given the independence which characterized both
denominations, could any such controls have been imposed.
The result was that both were served by a plethora of generally small, often overlapping and competing institutions of
variable quality. Their financial security, even in the case of
some of the older, better endowed foundations, had always
been quite precarious. Apart from board and lodging students at Congregational academies in the first half of the
century were required to pay between £20 (Homerton in the
1820s) and £30 (Airedale and Cheshunt) a year for tuition.
Given that most institutions had not more than about a
dozen students a year and that tutors' salaries were
generous—the Theological Tutor at Cheshunt got £200 a
year in the 1820s, his equivalent at Airedale £250—it is easy
to see why even larger colleges like Highbury lived very
much hand to mouth.[7] In 1842 the Highbury *Report* pointed
out that while the current year's deficit of £700 had been
eliminated by dint of stringent economies, there still remained an accumulated debt of £714 to be paid off.[8] All
colleges, no matter how large or small, depended very heavily for their financial viability on the generosity of individual

[7] These details of salaries are from 'Allowances to W. Kemp', Sept. 1821, Cheshunt College Archives, C9/6/8, Westminster College, Cambridge; Airedale Independent Academy, *Report* (1826), 8.
[8] Highbury College, *Report* (1842), 3.

subscribers to supplement what could be raised from student fees and preaching tours undertaken by students and staff alike. Hoxton and Highbury, for instance, were frequently helped out by the extensive financial generosity of the Wilson family.[9] In 1827 Bristol Baptist derived over half of its income from donations given by private individuals or single congregations. This was just about adequate while nonconformity was still expanding and thus sustaining both the demand for college trained men and the financial resources to support the training institutions, although some of the Baptist colleges were experiencing financial difficulties even in the 1840s. It was in the second half of the century that the financial problems began to mount, however.

Apart from the stimulus provided to the Baptists by the revival of 1859–60, nonconformity was no longer expanding so rapidly into new areas of society and winning new converts. But demands on individual nonconformist pockets were increasing. Over and above any local needs, denominational authorities appealed repeatedly for finance, not just for college expansion but also to underwrite the mid-century chapel building boom, extend missionary activity, upgrade ministerial salaries, establish pension funds, and support growing central bureaucracies. The resentments that such demands could sometimes engender were encountered by an unfortunate Abergavenny student who had undertaken a preaching tour in Wales during the 1880s to raise funds for his college. One local Baptist Association chairman, he reported, 'sent forth a cataract of words upon me, denouncing denominational colleges, stating . . . that he would subscribe no more to institutions that had no object in view but to keep tutors in good livings'.[10] Henry Reynolds, Principal of Cheshunt, claimed in 1879 that 'the general interest in our work has been at the lowest point possible for our continued existence'.[11] The adverse effects of this situation were felt most in the smaller colleges. Cheshunt's finances were so

---

[9] For the contribution of Thomas Wilson see the memoir by his son: J. Wilson, *Memoir of the Life and Character of Thomas Wilson Esq.* (1849).

[10] D. M. Himbury, 'A Student on Collecting Tour in 1885', *Baptist Quarterly*, 17 (1957–8), 159.

[11] *Henry Robert Reynolds DD, his Life and Letters. Edited by His Sisters, with Portraits* (1898), 315.

strained that it could not afford to replace the principal
when he resigned in 1905. But even the larger colleges were
feeling the pressure by the turn of the century. By 1907
private donations provided only a quarter of Bristol's annual
income.[12] At Hackney, P. T. Forsyth's years as principal
(1901–22) were dogged by constant financial problems.[13]
· With finances under such pressure in some colleges
efficient use of resources was clearly called for, particularly
when the existing structure was also judged to be educa-
tionally defective. At a time when the demand was for better
quality training it was indefensible, as A. L. Bowser, Principal of Midland Baptist College, argued, for a single individual to be expected, as he was, to act as principal, and
as professor of biblical languages, theology, and church
history.[14] Proposals for rationalization filled the columns of
the Baptist and Congregational press and occupied the discussions of delegates at annual assemblies. A Rawdon student
suggested halving the number of Baptist colleges.[15] J. H.
Shakespeare made a similar suggestion for amalgamation
at the Baptist Union conference in 1891. Witton Davies,
another college principal, recommended the establishment
of a board of management, central funding, and a tiered
system of admission which would take in students at a level
appropriate to their educational background and pass them
up to higher institutions over a period of years.[16] Similar
ideas were floated among the Congregationalists but local
loyalties and college traditions were in many cases too
strong to allow of any very radical steps in this direction.
'The tendency of each College', said a Cheshunt memoran-
dum in 1902, 'is to fight for its own hand ...'[17] It is true that
Western College merged with the Bristol Theological Institute in 1897 but Yorkshire and Lancashire colleges got no
further than preliminary discussions in 1906. Financial

[12] N. S. Moon, *Education for Ministry: Bristol Baptist College, 1679–1979* (Bristol, 1979), 145.
[13] S. Cave, 'Dr P. T. Forsyth: The Man and His Writings', *Congregational Quarterly*, 26 (1948), 111.
[14] W. J. Avery, 'The Late Midland College', *Baptist Quarterly*, 1 (1922–3), 33.
[15] *Baptist*, 15 July 1892.
[16] Midland College, *Centenary Report* (1896–7), 6–7.
[17] Cheshunt College, Trustees Minute Book, 3 June 1902, Cheshunt College Archives, C1/19, Westminster College, Cambridge.

pressures helped to promote an amalgamation of some Welsh Baptist institutions but co-operation between Rawdon and Midland lasted only briefly. Talks of a link between New College and Spring Hill also came to nothing. For the rest, there was some shared teaching, for example between Hackney Congregational and Regent's Park Baptist.

The college crisis was not merely a matter of finance and organization, however. It was also a problem of manpower. In 1876 one college principal confided in Eustace Conder that the situation in the colleges was 'most grave and anxious ... supply is very deficient, both in quantity and quality'.[18] It was an anxiety that was to increase as growth rates continued to decelerate, and denominational leaders tried to stem the losses by improving the quality and supply of ministers. The problem of supply did not become acute among the Wesleyans until the immediate pre-war years but even in 1901 the annual Pastoral Address of the Conference was sounding a warning note: 'We would affectionately invite young men of piety and culture amongst us, prayerfully to consider whether the call to the service of the Lord Christ which they have received might not include a call to the work of the ministry.'[19] The other Methodists were suffering more severely. In 1914, only twelve men applied for the ministry in the United connexion, while the number of recruits for the Primitive ministry was only half of what it had been in 1900. Falling numbers hit the Congregationalists hardest of all. Lancashire Independent College's average annual intake of students fell by half between 1840–69 and 1900–10.[20] At Cheshunt the annual intake averaged 7.8 students between 1847 and 1855. Between 1900 and 1910 it was down to 4.5 a year and the college, which had won the theological colleges' football tournament in the 1890s, could not field a team at all in the first years of the twentieth century.[21] Baptist experience was more mixed. Admissions to the most popular college, Spurgeon's, rose from 21.4 a

---

[18] *Congregational Yearbook* (1876), 131.
[19] Wesleyan Conference, *Minutes* (1901), 419.
[20] Calculated from LIC, Register of Students, A–Z, Northern College, Manchester.
[21] Cheshunt College, Admissions Register, 1847–85, and 1900–10, Cheshunt College Archives, C6/5, Westminster College, Cambridge.

year between 1860 and 1869 to 26.1 between 1880 and 1889.[22] At Bristol, on the other hand, the annual intake declined from six between 1840 and 1869 to just over four after 1900, and total student numbers began to decline steadily after 1899.[23]

Because we are dealing essentially with matters of past human motivation it is difficult to know exactly why recruitment began to decline. It would certainly be unwise to isolate any single cause, especially as the Church of England was suffering from a similar problem. In 1908 the Lambeth Conference set up a special commission to investigate why recruitment had fallen from 870 new priests in 1885 to 650 by 1900.[24] What can be done, however, is to construct a framework of explanation which combines several different contemporary trends. In the early nineteenth century the ideas of divine call to the ministry and the necessity of encouraging individual conversion were undoubtedly very strong motivators to ministerial careers, especially among the Methodists and Baptists, a little less so, perhaps, for the Congregationalists. Thus James Thorne recalled of his summons to the ministry: 'My love for souls daily increased, and at the same time I cared not for anything in this world. I saw its vanity, and all my desire was to get holiness myself and promote it among others ...'[25] Henry Hebron, a Primitive Methodist, wrote to a friend in 1831 that 'we are praying hard for a revival ... I feel a greater desire than ever to be useful in bringing souls to God. O that I had more fruit for my labours.'[26] Similarly, Mr Pollard told the Homerton Committee in 1836 that he wished to become a minister because, having been saved himself, he 'immediately felt a desire that others might be brought to an experimental acquaintance with the same great and momentous subjects'.[27] Even when religious convictions became rather less certain

[22] Calculated from lists in Spurgeon's College, *Report* (1860–9; 1880–9).
[23] Calculated from the index of students kept at the Baptist College, Bristol. For total student numbers see J. Munson, 'The Education of Baptist Ministers, 1870–1914', *Baptist Quarterly*, 26 (1976), 324.
[24] A. J. Russell, *The Clerical Profession* (1980), 242.
[25] F. W. Bourne, *The Centenary Life of James Thorne of Shebbear* (1985), 29.
[26] Anon., *Earnest Men: Sketches of Eminent Primitive Methodists* (1872), 79.
[27] R. Pollard to the Homerton Committee, 1836, DWL. NCA. 307/5/1/.

in the late nineteenth century there were still those, for example most of the students at Spurgeon's College, who clung to the belief in the existence of hell and the need for personal salvation.

Of course, less well-defined theological outlooks did not necessarily deter men from going into the ministry but at the spring assembly of the Baptist Union in 1914 the Principal of Regent's Park quoted with some despair the findings of an American scholar, Johnson Ross: 'It is getting to be an appalling feature of the present generation, that young persons seek to enter upon the work of the missionary, or the minister, who have apparently no religious interest ... they just want to *do something* ...'[28] But for others who had also embraced the gospel of good works the imperative to enter the ministry might well have seemed less urgent. Salvation was a message to be preached, good works were actions to be done and while, as Principal Gould's comments indicate, it would be wrong to make too clear a distinction between the speakers and the doers, it is apparent that many contemporaries believed that preaching was the primary task of a minister, whereas anyone could undertake good works.[29] Both inside and outside the Church specialist agencies concerned with welfare, recreation, and education sprang up, agencies to which the young nonconformist could perhaps feel just as called as his grandfather had been to the ministry. W. T. Stead, for instance, himself the son of a Congregationalist pastor, was persuaded that journalism could be as potent a medium as the pulpit for the propagation of Christian righteousness.[30] Furthermore, his career showed that by the late nineteenth century the ministry was no longer the only road to prominence within the Church. In virtually all the main nonconformist denominations there were lay figures as well known and as powerful as the leading ministers. Wesleyanism had its Lunn and Perks, Primitive Methodism its Hartley, Congregationalism its Spicer.

---

[28] *Baptist Handbook* (1914), 285.
[29] See, for example, the comments made by W. F. Adeney when he retired from the Lancashire Independent College: *Christian World*, 1 May 1913.
[30] J. O. Baylen, 'The "New Journalism" in Late Victorian Britain', *Australian Journal of Politics and History*, 18 (1972), 368.

Declining recruitment was, however, more than merely a question of changing perceptions of the minister's role. For some, the ministry was no longer as attractive a career as it had once been, in terms of either income or status. That such apparently ignoble motives did attract some men into the ministry was suggested by the *Congregational Magazine* in 1844. Young men, the paper claimed, were going forth 'not so much as labourers in the vine-yard of Christ as inquirers for an easy place, a good salary, and respectability'.[31] But by the end of the century, if the evidence of the denominational press is to be believed, it was widely held that ministerial incomes and conditions were, on average, much inferior to those available elsewhere, especially in the mushrooming white-collar sector which was freely blamed by contemporaries for the fall in ministerial recruitment. Certainly among Anglicans the evidence suggests that the sons of clergymen were increasingly opting for these better paid alternatives, rather than following their fathers into the priesthood.[32] Unfortunately, there is no comparable evidence available for the general body of nonconformist ministers' children, except for some material relating to the careers followed by boys who attended Kingswood School, the institution for the sons of Wesleyan ministers. This information is analysed in Table 3.2 and appears to suggest a marked similarity of experience as between Wesleyans and Anglicans. First of all, there was a consistent diminution in the number of sons going into the ministry, a trend which became more pronounced after 1890. Secondly, even if we discount those going into the white-collar sections of 'business', the proportion of those who found employment in strictly white-collar occupations—teaching, the civil service, banking, journalism, accounting, and clerical work—increased from 20.3 per cent in 1840–9 to 37 per cent in 1890–8.

This evidence relates only to the Wesleyans and cannot be substantiated for other denominations. However, Table 3.3

[31] *Congregational Magazine* (1844), 127.

[32] For the Anglican evidence see A. P. M. Coxon, 'Patterns of Occupational Recruitment: the Anglican Ministry', *Sociology*, 1 (1967), 73–9; and A. G. L. Haig, *The Victorian Clergy. An Ancient Profession under Strain* (1984). 305 ff. For an example of nonconformist concern, which is discussed more fully in Chapter 4 below, see the remarks made by Stowell Brown in *Baptist Handbook* (1879), 64.

TABLE 3.2. Subsequent Careers of Kingswood School Boys, 1800–98

Years of Leaving	1800–9	1810–19	1820–9	1830–9	1840–9	1850–9	1860–9	1870–9	1880–9	1890–8
Total Leaving	75	95	120	243	194	262	283	326	539	411
Number of known jobs	26	28	52	131	122	150	192	280	459	217
As a percentage of the total leavers										
Wesleyan Ministry	20.0	10.5	12.5	14.4	14.4	10.6	12.7	12.2	12.2	3.1
Anglican Ministry	1.3	1.0		4.5	5.7	1.5	5.6	3.9	1.4	
Other Ministry		1.0			0.5	0.7	0.3	0.9	0.5	0.2
As a percentage of those whose subsequent jobs are known										
Farming				3.0	1.6	2.0	7.3	0.7	3.5	5.5
Medicine				11.5	4.0	10.6	3.6	5.7	6.1	1.8
Law				1.5	2.5	2.6	4.7	4.6	3.2	8.3
Pharmacy				6.1	6.6	8.0	0.5	5.4	7.6	3.2
Architect								1.1	1.9	3.2
Dentist					0.8	2.0	1.6	0.3	0.4	2.3
Engineering				0.7	2.4	1.3	1.0	4.6	3.9	10.1
Sea					0.8	2.0	3.6	1.8		0.4
The Arts				0.7		0.6	0.5	0.3	1.0	0.5
Business				26.7	27.0	28.6	25.0	18.9	21.3	22.1
Education				9.1	10.6	5.3	10.9	15.0	15.4	11.5
Civil Service					1.6	4.6	4.1	5.3	3.0	5.0
Banking					0.8	1.3	1.5	5.3	5.9	8.7
Journalism				0.7	2.4	1.3	1.5	1.0	1.0	0.4
Accounting				0.7	0.8	2.0		1.8	1.3	4.1
Clerical				2.3	4.1	4.6	3.1	3.5	5.7	7.3
Miscellaneous				1.5	0.8		3.1	4.3	1.5	1.8

Source: Based on 'Registers of Names, 1748–1897, pp. 1–127', in A. H. Hastling et al., *The History of Kingswood School* (1898).

indicates clearly that, despite the growing tendency for Wesleyan sons not to follow their fathers, the proportion of ministerial sons in the ministry actually increased. This suggests that the ministry was becoming even less attractive to the generality of nonconformist youth. Nor was this just a matter of salaries. It was also evident that the status which nonconformist ministers had enjoyed in earlier times was changing by the end of the century. It was no longer an automatic concomitant of the ministerial office but appeared to depend more and more on the personality of the incumbent. Ministerial education needed to be improved, said the chairman of the Hackney College committee in 1895, because respect for the actual office was much diminished and people would no longer listen simply because a man had a title.[33]

Concern with the failing supply of ministerial recruits was coupled with alarm about an apparent deterioration in quality, an alarm also being expressed in contemporary Anglican circles.[34] Now it may be that this was a reflection of the rising proportion of men, especially among the Baptists and Methodists, being drawn from social classes IV and V (see Chapter 1, above). On the other hand, any qualitative decline might have been more apparent than real, representing not a catastrophic fall in standards but rather the rise in levels of education in the population at large. After all, as we saw in the previous chapter, standards had not been uniformly high in the past. Yet there is no gainsaying the evidence of alarm, however realistic its basis. As early as 1876 Baptist leaders were drawing attention to the 'lessened number and lower quality of the men who seek ... admission to our ministry'.[35] Principal Whitehouse told the Cheshunt Trustees in 1902 that many students were being admitted to the colleges without any regard for their educational suitability.[36] P. T. Forsyth found the students at Hackney to

[33] *Independent and Nonconformist*, 20 June 1895.
[34] Thus Hensley Henson in 1913 agreed with Bishop Westcott's complaint that increasingly it was 'second rate stuff' that was taking holy orders: D. L. Edwards, *Leaders of the Church of England, 1828–1944* (Oxford, 1971), 334.
[35] *Baptist Handbook* (1876), 95.
[36] Cheshunt College, Trustees Minute Book, 3 June 1902, Cheshunt College Archives, C1/19, Westminster College, Cambridge.

TABLE 3.3. Proportion of Ministers with Ministerial Fathers (%)

	1840–69	1850–79	1860–89	1870–99	1880–1909	1890–1919
Baptist			7.2	9.8	14.4	Not valid
Congregational	14.7	14.8	13.8	18.7	21.5	20.4
Wesleyan		6.6	6.9	12.0	12.2	12.8

be of generally low calibre and urged the churches to find
ways of sending better men forward for the ministry.[37] He
found some support from the editor of the *Christian World*
who claimed that many serving Congregational ministers
should never have been allowed into college in the first
place.[38]

It was among the Methodists, however, that concern with
quality was paramount. The Primitives had been exercised
on this score for some years. In 1906 almost two in five of the
ministerial applicants were rejected and the following year
the connexion accepted only thirty-two of the ninety-five
men who applied. Principal Jones Davies of Hartley made
few friends for speaking out so openly but he was merely
airing publicly what many Primitives had known privately
for some time. He was getting poor men, he said, and could
not make brains out of wool or a peal of bells out of cracked
metal.[39] Many Wesleyan ministerial students, said George
Findlay, a tutor at Headingley, had no more than the most
elementary education with the result that college professors
were having to do the work of secondary school masters.
He reckoned that two-thirds of their trainees fell into this
category and in 1902 the Didsbury Committee urged that the
whole system of ministerial training should be reorganized
because so many of the candidates lacked the basic rudiments of education.[40] In 1912, well after the Headingley
Committee had lent its support to the Didsbury campaign,
J. W. Lightley, a college tutor, was deploring the fact that
many of the newer students 'betrayed a scanty acquaintance

[37] Cave, p. 111. See also Forsyth's letter to *Christian World*, 24 Oct. 1901.
[38] *Christian World*, 7 Nov. 1901.
[39] Ibid. 20 June 1912.
[40] Didsbury Management Committee Executive Minutes, 24 Sept. 1902, Didsbury
College Archives, A1/2/3, Wesley College, Bristol.

with the elementary facts of the English Bible'.[41] Some general enquiries were instituted and in 1912, a year after the Wesleyans turned down 40 per cent of their applicants, an examination was prescribed to ensure minimum levels of education for all ministerial candidates.

The third main element in the college crisis of the late nineteenth century—again one that had its counterpart among the Anglicans—concerned the actual content of the college courses. There was first of all the question of the attitude to be adopted towards the new works of biblical scholarship and science which together appeared to undermine the doctrine of biblical infallibility. The Methodist response was initially hostile and always remained suspicious. A. S. Peake, who did much to modernize the syllabus at Hartley, recalled that when he first went to Manchester in 1891 it was 'antiquated' and 'most inadequate'.[42] Although the Wesleyans commissioned the Revd W. H. Dallinger to try and develop some reconciliation between Christianity and evolutionary theory, Dallinger's acceptance of Darwin's views was exceptional. As late as the 1880s the editor of the *Wesleyan Methodist Magazine*, Benjamin Gregory, still accepted the verbal inspiration of the Bible. It was hardly surprising, therefore, that one Wesleyan claimed to have left college in 1887 'without ever having so much as heard of the "Problem of the Old Testament"'.[43] Another confessed later that he and his peers had been

sublimely unconscious of the movements of destruction and reconstruction which the historians can now see were already at work. The Darwinian hypothesis did not disturb the Didsbury of my day. Karl Marx was never mentioned, and as for Biblical criticism, all we knew was that Wellhausen, Ewald, and Kuenen were slain three times a week by our Theological Tutor .... we were behind the times ... and lived in strange ignorance of what was transpiring in the world of thought.[44]

[41] Headingley Management Committee Executive Minutes, 18 Dec. 1912. Headingley College Archives, B1/3/2, Wesley College, Bristol.
[42] L. S. Peake, *A. S. Peake: A Memoir* (1930), 103, 110.
[43] F. H. Cumbers (ed.), *Richmond College, 1843–1943* (1943), 72.
[44] Brash and Wright, p. 97. Anglicans suffered in the same way: see B. Heeney, *A Different Kind of Gentleman. Parish Clergy as Professional Men in Early and Mid-Victorian England* (Hamden, Conn., 1976), 41. See also D. Bebbington, 'The Persecution of George Jackson: a British Fundamentalist Controversy', *Studies in Church History*, 21 (1984).

W. T. Davison, a Richmond tutor, was investigated by a special committee of the Theological Institution because complaints were made that he was not sufficiently critical of the findings of the modern biblical scholarship. Again, when the appointment of George Jackson as resident tutor at Didsbury was mooted in 1913, considerable opposition erupted within the connexion from those who felt that Jackson's Fernley Lecture of 1912 had appeared to accept, albeit to a modest degree, biblical criticism. Nationally, there was a great deal of theological conservatism well entrenched within Wesleyanism, especially among ordinary chapel members. It was such a conservatism that caused one old man to vow that he would never again sit under the ministry of Raymond Preston, a minister who, in his eyes, had fallen from grace completely by playing cricket.[45] But even the most conservative must have been aware, however vaguely, of the challenges presented by the new modes of scientific and theological thought. They were challenges that Methodist ministers were singularly ill-equipped to meet. What was the point, demanded one irate 'ex-Methodist' of continuing to train ministers on Wesley's sermons and his *Notes on the Old Testament*? 'The doctrinal standards of 150 years ago are not applicable to modern conditions.'[46]

Baptist response to the new scholarship was rather more mixed but equally divisive within the denomination. In 1870 the current president of the Baptist Union said that to the best of his belief Baptists were 'freer than most others from the mournful scepticism by which multitudes are shaken'.[47] Yet Regent's Park was shortly to expel students for embracing modernist views, while T. G. Rooke, Principal of Rawdon from 1876, took a liberal view of biblical criticism. So, too, did Thomas Goadby of Midland College. If the Didsbury tutors were busy slaying Ewald, Goadby just as enthusiastically extolled his virtues, believing that the new learning should be discussed and incorporated, 'a truer exegesis as the basis of a broad evangelical faith'.[48] It was this sort of

[45] W. K. Greenland, *Raymond Preston* (1930), 58.
[46] *Christian World*, 21 Sept. 1911.
[47] *Baptist Handbook* (1871), 14.
[48] B. and L. Goadby, *Not Saints But Men; or the Story of the Goadby Ministers* (1906), p. xi.

approach which so alarmed the most fervent Baptist champion of evangelical orthodoxy, C. H. Spurgeon. In 1887 he left the Baptist Union, accusing some of its members of compromising evangelical truth. His college stood as the bastion of traditional orthodoxy and the founder's views naturally communicated themselves to the bulk of his students. A survey of 1888 revealed that very few of them had been 'infected with the heresy that is working such sad havoc ...', the significance of this lying in the fact that by 1891 over a fifth of all Baptist ministers had been trained in Spurgeon's.[49]

It was the Congregational colleges that were most disturbed by the impact of the new theology, however. The first serious dissensions had occurred as early as 1851 when New College expelled three men, including W. H. White (Mark Rutherford), for questioning whether the whole Bible was equally inspired. Samuel Davidson was more or less compelled to resign his tutorship at Lancashire because he also had doubted the Mosaic authorship of the Pentateuch. Archibald Duff of Yorkshire was rather more fortunate, surviving a college investigation into his views on the Old Testament. On the other side, Reynolds and Whitehouse at Cheshunt and A. E. Cave at Hackney took a conservative stance. It was another college principal, P. T. Forsyth, who admitted in 1905 that 'as a whole we have never really faced the spiritual situation created by the collapse of Biblical infallibility for communities that had long ago repudiated the final authority of the Church'.[50] Forsyth himself worked to emphasize the dynamics of personal conviction and church order which did much to hold Congregationalism together during these difficult years but there is little doubt that the denomination's colleges were in a state of some disarray. Whether they ignored or incorporated the new learning they could not avoid criticism from some affronted party. There was an added significance to this in that the colleges acted—as, to a lesser extent, Wesleyan and Baptist institutions did also—as barometers of denominational health. They were resource

---

[49] T. Medhurst to D. Gracey, 11 Feb. 1888, Spurgeon's College Archives, Cupboard A1. The Spurgeon's material has not been formally catalogued.
[50] *Congregational Yearbook* (1906), 73.

centres for both manpower and scholarship, while their heads were figures of major importance in the lives of their respective denominations.

Criticism also came on an even wider front about the inappropriateness of the colleges' training for the late nineteenth century. Anglicans like Charles Masterman were making similar complaints about their Church's training programmes, suggesting that college trained priests knew nothing of science, economics, or social conditions.[51] Nonconformist critics were equally voluble. In a series of articles and essays George Findlay, a Headingley tutor, drew attention to this defect of Wesleyan preparation. Since the Theological Institution had been established and the curriculum defined, he argued, the whole emphasis of life in Britain had shifted to the urban, industrial centres. It was there, he argued, that thought was keenest and social problems most acute, yet ministerial training made no allowance for it. As a result, he continued,

Christian ministers in our large towns will find themselves at a loss without some exact knowledge of economic and industrial questions ... if ministers were more familiar with these matters and more in touch by study as well as sympathy with the wants and thinkings of the labouring multitude, we should not have so much occasion to grieve over our empty churches ...[52]

Yet when S. E. Keeble suggested in the 1890s that sociology be added to the colleges' curriculum he was told that the Institution's General Committee thought such a step premature. Henry Bisseker expressed a common view when he argued instead that acquaintance with such practical matters was best made during rather than before the career. Introducing such questions into college courses would lead inevitably to consideration of their solution and this, he feared, would produce internal dissension.[53] By 1909, however, Conference had accepted completely the need for the curriculum to contain 'the systematic study of social

[51] C. F. G. Masterman, *The Heart of England* (Harvester ed., 1973), 44.
[52] G. Findlay, 'The Better Education of the Ministry', *London Quarterly Review*, 98 (1902), 112–13.
[53] *Methodist Recorder*, 5 Jan. 1911.

facts and problems'.[54] Pastoral training had been included in the Ranmoor courses right from the college's inception and United Methodists were, therefore, rather better served in this respect. Surprisingly perhaps, it was virtually non-existent among the Primitives. When Jones Davies published his lectures on the work of the ministry in 1910, the first nine chapters were devoted to the minutiae of sermon preparation. The second half of the book, which was intended to cover the pastoral aspects of ministry, concentrated almost exclusively on matters of church organization and administration. Only three chapters dealt with pastoral care as it would now be understood.[55] Probably this was why a connexional committee, appointed to examine the content of ministerial training, reported in favour of a greater emphasis on pastoral work. Once again, however, finance proved the insuperable barrier to extending the courses and staffing in the recommended directions.

Similar complaints surfaced among the Baptists and Congregationalists as well. Pye Smith had included pastoral theology in the Homerton curriculum but its relevance by 1900 was questionable, certainly to one Congregational pastor who accused the colleges of filling their men with antipathy to visitation. 'We want in every college a Chair of Pastoral Theology. Our young men can do with a little less comparative religion, and a little more knowledge as to how to deal with the men and women of England today ... Congregational and Baptist churches are in supreme need of devoted pastors.'[56] True perhaps, but it is doubtful if much good would have been achieved if the patronizing approach of one Rawdon student was typical. Urging greater visitation, he pressed his audience to remember 'the pleasure it affords them, one and all, to grasp your hand, to hear your voice in their sometimes humble homes ...'.[57] At Cheshunt the students virtually compelled the principal to resign in 1905 because, they complained, his lectures were 'not sufficiently in touch with their practical requirements as

[54] Wesleyan Conference, *Minutes* (1909), 63.
[55] W. Jones Davies, *The Minister at Work* (1910).
[56] *Christian World*, 12 Sept. 1895.
[57] J. Thew, 'Ministerial Life and Work', *Baptist Magazine*, 82 (1890), 347.

students for the ministry'.[58] Even at Midland College, which—untypically—offered economics to its students, this sole concession to the practicalities of late century urban and industrial life was swamped in an otherwise traditional curriculum concentrated heavily on the arts, languages, and Scripture. A visitor to Rawdon in 1903 warned that because the colleges were unduly emphasizing the academic, they tended to neglect the study of people. As a result, he concluded, 'men often enter the ministry a good deal crippled in this direction'.[59] This was certainly the perception of most contemporaries, notwithstanding the contrary evidence provided by the experience of Mansfield College. In its first five years of existence, students at this Congregational foundation in Oxford won sixteen university prizes, out of all proportion to their numbers. One former student, Basil Martin, likened it to a monastery, 'a community of devout and scholarly men engaged in hard reading and bent on winning University prizes and distinctions.'[60] It was not an inappropriate metaphor, since the college's settlement in east London subsequently provided many of the pastoral services which in an earlier time might have been offered by monastic communities.

It was suggested in Chapter 1 that a disproportionate number of men entering the late nineteenth-century ministry were from rural backgrounds. While the distinction between town and countryside should not be drawn too starkly, men from such backgrounds could not always have been very well prepared by their own experience for the realities of urban ministry. Perhaps this was why Charles Brown's presidential address to the Baptist Union in 1909 contained the suggestion that ministerial training be remodelled to include 'two or three years in business where they may be compelled to earn their own living, and become acquainted with the struggles and temptations of ordinary life'.[61] Table

[58] Cheshunt College, Trustees Minute Book, 5 Mar. 1903, Cheshunt College Archives, C1/19, Westminster College, Cambridge.

[59] R. Gray, 'Some Conditions of a Successful Ministry', *Baptist Magazine*, 96 (1904), 310.

[60] W. T. Davies, *Mansfield College* (Oxford, 1947), 23.

[61] *Baptist Handbook* (1909), 253.

3.3 shows that there was also a growing proportion of entrants to the ministry from ministerial homes which, again, did not always provide a good understanding of the life style of ordinary people. William Dawson, son of a Methodist minister, found himself unable to deal adequately with pastoral problems during his own ministry because 'I had no data concerning the lives of ordinary men. The only lives which I knew by actual observation were highly specialised.'[62] It is a comment which serves to illustrate both the need for proper pastoral training and the colleges' failure to provide it.

The concern with pastoral inadequacy was undoubtedly one result of the Church's growing realization that it had little effective contact with the working classes, and it reflected also perhaps the fears of the middle classes in general about the potentially explosive consequences of neglecting urban social problems. That the critics of nonconformist training were thus arguing the case for supplementing the scholarly attributes of ministry with instruction in pastoral technique was perhaps indicative of some vitality in the Church. Yet relatively little was done by the various denominational authorities to respond to the critics. It may legitimately be asked why. Most obviously, there was in fact no real, positive pressure to do anything at all radically or urgently. None of the major denominations was currently suffering from an actual shortage of manpower. Indeed, the total number of ministers continued to increase fairly uniformly until the time of the First World War, as Table 3.4 shows. The Methodists could always make up any shortfall with lay preachers while there was talk of over supply among both the Baptists and Congregationalists.[63]

In the absence of any acute manpower shortage, therefore, the practical obstacles to reform remained immovable. There was, first of all, the inherent paradox of the task. Colleges were being asked simultaneously to broaden the curriculum and improve the training of students at a time

---

[62] W. J. Dawson, *Autobiography of a Mind* (1925), 43. J. G. Pike recalled that his father, a Baptist minister, 'allowed us to mingle very little with other children', *General Baptist Repository*, 2 (1855), 355.

[63] This is discussed at length in Chapter 4, below.

TABLE 3.4. Number of Ministers at Selected Dates

	Wesleyan	Primitive	United	Baptist	Congregationalist
1871	1649	790	555	—	2503
1881	1910	924	645	—	2830
1891	2018	883	651	—	—
1901	2238	962	719	2000	3083
1911	2478	1094	845	2107	3093
1921	2474	1059	715	2049	—
1931	2568	1092	691	2000	2843

Source: Figures taken from R. Currie, A. Gilbert, and L. Horsley *Churches and Churchgoers: Patterns of Church Growth in the British Isles since 1700* (Oxford, 1977), pp. 204–10.

when both numbers and quality were deteriorating. Any serious attempt by the Congregational and Baptist colleges to raise entry standards would have led to some institutions losing their viability altogether, particularly as in both denominations it was possible to enter the ministry without going to college at all. Appropriate qualifications could be obtained simply by taking written examinations, usually at county union level. Then there was the consideration that any fundamental reorganization of facilities and extension of the training programme would have involved financial outlay to pay for more staff at a time when college finances were already under pressure. In the last years of the nineteenth century nonconformists had raised large sums to support the extension of missionary work, new chapel buildings, better ministerial salaries, and improved provision for retired men and their widows. They do not appear to have been so keen to support ministerial colleges, however. One alternative, certainly for the Baptists and Congregationalists, was to improve income by admitting more students— thus lowering the quality and undermining the attempt to improve standards. This was a danger to which Principal Whitehouse had drawn attention in 1902. A college, he said, might be tempted 'to increase the number of students in order to justify its own existence, and this increase is frequently made without duly considering the qualifications of those who enter'.[64] The Old Dissenters also had the problem

[64] Cheshunt College, Trustees Minute Book, 3 June 1902, Cheshunt College Archives, C1/19, Westminster College, Cambridge.

that all their colleges were independent, existing to serve the churches, not their respective central unions. The process of reform, therefore, was likely to be obstructed by college committees determined to preserve their own heritage, their own buildings, and their own burden for a particular locality. In any case, Congregationalists and Baptists were committed to the principle of individual autonomy and were deeply suspicious of any centralizing tendency, although it is clear that successful reform could come only from some centrally directed plan.

The Methodists, of course, were not hampered by any such reservations although, like the Old Dissenters, their attentions were perhaps somewhat diverted from reform by the education controversies which marked the birth of the twentieth century. In both cases, too, there was an emotive element in the opposition to change. Colleges were more than simply academic institutions and the sense of loyalty, community, and fellowship which they engendered in the minds of most of their students, provided a formidable psychological barrier to radical restructuring. Connexional reunion also claimed a very high priority among late Victorian Methodists. The Bible Christians, the New Connexion, and the Free Methodists successfully crowned years of discussion when they formally amalgamated in 1907, and other mergers were under active consideration. Such structural changes would quite clearly have implications for the provision of ministerial training facilities and there seemed little point in undertaking fundamental reform until such time as the future shape of Methodism was settled more firmly.

There was, however, a further dimension to the college crisis and one which also helped to prevent any radical reforms, though the courtesies of etiquette prevented it from being very openly discussed. The *Independent and Nonconformist* perhaps came closest in 1892. Commenting on the reaction of Principal Reynolds to certain reform proposals which had been quite widely aired, the paper suggested that he seemed to 'shrink from the prospect of any drastic changes in our academic system'.[65] Some years earlier,

---

[65] *Independent and Nonconformist*, 27 May 1892.

Samuel Newth of New College had shown himself to be rather sensitive to this suggestion that the college staffs were reluctant to sanction change and were thus perpetuating an indefensible system. 'It may be needful for the information of some', he told the Congregational Union assembly in 1880, 'that I should emphasise the fact that all the successive improvements made in our college plans during the past forty years have been made at the instance of the professors and committees of the colleges, and that in no single case has the suggestion of the measure come from a source outside themselves.'[66] He protested too much. There is no doubt that in the end much of the criticism of ministerial training in the late nineteenth century came down to an implied attack on the individuals responsible for it, and it is to them that we now turn.

When Samuel McAll accepted the post of principal at Hackney in 1860 he acknowledged his own sense of unworthiness for a position which, he said, entailed much greater responsibilities than those involved in pastoring a single congregation because it concerned the instruction of those 'who may become centres of influence to others, probably through many future years'.[67] This general point has been confirmed by studies of twentieth-century Anglican training establishments and there is ample evidence that similar influences were exerted in nonconformist colleges and academies of the previous century.[68] Thus the teaching of W. F. Slater of Didsbury was later described by one student as 'deep and abiding'.[69] G. P. Gould, himself an eminent principal of Bristol Baptist College, paid a glowing tribute to Fred Gotch, one of his predecessors to whom he reckoned himself 'more deeply indebted ... than to any other man I have ever known for his influence on my mind, its modes and habits of thought'.[70] Often, as McAll had

---

[66] *Congregational Yearbook* (1881), 109.

[67] S. McAll to Hackney Committee, 1 Feb. 1860. 'The Village Itinerancy', Minutes of Committee commencing 1859, DWL. NCA. 70.

[68] For the impact of college life on Anglican students generally see R. Towler and P. Coxon, *The Fate of the Anglican Clergy* (1979), *passim*.

[69] Brash and Wright, p. 108.

[70] G. P. Gould, 'In Memoriam: Rev F. W. Gotch, LLD', *Baptist Magazine*, 82 (1890), 304.

implied, such influences could last a lifetime. Thus Ryder Smith of Handsworth cast a spell over one of his students 'which, I am happy to say, remains to this day and will endure'.[71] If such assessments tended sometimes to a pardonable hyperbole, they cannot all be dismissed out of hand as mere concessions to polite convention or as distortions produced by the passage of time. Students were by no means blindly uncritical of their mentors. William Stowell was forced to resign from Cheshunt in 1856 because his overzealous approach to discipline unduly antagonized the students. Further, the students expressed themselves 'disappointed in the expectation that during their stay at the College they should have found in the President a Pastor who would have cared for their spiritual improvement'.[72] The mathematics tutor at Bristol was later described by one student as 'deplorably weak ... not the man for the job'.[73] A Wesleyan student was highly critical of virtually everything about Richmond but reserved his most trenchant censures for the house governor: 'Most lamentable of all was the so-called "class meeting" which met weekly under the leadership of the Governor. What should have been the peak of a week's experience was for many of us its nadir, so ghastly in its unreality was it.'[74]

College staffs certainly believed that they were in a position to influence their charges and it is important to remember that in the nineteenth century they generally exercised a very high degree of personal supervision over their students. W. H. Hunt remarked on the freer regime which appeared in the Wesleyan colleges after 1918, suggesting in 1943 that 'I don't think the men are *now* required to "consult the Governor." about some things as they were then'.[75] Students' personal affairs were closely monitored and the Didsbury and Headingley minute books contain numerous references to individuals who were disciplined for breaking off roman-

---

[71] Cumbers, p. 118.
[72] Cheshunt College, Governors' Minutes, 23 Apr. 1855, Cheshunt College Archives, C1/8, Westminster College, Cambridge.
[73] G. Hawker, *Records and Reminiscences* (1922), 14.
[74] Cumbers, p. 72.
[75] Ibid. 67. My italics.

tic attachments.[76] Such control was reinforced by the fact that the colleges were generally quite small, permitting the establishment of close and intimate links between staff and students. Thus it was written of Henry Reynolds, Principal of Cheshunt, that

From the moment of every student's entry—not merely until the day of his leaving—but, as we gather, in most cases, so long as that student ... lived, Henry Reynolds watched over him with fostering care. It is in our brother's letters to these former pupils, coupled with letters from many of them, that we find the great work of his life exhibited ...[77]

Such closeness was further reinforced by the prevailing philosophy of education which did not encourage students to question tutors' opinions. This was why Dr Vaughan was able to get away at Lancashire for so long with 'repeating over again to successive generations of students lectures which had never had very much contact with reality and had certainly never grown beyond their first inception'.[78] A former student of Thomas Crisp's at Bristol claimed that his teacher was content only if students reproduced in examinations the material he had given them in his lectures: 'Somehow he did not perceive that this was not the most effective mode of teaching, and was more an exercise of memory than an incentive to our own powers of thought'.[79] It is true that this obsession with orthodoxy was weakening by the end of the century, especially in some of the Congregational institutions (New College had a reputation for heterodoxy), but even then Dr Scott of Lancashire was so disturbed by one of his student's radical views about the person of Christ that he took to praying for him openly at the college's public evening service.[80] There is even a hint that some candidates were

[76] Andrew Moffatt, for example, lost two years' seniority because he entertained 'Improper views in regard to the relationships between persons engaged to be married', Didsbury Management Committee Executive Minutes, 19 May 1905, Didsbury College Archives, A1/3/1, Wesley College, Bristol. In March of the same year two other students were similarly disciplined for breaking off engagements. Ibid. 9 Mar. 1905.

[77] Reynolds, p. vi.

[78] F. J. Powicke, *David Worthington Simon* (1912), 33.

[79] F. Trestrail, *Reminiscences of College Life at Bristol, During the Ministry of Robert Hall, 1825–1831* (n.d.), 22.

[80] W. A. Lupton to C. Surman, 22 Mar. 1936, LIC, Registers of Students, K–M, Northern College, Manchester.

turned down by the colleges because they were judged to be insufficiently open to tutors' influences. At least, Hackney rejected one man in 1880 because he was twenty-seven years old and 'judging from his papers his mind and his opinions are too "set" ...'.[81]

It seems likely, therefore, that a systematic investigation of these ministerial educators will throw some further light on the causes of, and the failure to resolve, the late nineteenth-century college crisis. The tables which follow are based on an examination of the college principals only. Partly, this is to keep the number of individuals down to manageable dimensions but the rationale for such an approach is not only statistical. Principals were ultimately responsible for setting the general tone of their institutions, usually taught theology and had the pastoral oversight of the students. In most cases, theirs was the primary influence. 'There is perhaps no position in the appointment of the Wesleyan Conference', the *Wesleyan Methodist Magazine* had suggested in 1878, 'which, rightly apprehended, devolves more serious responsibilities than that of the Governorship of any one of the theological colleges.'[82] Thirty years later George Findlay made the same point, saying that it was to the post of principal that 'the greatest weight is justly attached'.[83] This was also true in the Old Dissenting colleges where, as W. T. Whitley acknowledged in 1923, 'the personal influence of the head was all important over the members of his "family"'.[84] Except in the case of the non-Wesleyan Methodist connexions, where the total number of individuals is in any case very small, those who served for less than three years have been excluded on the grounds that their influence could not have affected many students. This leaves a total of 54 Congregationalists, 40 Baptists, 11 Primitives, and 9 United Methodists, whose terms of office were completed between 1815 and 1939.[85]

[81] S. Newth to J. Farrer, 3 Aug. 1880, DWL. NCA. 219/95.
[82] *Wesleyan Methodist Magazine*, 2 (1878), 346.
[83] G. Findlay, *The Education of the Wesleyan Ministry* (1903), 26.
[84] W. T. Whitley, 'Our Theological Colleges', *Baptist Quarterly*, 1 (1922–3), 26.
[85] This includes the principals of the four branches of the Wesleyan Theological Institution, the Primitive colleges at Sunderland and Manchester, the New Connexion's Ranmoor, and the Free Methodists' Victoria Park. The Baptist institutions are

For the purposes of analysis the period has been divided into five equal segments and each individual allocated to that which covered his period of office. Where any man's time overlaps the terminal dates by three or more years, he has been included in all the appropriate groups. Thus A. M. Fairbairn, Principal of Airedale between 1877 and 1886, and of Mansfield College until 1909, has been included in two periods, 1865–89, and 1890–1914. John Morris, President of Brecon from 1854 until 1896, appears in three periods, 1840–64, 1865–89, and 1890–1914. Table 3.5 analyses the principals' birthplaces. It is immediately apparent that a high proportion of men, especially among the Baptists and Congregationalists, was drawn from the Celtic fringes. Between 1890 and 1914 slightly more than half of the latter and rather under half of the former came from peripheral areas of the British Isles. This is in line with the high numbers originating in rural districts which were to some extent synonymous with the Celtic areas. The Wesleyans also relied heavily on men with rural roots. If we include the English market towns it would appear that in the three largest and most influential nonconformist denominations never less than half of the training college principals came from rural society. Even in the late nineteenth century, when increasing concern was being expressed about the relevance of college courses, much ministerial education was still in the hands of men whose values, ideas, and attitudes had been formed in environments very different to the urban, industrial world in which the majority of ordinary people lived. In this respect they tended to mirror the backgrounds of the students themselves.

Indeed, as Table 3.6 suggests, the principals themselves often had had very little contact with the secular world at all, although there are clear differences between the various denominations. Once again it was the Congregationalists

Abergavenny, Bangor, Bristol, Cardiff, Haverfordwest, Horton, Llangollen, Manchester, Midland, Pontypool, Spurgeon's, Stepney, Rawdon, and Regent's Park. Among the Congregational colleges, Airedale and Rotherham are included as the precursors of Yorkshire College. The rest comprise Cheshunt, Coward, Hackney, Highbury, Homerton, Hoxton, Lancashire, Mansfield, New, Paton Congregational Institute, Spring Hill, Western, Wymondley, and the Welsh colleges at Brecon and Bala-Bangor, though the latter trained some Baptist and the former some Presbyterian men as well.

TABLE 3.5. College Principals: Places of Birth

	1815–39					1840–64					1865–89					1890–14					1915–39				
	W	P	U	B	C	W	P	U	B	C	W	P	U	B	C	W	P	U	B	C	W	P	U	B	C
Rural Wales				2	2					4					4	4	1			3	2			2	2
Urban Wales										1				1					1	2	2	1		1	1
Rural Scotland					1				1	2					1					2					2
Urban Scotland						1				1					1				1					1	1
Ireland													1	1		1		1				1			
Isle of Man					1				1	1															
Abroad											1				2	1					1	1		1	1
Rural England				4	3	1			1	4	4	1	1	5	4	2		1	3	3	1	1		1	
Urban England				1	1	1			1	4	1	2	2	1	2	1		1	1	1	3		2	1	3
Market Town				3	2	1			2	6	1	1	1	3	4	5	2	1	1	3	4		1	1	2
London					1					2				1	2				3	2	1				1
Total Celtic				2	3				3	3		1	1	5	4		1		1	3	5	1	1	4	7
Total Rural				9	7	2			10	15	5	2	3	8	13	7	3		9	13	5	2	1	5	6
Unknown	1																			1					
Total number	1			10	11	3			12	24	6	4	5	18	18	10	5	4	15	23	10	2	2	8	11

W = Wesleyan.   P = Primitive.   U = United Baptist.   B = Baptist.   C = Congregational.

TABLE 3.6. College Principals: Personal Backgrounds

	1815–39					1840–64					1865–89					1890–14					1915–39				
	W	P	U	B	C	W	P	U	B	C	W	P	U	B	C	W	P	U	B	C	W	P	U	B	C
Ministerial father				1	1					1	6	1	1		2	6	4		1	8	6			1	3
Worked prior to ministry	8	10	1			7	14	3			2	11	11			5	1	1	8	12	7	2	1	3	3

and Wesleyans who after 1890 had a relatively high proportion of principals born in ministerial homes where the outlook was most likely to be rigidly controlled by the demands
of chapel propriety and from which 'worldly' influences
were carefully screened. The resulting atmosphere of religious intensity can be seen from David Simon's experience,
for example. Sundays started with family prayers, and then
it was off to chapel for Sunday school and morning service.
A second dose of Sunday school followed lunch, and tea was
followed by evening service. Afterwards there was another
prayer meeting, and the day closed with family prayer.
'Father would not allow dish-washing on Sunday.'[86] In the
crucially important years at the end of the century about a
third of Wesleyan and Congregational principals had ministerial fathers, a proportion which increased among the
Wesleyans in the years after 1914. Sometimes this narrow-
ness could be further reinforced by education at one or other
of the various denominational schools catering for ministers'
sons. W. F. Moulton (whose son was to become Principal of
Didsbury in 1919) was at Woodhouse Grove between 1846
and 1850 and later recalled that he had been 'often struck
with the remembrance of our isolation from the world, in
which the stirring events of our time were happening. A newspaper seldom reached us ... '[87] Thus at the very time when
the chapel's dominance of much social and recreational
activity was being undermined by the growth of commercial entertainment and a steadily expanding range of
alternative leisure and educational facilities, ministers, who
were themselves increasingly drawn from clerical homes in
which upbringing could be very restrictive, were increasingly likely also to be educated by men from similarly limited
backgrounds.

It was, of course, not inevitable that upbringing in a ministerial home should have been intellectually, socially, or
culturally confining. Many of the principals came from leading dissenting families whose interests and activities stretch-

[86] Powicke, p. 6.
[87] J. Craig, 'Woodhouse Grove in John Lockwood Kipling's Day', *Kipling Journal*, 40 (1973), 12. H. A. Scott, 'My Early Life and Ministry', *Methodist Magazine* (Feb. 1912), 107, said that at Kingswood in the 1860s 'we were kept in close bounds'.

ed into most aspects of respectable secular life. Usually, they had been intimately involved since childhood in the lives of the churches which their students would serve. Furthermore, any limitations which were imposed by a childhood spent in a ministerial home could be offset by some secular work experience. Principal Garvie certainly acknowledged the value this had been to him: 'I am now grateful that I had this experience of the ways and works of the world of business, and gained the discernment I now have into human disposition and character under the test and stress of the existing economic system.'[88] Yet the proportion of Congregational principals who had ever had secular work fell continuously through the century as more and more of them went directly into ministerial education. This trend did not appear among the Baptists until the time of the First World War, while the proportion of Wesleyans with work experience remained fairly steady at about 50 per cent until the First World War. Even so, except among the Baptists, most of the work experience was gained, as Table 3.7 points out, in commercial or educational establishments, not in heavy industry. Garvie's job was in a Glasgow draper's shop. This was the world of Kipps and Mr Polly, whose horizons were bounded by the counting-house desk and the retail counter. It was dismissed by Charles Masterman as the world of the suburbans, 'easily forgotten ... a homogeneous civilisation — detached, self centred, unostentatious ...'.[89] Giving evidence to the Royal Commission on Labour (1893–4) the Secretary of the National Union of Shop Assistants pointed out that 'the average warehouse clerk and assistant goes into business at an early age. Indeed, from the time he goes in as a rule he is shut off from all communication with the world and he does not know really the changes that are taking place around him. He does not read the daily papers ... and knows nothing of the outside world.'[90] In many cases, therefore, the principals could do no more than reinforce the

---

[88] A. E. Garvie, *Memories and Meanings of My Life* (1938), 63.
[89] C. F. G. Masterman, *The Condition of England* (1909), 56–7.
[90] Quoted in R. McKibbin, 'Work and Hobbies in Britain, 1880–1950', in J. Winter (ed.), *The Working Class in Modern British History: Essays in Honour of Henry Pelling* (Cambridge, 1983), 141.

TABLE 3.7. College Principals: Occupations Prior to Ministry

Type	1815–39					1840–64					1865–89					1890–14					1915–39				
	W	P	U	B	C	W	P	U	B	C	W	P	U	B	C	W	P	U	B	C	W	P	U	B	C
Unknown					3					3				3			1			1	1				1
Retail									1	2		1		4	1				1	2					1
Industry				2	3				3	4		1		2	5	1			3	4				1	1
Education				5	1	1			2	3	2			1	4	2	1	1	1	2	6	1		2	
Clerical									1	1	1			1		2			1	1		1			1
Professional														1					1	1					
Agricultural				1	1					1					1										

somewhat blinkered lower-middle-class views which many of their students were likely to have possessed already. The complacency could be quite staggering. When the Principal of Mansfield College spoke at the Hackney anniversary meetings in 1912 he claimed that 'there were scores of ministers who had more knowledge of the working class than so-called labour leaders'. He then added that he told his students to 'preach to the half witted servant girl in the gallery, and if she could understand the others would'.[91] Even if the principals' exposure to secular work was potentially more fruitful than contemporary evidence might suggest, the experiences were generally too brief to be of much long-term significance. The average age at which they commenced their own ministerial careers hovered constantly between nineteen and twenty-one.

Table 3.8 shows that both Congregational and Baptist principals tended to take up senior ministerial training posts rather earlier in life than their Methodist counterparts. They thus took to the educational process a rather briefer personal acquaintance with the practicalities of ministerial life, though at least one, D. Miall Edwards, thought that eight years 'in the field' was sufficient. Applying for a post at Brecon Memorial College in 1909 he referred to his own experience: 'I venture to think that my eight and a half years in the active ministry have given me a better appreciation of the truth and power of the Christian Gospel than a merely academic knowledge could give.'[92] It is true, too, that it was common practice in the first half of the century for college principalships to be combined with the pastorates of nearby congregations. This was the case at Homerton and Hackney, while the headship of Bristol Baptist College was linked to the pastorate of Broadmead Baptist chapel.

In complete contrast, Joseph Entwisle, first house governor of the Wesleyan Theological Institution, was sixty-seven years old when he was appointed and he had travelled for forty-seven years in the itinerancy. Yet of all denominations the Wesleyans were most critical of their college

---

[91] *Christian World*, 20 June 1912.
[92] 'Application of the Rev D. Miall Edwards and Testimonials in His Favour' (1909), p. 6, Brecon Memorial College, Correspondence, National Library of Wales.

TABLE 3.8. College Principals: Ages at First Principal's Appointment

Age	1815–39					1840–64					1865–89					1890–14					1915–39				
	W	P	U	B	C	W	P	U	B	C	W	P	U	B	C	W	P	U	B	C	W	P	U	B	C
30–4				2	4				3	6				4	4				2	1				1	1
35–9				4	1				2	3				4	4				1	6					3
40–4				3					3	4				3	5			1	3	5			1	1	2
45–9				1	4	1			3	6	1		2	3	1			2	7	5	1			3	3
50–4					1					2	3			1	3	1	2	1	1	1	1	1		1	1
55–9					1		2		1	2	4	1	2	2		4	1	1	1		3	1	1		1
60–4						1	1		1	1	5	2	1	1	1	5	2			1	5	1		2	2
65+	1					1	1		1																

system and it does not appear that their principals derived much benefit from their much longer periods of active work. This is puzzling, if only because the peripatetic nature of the Wesleyan ministry *should* have given them useful experience in a much wider variety of pastoral situations than those to which men in other traditions were generally exposed. This, at least, was the theory. G. Stringer Rowe's credentials for the Headingley post, for instance, were thought to include 'an intimate knowledge of Methodist History and Polity and the ripe experience gained during 33 years successful work in our leading circuits'.[93] It seems inconceivable that nothing should have been picked up by men who spent so long in the ministry themselves before turning to education, but by the end of the century the Methodist colleges *were* being criticized for failing to equip their students adequately. Perhaps the old men had lost something of their cutting edge by the time they entered college. Or perhaps it was simply that they were inadequate as scholars and teachers. Because of their shorter tradition of college training the smaller Methodist connexions could not look to a large pool of academically qualified men from whom to appoint but even among the Wesleyans, as Table 3.9 confirms, academic qualifications were not highly regarded until the immediate pre-war years. This was a shift of outlook which was symbolized in the change of nomenclature from 'house governor' to 'principal'. The preference for older, experienced ministers rather than for highly educated men might well have been encouraged by the latent antipathy, which survived for a long time among all varieties of Methodism, towards the whole concept of training. The longer traditions of ministerial training which prevailed among Congregationalists and Baptists enabled them to appoint relatively well qualified men right from the start of the century, as Table 3.9 reveals. Not until the First World War did the proportion of university trained Wesleyan principals reach the same levels as those in the other non-Methodist denominations. Yet, given that Congregational and Baptist colleges were just as

---

[93] Headingley Management Committee Executive Minutes, 23 June 1904, Headingley College Archives, B1/3/2, Wesley College, Bristol.

TABLE 3.9. College Principals: Highest Forms of Education Received

	1815–39					1840–64					1865–89					1890–14					1915–39				
	W	P	U	B	C	W	P	U	B	C	W	P	U	B	C	W	P	U	B	C	W	P	U	B	C
Elementary	1					1				1					1		3	3							
Grammar School				1	1	1					3		3			1	1				1				
Private tuition				1	1	1				1	2	1	1	1			1	1	1						
Academy/College				5	8				7	16		1	1	9	13	8	1	1	9	12	2	2	1	5	1
University				1	1				5	6				8	5	1	1	1	5	11	7	1	1	2	10
No. with degree				5	5				8	14		1	1	14	14	5	2	2	14	22	9	2	2	7	10

heavily criticized as the Methodists by the end of the century, it may be that the educational qualifications of the principals had little real importance.

The Methodist practice of appointing older men did have one small advantage. If a mistake was made then the incumbent's term of office was not likely to be long. As Table 3.10 shows, the principals of the Older Dissenting colleges tended to hold office for much longer periods than did the Methodists. John Morris presided at Brecon for forty-two years, a year less than his Baptist counterpart at Bristol, Thomas Crisp. In this situation there was always the possibility that individuals would become progressively less able to adapt to the demands of new knowledge and a changing social environment. At Regent's Park, Joseph Angus's outlook remained virtually unchanged for half a century. This longevity, it was suggested later (though with much gentleness), 'made it impossible for him to feel the pulsation of the recent and contemporary bloodstream. He could not help it that he was dwelling in a vanishing yesterday . . .'[94] Another of Angus's former students, who himself later served on the staff of the college, admitted that his mentor's great age and loss of mental vigour in his declining years had 'resulted in some decline in the efficiency of the college'.[95] A similar lack of flexibility had been apparent even earlier in Dr Vaughan of Lancashire Independent College: it was alleged that when some of his students began to attend lectures at the newly opened Owens College in Manchester, he experienced 'a flutter now of jealousy and again of alarm'.[96] The arrival of the relatively youthful William Henderson at Bristol in 1896 heralded a much more vigorous and modern approach to ministerial training than that which had been exhibited by his older and long-serving predecessors.

Of course, there was no inherent reason why long service *had* to isolate men from the outside world. Table 3.11 sets out to provide a proxy measurement of the extent to which college principals involved themselves in the wider world which existed beyond the college walls. It does this by counting the number of individuals who were involved in

---

[94] S. P. Carey, 'Regent's As I Knew It', *Baptist Quarterly*, 8 (1936), 139.
[95] A. J. D. Farrer, 'Forty Years of Regent's Park College', ibid., 10 (1940–1), 328.
[96] Powicke, p. 17.

TABLE 3.10. College Principals: Length of Time in Office

	1815–39					1840–64					1865–89					1890–14					1915–39				
	W	P	U	B	C	W	P	U	B	C	W	P	U	B	C	W	P	U	B	C	W	P	U	B	C
Under 4 yrs	1			2								2	1	1	1	1	1		1	2	4	2	1	1	1
5–9				3	1	2	1			2	1	1	1	6	5	2	3		5	6	4		1	1	3
10–14					7	2	1		3	5	3	1	4	3	5	4		2		4	2				3
15–19				3	5	2			1	2	1				2	3		2		2				3	3
20–4					4				1	2	2			1					4	2				2	3
25–9				1	2		1		2	5				2					2	2					
30–4															5					5					
35–9				2	1				1	2				1	2				1	1				1	1
40+				3	4				2	2				4	2				2	1					

Table 3.11. College Principals: Extra-Curricular Activity

	1815–39					1840–64					1865–89					1890–14					1915–39				
	W	P	U	B	C	W	P	U	B	C	W	P	U	B	C	W	P	U	B	C	W	P	U	B	C
Number involved				7	6				6	11		1		10	10	1	2	1	6	10	1			5	6
Total number	1		10	11	3				12	24	6	4	5	18	18	11	4	4	15	23	9	3	2	8	11

learned societies, political or pressure group activities, charitable and missionary societies, educational work, and local government work, such as serving on a local board of guardians. Such a table cannot be regarded as possessing any strict numerical accuracy, since our knowledge of such activities depends very largely on the whims of surviving evidence, particularly in the case of the majority of men who did not merit full-length biographies. But it does have some value in that it gives an approximate idea of the orders of magnitude involved.

It is the Baptists and Congregationalists who appear to have been most conspicuous. True, Thomas Goadby of Midland 'shrank from taking a prominent part in public life', but Henderson at Bristol, for instance, served on school boards, the council of Bristol University, and the committee of the Coventry Technical Institute, and he was a member of the Baptist Missionary Society.[97] William Edwards of the South Wales Baptist College was a temperance activist, a member of the Monmouth County Council, and active in Liberal Party politics. Similarly, about half the Congregational principals seem to have been fairly active in public life. The rest were like D. W. Simon of Yorkshire whose biographer has commented that there were few visible signs of him outside the college. It was his world and he 'confined himself to his duties as Principal and Tutor, seldom taking part in outside functions'.[98] It is difficult to generalize about the smaller Methodist connexions as the number of men involved is so small. What is striking, however, is the low participation among the Wesleyans—none at all until the late nineteenth century and then only about one in ten. Perhaps this was a reflection of the way the peripatetic system hampered any long-term habitual activity of this sort. But whatever the reason, the 'one defect' which an obituarist discerned in Principal Sherwood of Victoria College—'with what he called "affairs" he had little interest or knowledge'—would appear to have been generally true among the Methodists.[99]

On the whole, and with the possible exception that some of their men served rather long terms, the Baptists seem to

[97] *Freeman*, 29 Mar. 1889.
[98] Powicke, p. 215.
[99] *United Methodist Magazine*, 12 (1920), 174.

emerge from this analysis with the best equipped body of college principals. In general a higher proportion of them had experience of industrial life, and fewer of them came from ministerial homes. The Wesleyans were the most poorly served of all. While it is possible to point to individual exceptions, as a body their principals generally had little personal acquaintance with the industrial world. Their formative years were more likely to have been spent in areas with a predominantly agrarian ethos and more often in homes likely to have been circumscribed by the demands of ministerial propriety. Certainly, they appointed men of experience, but their advanced years may have robbed them of the vitality and flexibility which might have enabled them to cope more effectively with the demands being made upon their students. The Congregationalists, better equipped academically, generally younger than the Wesleyans, and with rather more experience of the world outside the chapel, fared little better. Long periods in office meant that they, too, perhaps tended to lose touch with the realities of ministerial life. Once again, there were some obvious and notable exceptions but we may perhaps bring forward Henry Reynolds as a representative college principal during the years of crisis. Born in rural Hampshire, he was a son of the manse. He never held a secular job but after studying with his father passed by way of Coward College to University College, London. This rather sheltered background was to some extent offset, not only by his wider family connections (his brother was a fashionable London physician) but also by two testing pastorates at Halstead and in Leeds. They lasted for only fourteen years, however, before he was appointed principal at Cheshunt. There Reynolds remained for thirty-four years, an active scholar but little involved in the outside world, apart from some spasmodic campaigning for the Liberal Party. It was a career which explained not only the appalling state in which Cheshunt College found itself by the turn of the century, but also, as the *Independent and Nonconformist* had hinted, the nature and persistence of the late Victorian crisis in ministerial training.[100]

---

[100] *Independent and Nonconformist*, 27 May 1892.

4

An Unsettled Ministry?

THE death of Charles Haddon Spurgeon in 1892 was an event of national impact. Even secular newspapers appeared with black-edged columns and filled their pages with reminiscences of the dead Baptist leader, prompting the editor of the *Christian World* to claim that 'the history of England during the past week has been mainly the story of Mr Spurgeon's influence ...'.[1] Because Spurgeon and men of similar eminence had appeared to be virtually permanent fixtures (Spurgeon had sustained a powerful ministry for over forty years), the sense of loss within the nonconformist community in Britain was enormous. For historians an undue concentration on the notable and the famous has led, in rather similar fashion, to an implicit assumption that the nineteenth-century ministry was a cohesive whole and something of a fixed entity.

Yet far from being a relatively static body of individuals whose composition changed only slowly with the natural rhythm of the recruitment and retirement of successive generations, the ministry was in a constant state of flux. In the early part of the century especially, there was a peripheral component of men who moved in and out of the Old Dissenting ministry as their economic circumstances permitted, while some of the individuals in the poorer Methodist connexions reverted to lay preaching when they got married. More significantly, however, there was a consistent and chronic haemorrhage of men out of the domestic pastoral ministry throughout the nineteenth century. Thus about half of the eighty-four preachers admitted to the Methodist New Connexion ministry between 1797 and 1814 had resigned

---

[1] *Christian World*, 11 Feb. 1892.

within six years.[2] Almost a third of the Wesleyans who entered the ministry between 1831 and 1851 were lost to the domestic pastoral body within four years, while half of the Baptists who began between 1861 and 1881 did not last for more than fourteen years (Table 4.1). One contemporary estimated that resignations alone were costing the Free Methodists four men every year in the 1880s.[3] These were losses of which the denominations themselves were vaguely aware but which did not seem to trouble them unduly until the last years of Victoria's reign. Somewhat paradoxically, perhaps, this was the very time when the leakage appeared to be becoming less severe but the concern can be understood if its context is remembered—falling church growth rates, the declining quality and quantity of ministerial recruits, and growing criticism of training methods. 'The number of ministers and probationers whose names have disappeared from the Roll in this year's "Minutes of Conference" is so large', commented the *Methodist Recorder* in 1912, 'as to be symptomatic of some serious disorder.'[4] Two years later the Annual Address to the Wesleyan Conference agreed that 'all is not well with us.... The situation is one of extreme gravity ...'[5] The United Methodists were equally disquieted. Despite the euphoria induced by the recent union the Annual Conference of 1911 could not 'persuade itself that all is well'.[6]

The basic statistics are set out in Table 4.1 which charts the cumulative losses of men at stated intervals since the commencement of their careers. Column A includes those Baptists and Congregationalists who, while still associated with their denominations and holding ministerial status, were entered in the year books as being without pastoral charge. Some of these were, in fact, retirements which had not been officially notified. Others were individuals who had taken up alternative occupations, mainly teaching, in which

[2] W. Townsend, H. Workman, G. Eayrs, *A New History of Methodism*, 2 vols., (1909), i. 501.
[3] *British Weekly*, 11 Feb. 1887.
[4] *Methodist Recorder*, 24 Oct. 1912.
[5] Wesleyan Conference, *Minutes* (1914), 459.
[6] United Methodist Conference, *Minutes* (1911), 160.

TABLE 4.1. Cumulative Loss to Ministry at Selected Intervals since Commencement of Career. Causes by Percentage

By Years	1831–51			1841–61			1851–71			1861–81			1871–91			1881–1901			1891–1911		
	A	B	C	A	B	C	A	B	C	A	B	C	A	B	C	A	B	C	A	B	C
Wesleyans																					
4	4.8	7.2	18.5	5.8	3.8	18.0	5.2	3.4	16.6	3.0	1.4	16.7	0.8	1.6	13.1	0.5	3.1	8.4	0.6	4.3	5.6
14	8.0	7.2	20.9	10.2	3.8	20.6	10.6	3.4	17.4	7.5	2.2	19.0	4.9	4.8	16.7	4.2	6.2	12.1	3.6	8.0	8.7
24	11.2	7.2	23.3	13.4	5.0	22.5	13.9	5.2	18.3	12.9	4.5	19.0	9.0	7.2	16.7	7.9	8.8	13.7	7.5	10.4	10.6
34	32.2	10.4	23.3	32.1	6.9	22.5	30.6	5.2	18.3	29.7	5.2	19.7	23.9	8.9	17.3	24.8	12.0	14.7	22.6	13.7	11.2
44	61.2	10.4	23.3	65.1	6.9	22.5	69.2	5.2	18.3	68.9	5.9	19.7	67.7	10.5	17.3	69.2	12.6	14.7	71.0	13.7	11.2
Primitives																					
4		1.9	38.0		3.1	47.7	0.9	6.4	41.2	0.8	11.2	27.4	2.2	12.2	15.5	1.1	12.9	10.7	1.2	5.1	10.2
14	1.8	3.9	56.7	3.0	5.5	58.1	2.7	9.1	49.4	2.5	12.0	36.1	2.2	13.3	24.4	2.3	14.0	19.9	3.7	6.3	16.6
24	5.8	3.9	61.5	6.2	6.2	59.7	6.4	9.1	51.3	5.9	12.9	37.7	5.5	13.3	26.6	4.6	15.2	22.2	7.6	7.6	17.8
34	19.5	3.9	61.5	17.0	6.2	59.7	16.5	9.1	51.3	16.2	12.9	38.6	21.0	13.3	27.7	21.1	15.2	23.4	23.0	7.6	17.8
44	30.3	4.8	61.5	30.6	6.2	59.7	37.5	9.1	51.3	43.9	12.9	38.6	53.2	13.3	27.7	54.0	15.2	23.4	67.8	8.8	17.8

United

Age	1831–56			1841–66			1851–76			1861–86			1871–96			1881–1906			1891–1916		
4	2.0	2.0	19.3	2.7	4.5	13.7	1.7	4.3	10.8	1.4	4.9	8.3	1.3	4.1	9.0	0.9	4.1	11.0	1.6	2.7	8.8
14	8.0	7.1	28.5	7.9	9.1	26.2	8.7	8.2	22.1	7.5	7.9	18.5	6.7	6.3	17.2	2.7	5.9	17.1	3.8	4.4	13.8
24	14.2	9.1	33.6	13.1	10.1	30.9	14.7	9.0	27.4	13.3	8.8	22.3	11.8	7.1	20.1	6.4	7.2	19.8	8.3	5.4	16.1
34	25.4	9.1	34.6	22.3	10.1	32.7	21.7	9.0	29.1	20.8	8.8	23.9	18.6	8.0	21.3	15.2	9.0	20.8	16.7	7.6	18.3
44	48.8	11.1	34.6	47.6	11.2	32.7	49.2	9.8	29.1	53.5	9.6	23.9	56.6	8.0	21.7	60.1	9.0	20.8	66.4	7.6	18.3

Baptist

Age	1831–51			1841–61			1851–71			1861–81			1871–91			1881–1901			1891–1911		
4				4.5	1.4	14.5	4.2	3.5	14.0	0.8	4.3	8.7	0.8	7.0	11.5	1.4	7.1	17.8	1.6	10.3	14.7
14				26.1	3.0	23.0	25.2	6.3	19.0	21.8	7.7	21.9	8.7	10.5	13.3	7.1	9.9	19.2	7.0	15.1	15.8
24				31.1	3.7	25.3	33.6	8.4	21.1	28.9	10.4	23.6	18.6	17.6	13.3	15.8	14.2	19.2	15.3	20.4	15.8
34				48.3	5.2	26.1	44.8	9.1	22.5	42.9	10.4	23.6	30.2	17.6	13.3	25.8	14.2	19.2	24.2	22.8	15.8
44				59.1	6.0	26.1	58.3	9.8	22.5	58.7	15.6	23.6	55.2	18.5	13.3	54.6	14.2	19.2	52.2	22.8	15.8

Congregational

Age	1831–51			1841–61			1851–71			1861–81			1871–91			1881–1901			1891–1911		
4				6.6	11.7	13.9	5.5	17.6	14.1	3.9	14.3	14.5	0.5	14.1	15.1	1.3	6.4	10.8	0.8	9.2	9.2
14				14.6	16.8	17.6	12.0	23.1	17.1	7.7	22.3	16.7	3.5	20.1	18.6	3.2	13.5	14.0	2.8	16.0	11.7
24				23.4	21.9	18.3	18.1	26.6	18.1	13.4	24.0	19.5	7.5	21.6	19.6	7.9	15.4	17.8	6.3	18.0	15.2
34				36.6	23.4	19.1	28.1	27.6	18.6	21.8	25.8	19.5	19.6	22.6	20.6	21.3	16.8	18.7	20.8	18.5	16.2
44				49.2	24.1	19.8	43.9	28.1	19.1	41.2	26.3	20.1	40.8	23.1	20.6	49.7	17.3	19.2	52.2	18.5	16.7

the retention of the ministerial title was thought to be advantageous. Its main constituent, however, can be most accurately described as 'natural wastage', meaning retirements and deaths. They will be more fully explored in Chapter 5, below. Column B counts those who were lost to the pastoral ministry in Britain, because they went abroad, were absorbed into denominational educational and administrative machines, or because they took up alternative and specialized forms of ministry, such as serving a missionary society or overseeing a cemetery chapel. It also includes those men who joined the ministry of other denominations. Column C contains all those who quit the ministry to take up secular work, as well as those who are described in the records as 'resigned' or whose names simply vanish.

Table 4.2 provides a finer disaggregation of the figures contained in column B of Table 4.1. It indicates that a small loss, but one whose significance gradually increased through the century, came through the siphoning off of experienced men into denominational administrative and educational activity. Of the Methodists, the Wesleyans had the largest loss of this type because they were the largest connexion with the longest history. Diversions from the Primitives' ministry were fewer, partly because of their more recent origin, partly because they sustained a growth impetus rather longer through the century. The United Methodist pattern was similar. The extension of the powers of both the Baptist and Congregational Unions in the second half of the century resulted in some increase in the proportion of their men pulled into administration but of those entering the ministry between 1891 and 1911 only about 1 per cent could expect to be an administrator and 3 or 4 per cent an educator within thirty years. Certainly, central administrative office was a diversion from the more immediate tasks of the pastoral ministry, as Charles Kelly found. Twice Wesleyan President and a member of many important central committees, he later described his life as a never-ending round of 'public services ... innumerable committees ... interviews ... enormous correspondence, advice to be given, disputes to be settled ...'.[7] In all denominations, however,

---

[7] C. H. Kelly, *Memories* (1910), 278–9.

administration and education accounted for only a very small proportion of the leakage from the domestic pastoral ministry.

The domestic ministry also lost men through a persistent, if somewhat erratic, flow overseas. Many of course went under the auspices of one or other of the various denominational missionary societies. Others from the Old Dissenting traditions were sometimes tempted to seek pastorates abroad. In commenting on the upsurge of men going to the United States in the 1870s both the *Baptist* and the *English Independent* warned against the assumption that ministerial life was in any way less onerous or more prosperous than in Britain. Both papers did concede, however, that men on typically small salaries would find the temptation hard to resist.[8] Probably equally significant for Congregationalists and Baptists, however, was the fluctuating level of opportunity at home. It was suggested in mid-century that the Congregationalists were over-producing ministers and certainly the decline in the proportion going abroad came in the 1880s, the very years when the domestic supply and demand came more nearly into line.[9] The proportion of Baptists going overseas continued to expand and the relevant 'push' factor was provided by the effect of Spurgeon's College on total ministerial output. The college report for 1879–80 indicates that of 511 men trained since 1856, 12.7 per cent had gone abroad. Of those who left in the next decade, 1880–89, almost a quarter left Britain within four years of completing their training and by 1915–16 a similar number, 23.3 per cent, of all the students at Spurgeon's since 1856, were listed as having emigrated.[10] Some few churches, perhaps, were reluctant to call Spurgeon's men because of doubts about their intellectual quality. Equally, at a time when theological certainties were increasingly in question, a few other Baptist congregations may have preferred ministers less closely identified with the champion of evangelical orthodoxy. More likely, however, the outflow of Spurgeon's students reflected their mentor's own high international

[8] *Baptist*, 26 June 1874; *English Independent*, 16 Jan. 1874.
[9] *Patriot*, 14 Nov. 1855.
[10] Spurgeon's College, *Reports* (1879–89; 1915–16).

TABLE 4.2. Cumulative Loss of Men by Cause to Domestic Pastoral Ministry (%)

By Years	1831–51					1841–61					1851–71				
	1	2	3	4	5	1	2	3	4	5	1	2	3	4	5
Wesleyans															
4	7.2					3.8					2.6	0.8			
14	7.2					3.8					2.6	0.8			
24	7.2					3.8	1.2				2.6	2.6			
34	7.2	2.4	0.8			3.8	1.9				2.6	2.6			
44	7.2	2.4	0.8			3.8	1.9				2.6	2.6			
Primitives															
4	1.9					3.1					6.4				
14	3.9					5.5					9.1				
24	3.9					6.2					9.1				
34	3.9					6.2					9.1				
44	3.9		0.9			6.2					9.1				
United															
4	1.0				1.0	4.5					4.3				
14	6.1				1.0	9.1					7.8				0.4
24	8.1				1.0	9.1	0.5			0.5	7.8	0.4	0.4		0.4
34	8.1				1.0	9.1	0.5			0.5	7.8	0.4	0.4		0.4
44	8.1		2.0		1.0	9.1	0.5	1.1		0.5	7.8	0.8	0.8		0.4
Baptist															
4						0.7			0.7		2.1			2.1	
14						2.3			0.7		2.8	1.4		2.8	
24						3.0	0.7		0.7		3.5	1.4		3.5	
34						3.0	0.7		1.5		3.5	1.4		4.2	
44						3.0	0.7		2.3		3.5	1.4		4.9	
Congregational															
4						8.8					14.1	0.5	0.5	2.5	
14						9.5					15.6	0.5	0.5	6.5	
24						11.7	0.7	0.7	8.8		17.1	0.5	1.0	8.0	
34						12.5	0.7	0.7	9.5		17.6	0.5	1.0	8.5	
44						12.5	0.7	1.4	9.5		17.6	0.5	1.5	8.5	

Notes: 1 Abroad
2 Denominational administration
3 Denominational education
4 Different type of ministry
5 Different denomination

1861–81					1871–91					1881–1901					1891–1911				
1	2	3	4	5	1	2	3	4	5	1	2	3	4	5	1	2	3	4	5
0.7		0.7			0.8		0.8			2.6	0.5				3.7	0.6			
1.5		0.7			2.4		1.6	0.8		3.7	1.0	1.0	0.5		5.0	1.2	1.2	0.6	
1.5		3.0			2.4	0.8	2.4	0.8		4.7	1.5	2.1	0.5		6.2	1.8	1.8	0.6	
1.5	0.7	3.0			3.3	1.6	2.4	0.8		5.2	2.6	3.7	0.5		6.9	2.5	3.7	0.6	
2.2	0.7	3.0			4.1	2.4	2.4	0.8		5.8	2.6	3.7	0.5		6.9	2.5	3.7	0.6	
11.2																			
12.0					12.2					12.9					5.1				
12.9					12.2					12.9		1.1			5.1		1.2		
12.9					12.2		1.1			14.1		1.1			6.4		1.2		
12.9					12.2		1.1			14.1		1.1			6.4		1.2		
					12.2		1.1			14.1		1.1			6.4	1.2	1.2		
					12.2		1.1												
4.9					4.1					4.1					2.7				
7.6			0.3		6.3					5.5			0.4		3.9			0.5	
7.6	0.3	0.3	0.3	0.3	6.3		0.4	0.4		5.5	0.4	0.4	0.9		3.9	0.5	0.5	0.5	
7.6	0.3	0.3	0.3	0.3	6.3	0.4	0.4	0.9		5.5	1.3	0.4	1.8		3.9	1.6	0.5	1.6	0.5
7.6	0.7	0.3	0.7	0.3	6.3	0.4	0.4	0.9		5.5	1.3	0.4	1.8		3.9	1.6	0.5	1.6	0.5
3.5			0.8		5.3	0.8		1.7		5.7			0.7	0.7	8.2		0.5	1.1	0.5
4.3	1.7		1.7		6.2	1.7		2.6		7.1		0.7	0.7	1.4	10.0		1.7	2.3	1.1
5.2	1.7		3.5		7.1	1.7	1.7	7.1		7.9		2.1	2.8	1.4	11.2	0.5	2.9	4.7	1.1
5.2	1.7		3.5		7.1	1.7	1.7	7.1		7.9		2.1	4.2	1.4	11.2	1.1	2.9	6.5	1.1
5.2	5.2		5.2		7.1	1.7	1.7	8.0		7.9		2.1	4.2	1.4	11.2	1.1	2.9	6.5	1.1
11.7	0.5	0.5	1.6		11.6		1.5		1.0	3.7		2.3		0.4	5.4		2.9		0.9
14.6	0.5	0.5	6.7		13.1		2.0	1.5	3.5	6.1	0.4	3.3	1.4	2.3	7.4	0.4	3.9	1.4	2.9
15.1	0.5	1.1	7.3		13.6		2.5	2.0	3.5	6.6	0.9	3.7	1.4	2.8	7.9	0.9	4.4	1.9	2.9
15.7	0.5	2.3	7.3		13.6		2.5	3.0	3.5	7.1	0.9	3.7	2.3	2.8	8.4	0.9	4.4	1.9	2.9
15.7	0.5	2.8	7.3		13.6		2.5	3.5	3.5	7.1	0.9	3.7	2.8	2.8	8.4	0.9	4.4	1.9	2.9

standing. He gladly responded to the numerous requests which came from abroad for his students. At home, Spurgeon's men often went to causes which existed on the very margins of economic viability and if they subsequently failed to build up a congregation sufficiently, an overseas call might have appeared as a welcome release. But whatever its precise causes, the propensity of Spurgeon's students to go abroad, coupled with the fact that by 1911 24 per cent of all Baptist ministers had been trained by him, must account for the upsurge of newly emigrating Baptists apparent in Table 4.2.

Finally, we can note the drift of men into the ministry of other churches. The outstanding feature here is that the Methodists suffered virtually no losses at all of this sort, a reflection perhaps of their rather tighter control and the solidarity afforded by a common loyalty to the teaching, if not always to the precise forms of church administration, laid down by Wesley. This should put into perspective the fears expressed in the 1840s and later that products of the Theological Institution might be tempted to succumb to the blandishments of the Established Church.[11] Baptists showed a similar loyalty to their denomination, although there is some indication of an outward movement, albeit a very small one, at the very end of the century. The doctrine of believer's baptism tended to set the Baptists apart, theologically speaking, from the ministry of the other churches, and the very few ministers who did join a paedo-baptist communion must have undergone some very fundamental change of belief. It is interesting in this context to note that in the 1890s Charles Booth reckoned that Baptists in general had a far deeper religious commitment than Congregationalists who, he believed, were already adopting a broader view of Christian truth.[12] Certainly it was the Congregationalists who suffered the greatest losses of men into the ministries of other churches. In the early part of the century there was a constant drift out, something like a tenth of all Congregational ministers joining other churches. If the total fell off

---

[11] See above, p. 77.
[12] Cited in A. Gilbert, *The Making of Post-Christian Britain: A History of the Secularization of Modern Society* (1980), 149.

somewhat thereafter, the denomination's distrust of formal theological creeds and the fact that their main differences with Methodism and Anglicanism concerned forms of church government rather than substantial points of belief, ensured that their men remained particularly vulnerable. W. A. Lupton wrote in 1936 that 'it would seem somewhat ironic that a Principal of a College who held such strong opinions about the Establishment, should have seen so many of his students enter its bosom'.[13] The principal to whom he referred was Dr Scott of Lancashire (1869–1902), about 3 per cent of whose students ended their careers as Anglican priests.[14] Other colleges had even worse records in this respect. Of the men who attended Western College between 1752 and 1901, 6 per cent entered the Anglican priesthood, and rather more than 8 per cent of those at Cheshunt between 1853 and 1903 took the same course.[15] Henry Reynolds freely blamed these losses on the malign influence of the biblical critics. Their findings had so undermined the concept of Scriptural authority, he told a friend in 1891, that Congregational students were being thrown 'into the arms of Rome, or, what is more unsatisfactory, into High Anglican ideas of the Church and of authority'.[16]

This takes us to the losses classified in Table 4.1 under column C, those whose cause is unknown. Why should about 17 per cent of Wesleyans and 14 per cent of Congregationalists have fallen out of the ministry within four years of starting in it between 1831 and 1881? Why did over 40 per cent of the Primitives who began between 1831 and 1871 not last for more than four years? It is likely that some few of these losses were in fact unnotified deaths or retirements, since the collection of such information depended very much on the assiduity of denominational yearbook editors and the

---

[13] W. A. Lupton to C. Surman, 22 Mar. 1936, LIC, Register of Students, K–M, Northern College, Manchester.

[14] Calculated from ibid. A–Z.

[15] The Cheshunt figures are calculated from information contained in O. C. Whitehouse to R. Lovett, 26 Apr. 1904, Cheshunt College Archives, C9/6/82, Westminster College, Cambridge. For the Western College figures see J. C. Johnstone, 'The Story of the Western College', *Transactions of the Congregational Historical Society*, 7 (1916–18), 109.

[16] *Henry Robert Reynolds DD. His Life and Letters. Edited by His Sisters, with Portraits* (1898), 455.

promptness of local denominational officers in providing it. Some were the product of moral lapses although chapel and connexional authorities naturally preferred to draw a discreet veil over such cases. Nevertheless the evidence is there. One Congregational minister was compelled to leave his chapel in 1828 because he had been guilty of 'irregularities and imprudences'. The problem, a correspondent confided in Thomas Wilson, was that his 'appetites are so strong, that when opportunity to gratify them occurs he has no more self control than a child ... he is and must be thought unfit for the Christian ministry'.[17] The Wesleyan Conference expelled the superintendent of Epworth circuit in 1847 even though he denied charges of intemperance. His denials were difficult to sustain in face of the evidence provided by invoices that in a six-month period between September 1846 and February 1847 he had received 132 bottles of porter, 4 bottles of sherry, 2 bottles of port, 1½ gallons of whisky, 9 gallons of brandy, and 16½ gallons of gin.[18] Alexander Bell of the York circuit admitted that he had been imprudent to kiss a lady goodnight in his bedchamber but he denied exposing himself to the maidservant.[19] Such misdemeanours probably diminished as the colleges exercised a growing control over the admission of men. Even so, when one New Connexion Methodist calculated that fifty-nine had left out of the 240 who had entered his church's ministry between 1856 and 1888, he adduced 'dishonourable reasons' in the case of about a third of them.[20]

For another small number, although there is no way now of knowing exactly how many, leaving the ministry must have been the result of changed views or the realization that a vocation had been mistaken. Individuals in this category have, however, left few written records. Susan Budd's study of secularists suggests that typically they lost their faith sometime between the ages of thirty and forty, and the few accounts we do possess of ministerial dropouts tend to sug-

[17] The Revd Alliott to T. Wilson, 18 Jan. 1828, DWL. NCA. 331/15.
[18] W. Vevers to J. Bunting, 11 Mar. 1847, W. R. Ward, *Early Victorian Methodism. The Correspondence of Jabez Bunting, 1830–1858* (Oxford, 1976), 347.
[19] F. Jobson to J. Bunting, 17 May 1849, ibid. 373.
[20] T. Hudson, 'Our Ministry', *Methodist New Connexion Magazine* (1888), 9.

gest a similar age profile.[21] For example, J. F. Makepeace
had been in the Baptist ministry for some time before he
finally found the Calvinism of his deacons too much and
resigned, resolving his own spiritual turmoil about the nature of authority by becoming a lay member of the Catholic
Church.[22] Even more tragically, perhaps, both for the Church
and the individuals concerned, there were those—estimated
at 'scores' in 1937—who realized that they had mistaken
their vocation but who were obliged to remain in it for the
want of any suitable alternative employment.[23]

On the other hand, it is clear from Table 4.1 that the bulk
of men dropped out within the first few years of ministerial
life, confirming Bishop Brooks's feeling that 'it is the first
five years after college which are the most decisive in a
man's career'.[24] Brooks's comments appeared in an article
about ministerial training and it seems likely that the inadequacies of training noted in the previous chapter may
well explain some of the losses in the 'unknown' category,
although the evidence is by definition, circumstantial rather
than explicit. Ten per cent of the Wesleyan students who
completed their training in 1892 did not even go into the
ministry.[25] A. M. Fairbairn found the transition from Congregational college to chapel life traumatic in the extreme.
'It was', he recalled later, 'a season of mental storm and
doubt, when the very foundations of faith seemed to be
shaken ... life seemed a ruin, all its plans had been thrown
down.'[26] Similarly, David Simon underwent a lengthy
period of intellectual turmoil when he left Lancashire College for his first pastorate and had to reconcile his college
learning with the realities of congregational life. Both Fairbairn and Simon survived to enjoy successful careers as
ministers and college principals. The evidence of Table 4.1
indicates that quite a few did not negotiate their early years

[21] S. Budd, *Varieties of Unbelief* (1977), 105 ff.

[22] J. F. Makepeace, *All I Could Never Be* (Oxford, 1924), 60.

[23] H. E. Berry, 'Concerning the Paid Ministry', *Congregational Quarterly*, 15 (1937), 180.

[24] Quoted in P. Evans, 'The Ideal Training for the Ministry', *Baptist Quarterly*, 2 (1926–7), 69.

[25] Wesleyan Conference, *Minutes* (1892), 156.

[26] *Congregational Yearbook* (1913), 165.

in the ministry so successfully. Among them was W. J. Dawson who discovered that his training as a 'seller of rhetoric' did nothing to alert his middle-class congregations, all 'suburban smugness and stagnation', to the needs of the London poor.[27]

Dawson was a Wesleyan, and among the causes which might be further adduced for the high losses sustained by the Methodists must be the burdens imposed by the system of itinerancy. All the connexions moved their men regularly at the direction of a central stationing authority. The maximum period which a Wesleyan could spend in one circuit was three years. The New Connexion initially had a two-year maximum for single men, three years for those who were married, but after 1868 a man could be invited to stay up to five years with the agreement of two-thirds of the Quarterly Meeting. The Free Methodists had similar arrangements and the Bible Christians also permitted some exceptions to their three-year rule. The effects of these relaxations are seen in Table 4.3 which plots the lengths of pastorates held by Methodists over the period 1831 to 1911. Of those men entering the ministry between 1871 and 1891 a quarter of the Primitives and rather more of the United Methodists remained in a circuit for more than three years. The Wesleyans were less responsive to the criticism which emerged in mid-century about the restrictive effect of the three-year maximum. Certainly more of their men did the three-year maximum (63.5 per cent as against 29.6 per cent of Primitives and 20.6 per cent of Uniteds in 1871–91), but fewer than one in twenty did any more. To some extent their hands were tied since the three-year rule had been laid down by Wesley's Deed of Declaration and could be changed only by an Act of Parliament. Right through to the outbreak of war in 1914 there was a constant groundswell of complaint from those in the connexion who believed that nobody could hope to gain the 'confidence and love of poor fallen people who only appears in the same pulpit once a month in the morning, and once a month in the evening, and that for the short space of three years'.[28] Yet the committees which the

[27] W. J. Dawson, *Autobiography of a Mind* (1925), 314.
[28] *Methodist Times*, 29 Apr. 1886.

TABLE 4.3. Length of Methodist Pastorates (%)

Wesleyans / Primitives	1831–51	1841–61	1851–71	1861–81	1871–91	1881–1901	1891–1911
Wesleyans							
Under 1 yr							
1 yr	24.8	24.1	21.7	19.8	17.5	15.4	14.7
2 yrs	28.8	24.7	19.9	16.7	14.1	13.2	13.1
3 yrs	46.2	50.7	57.6	61.4	63.5	56.2	50.6
4 yrs	0.1	0.1	0.3	1.2	2.9	8.6	11.2
5 yrs			0.1	0.3	0.9	3.2	5.0
More than 5 yrs		0.4	0.4	0.6	1.1	3.4	5.4
Primitives							
Under 1 yr	0.2						
1 yr	38.2	33.3	21.3	21.6	20.5	19.6	12.7
2 yrs	38.1	37.4	34.2	28.0	24.8	23.2	15.8
3 yrs	16.6	20.6	27.4	28.6	29.6	29.4	24.7
4 yrs	5.6	6.5	12.8	13.8	15.6	15.0	21.0
5 yrs	0.7	1.8	3.0	4.4	4.7	6.2	13.4
More than 5 yrs	0.6	0.4	1.3	3.6	4.8	6.6	12.4

United	1831–56	1841–66	1851–76	1861–86	1871–96	1881–1906	1891–1916
Under 1 yr	0.7	0.2	0.2	0.1			
1 yr	43.8	35.7	30.7	29.0	26.9	23.6	19.9
2 yrs	29.2	26.9	26.9	25.6	25.3	23.1	23.6
3 yrs	15.7	21.4	22.8	22.3	20.6	18.4	18.2
4 yrs	7.6	10.4	12.3	13.6	14.7	15.3	14.7
5 yrs	1.9	3.4	4.2	5.5	7.1	10.3	11.8
More than 5 yrs	1.1	2.2	3.0	3.9	5.4	9.3	11.8

Wesleyans set up periodically to investigate the matter appeared as unresponsive to the demands for change as did those committees charged with investigating the content of ministerial training. All that emerged was a rather weak recommendation to continue with the present policy of permitting special exceptions to the rule, mainly in inner city areas.

More germane to the present discussion, however, is the effect that the itinerant system had on the ministers themselves. Family men were perhaps the hardest hit since the frequent upheavals disrupted children's schooling and discipline. Commenting on the frequency with which ministers' offspring turned out to be rebellious the New Connexion *Magazine* blamed the 'necessities of the itinerant system [which] deprived them of a home when they were most susceptible of influence for good or evil'.[29] Boarding-school was the usual solution for boys and the Wesleyans opened Woodhouse Grove and Kingswood for just this purpose. But one man's testimony illustrates amply the price that the children often paid. In his six years at the school he claimed that 'he had never seen either his father or his mother, and had so completely forgotten their appearance that their personal identity had become a mere matter of trust in their testimony'.[30] Another believed that during his time at Woodhouse Grove between 1813 and 1819 he had been thrashed every single day. There was a price for parents, too. Tidying up the nursery after his sons had departed for Kingswood, S. R. Hall wrote to his wife that 'everything seemed to tell of other days and early scenes, and then my heart failed me; then I pictured the dear boys as finally separated from my home . . . till I could endure it no longer'.[31] Samuel Sellars appealed in some anguish to Conference when he was posted to Cornwall in 1858. Did the Conference mean, he pleaded, 'to tear his body and soul asunder by forcing him from his children, some of whom were settled in the north'?[32]

Apart from such emotional stresses the itinerant system made considerable physical demands upon the travelling

[29] *Methodist New Connexion Magazine* (1873), 387.
[30] J. R. Gregory, *Benjamin Gregory DD* (1903), 30.
[31] T. Nightingale, *Life of S. R. Hall* (1879), 61–2.
[32] S. Sellars, *The Quaint Preacher* (1892), 69.

preachers. The removal from one circuit to another was a frequent and sometimes difficult experience, especially in the days before the railway modified the hardships of passenger travel. Benjamin Gregory's posting to a Norfolk circuit in 1825 involved a 250-mile journey from Yorkshire in a hired wagon which got lost in Cambridgeshire and took eight days to complete the journey. Certainly the railways made such transfers far easier, but David Waller, who served in the Wesleyan ministry between 1857 and 1911, could still write later that 'the plucking up and replanting ... is a sore trial and tries me more each removal'.[33] Nor were such matters necessarily any more relaxed once a new settlement had been effected. Distances within circuits, especially in the first half of the century, were often considerable and also made severe demands on the individual's physical resources. Louth circuit in 1836 covered 264 square miles and contained forty-nine preaching places, served by just three preachers. Chester was 760 square miles in area, had twenty-three preaching places, and no railway when William Cooke went there in the 1840s. He covered the circuit on foot, reading as he went and protecting himself from the elements by means of an umbrella. Charles New's typical week in the Cornwall circuit in the 1860s began on a Sunday with a three-mile walk to take a morning service, followed by a further mile's journey to preach in the afternoon. In the evening he preached again and then walked home. The next day entailed a five-mile walk to an outlying preaching station. On the Tuesday he covered 28 miles, on Wednesday a further 8, on Thursday 6, and on Friday another 5. On the Saturday he walked home to take his class meeting and then set off to cover another 7 miles to fulfil two further engagements. A weekly coverage of 70 miles was perhaps more typical in scattered rural areas but one obituary in the *Wesleyan Magazine* for 1854 reported that Charles Radcliffe, who had travelled for thirty-eight years, had in that time preached 11,325 sermons and travelled 60,637 miles, a weekly average of almost six sermons and 30 miles.[34]

There is evidence that some men found these physical

[33] A. E. Sharpley, *Life of David James Waller* (1913), 70.
[34] *Wesleyan Methodist Magazine*, 77 (1854), 1068.

demands daunting, especially as they grew older. Writing to
Jabez Bunting in 1831, for example, the Revd W. Leach
asked for a circuit 'without so much travelling as I have had
lately. The Bristol South Circuit is rather fagging. ... I have
had an invitation to Burslem ... is it not a very hard circuit? 1700 members and only two preachers ...?'[35] The
Revd J. Shipman wrote to Bunting in similar vein in 1834.
He was, he said, content to leave the matter of his next posting to the president, the Conference, and God (apparently
in that order) but he 'felt objection to some adjoining circuits because the walks would be too much for me'.[36] A
few years later J. H. James, a younger but sickly individual,
was attracted by the possibilities of Camelford where 'the
chapels are small, the air good, the labour very moderate
and there is a circuit horse'.[37] Doubtless the provision of a
horse reduced the amount of physical exertion required,
while the further reorganization of circuits and the development of mechanized transport later in the century must also
have served to ease the burden. But the physical effort remained considerable, especially in rural circuits. Even into
the twentieth century there were areas of Wales which could
be covered adequately only on foot. It seems probable that
these heavy exertions forced some men out of the ministry
altogether. Certainly, as we shall see in Chapter 5, they were
enough to induce a high level of physical and mental break-
down. Constant removals and travel, said the Revd J. Bell,
called for 'the exercise of faith—it frequently makes us fail
when we think about it'.[38]

On top of this, Methodist preachers were expected to exercise pastoral care over flocks that could be widely scattered.
The Primitives actually laid down a norm of five pastoral
visits per day (except Sundays) and there was a general
expectation on the part of congregations that they would be
the recipients of regular ministerial visits. Most of the surviving biographies contain accounts of visitation records
verging on the heroic, but a valuable corrective is provided

[35] W. Leach to J. Bunting, 14 Feb. 1831, Ward, *Victorian Methodism*, 7–8.
[36] J. Shipman to J. Bunting, 2 July 1834, MAM. PLP. 97–8–10.
[37] J. H. James to J. Bunting, 13 July 1839, ibid. 61–4–17.
[38] J. Bell to Miss Bell, 17 May 1826, ibid. 8–6–2.

by a careful perusal of the Methodist press. Within Wesleyanism there was chronic discontent about the alleged
lack of visitation, sentiments which occasionally erupted
publicly, and it is apparent that dissatisfaction on this score
was a contributory cause of the disruptions which occurred
in the 1840s, hence the *Watchman*'s comment that 'pastoral
visitation is confessedly the great desideratum of the present
age'.[39] In one sense the Methodists were victims of their own
success. The Wesleyans, for example, had one minister for
every 205 members in 1800, but only one for every 229
members by 1845.[40] Still, the attacks were enough to sting
at least one minister into reply. Wesleyans, argued James
Kendall, could not visit so frequently because they were
primarily preachers and needed to study and to concentrate
on connexional business.[41] It was hardly surprising, therefore, that twenty years later the *Methodist Recorder* was still
harping on the subject, complaining that it remained a matter of concern throughout Wesleyanism that visitation was
so neglected.[42] By this time, too, the Primitive laity was
expressing similar discontents. One letter writer complained
that he had not been visited for a year, another that he had
received just four visits in the space of nine years, and the
suggestion that inadequate visitation lay behind falling
membership rolls was one which attracted considerable
support.[43]

Another congregational demand which added to the pressures under which Methodist ministers worked was the
financial one. Rapid expansion in the early years of the
century, combined with economic difficulty in the post-
Napoleonic years, left Wesleyan circuits with considerable
burdens of debt. A popular minister, it was frequently
argued, could boost membership, thereby providing extra
income to offset the liabilities. Impecunious circuits were
thus tempted to petition Conference for men particularly

[39] *Watchman*, 31 Mar. 1852.
[40] J. Kent, 'The Wesleyan Methodists', in R. Davies, A. George, and G. Rupp, *A History of the Methodist Church in Great Britain*, 3 vols. (1965–83), iii. 227.
[41] J. Kendall, *Remarks on Pastoral Visiting Among the Wesleyans* (1852), 3.
[42] *Methodist Recorder*, 19 June 1874.
[43] *Primitive Methodist*, 10, 24, 31 July 1873.

gifted in this area, or, indeed, to be rid of those who were not. This was a practice which did not please everybody:

Sometime the cry is, 'We *must* have some flaming men: what do you think of Mr Such-a-one? To be sure there are several things about him I do not like; but our chapel has a great deal of debt upon it; they say he is a dashing orator; or, he is a rousing fellow, he'll help us to let our seats ...'[44]

Bunting's correspondence is full of preaching invitations whose underlying motivation is quite clear:

The debt as you know is fearful—but our friends are trying to conquer the difficulty—We are now about to try to raise £500— three persons have promised £150 and if you will only give us the promise of your cheering presence and your valuable services for one Lord's Day—the promise will put life into our movement and ensure success to our efforts.[45]

Mammon was similarly struggling to assert himself in the Revd T. Roberts's mind when he contacted Bunting in some concern about a member of his circuit who had just married his dead brother's wife. Some men, Roberts felt, might believe such a liaison to be unscriptural. But, he continued, 'When I look at his liberality to every Fund of Methodism— his standing as a member of the Society—the offices he fills ... and that his name appears on several pages of our minutes, I cannot but regard it as a case requiring cautious treatment.'[46] Such problems were exacerbated by the mid-century building boom. Between 1850 and 1864 the Bible Christians erected 300 new chapels, the Primitives rather more. This produced a fresh round of debt, the redemption of which seemed to absorb energies and time which, it might have been felt, would have been better directed into the redemption of lost sinners. The Revd Withington spent five months, for example, trying to raise funds to pay off his chapel debts. He visited several local chapels in an attempt to get support, went up to London in order to stake a claim on the Conference Chapel Fund, and begged help from people of

[44] J. Crowther, *Strictures on Petitioning for Preachers Among the Methodists* (1809), 6.
[45] W. Bythway to J. Bunting, 14 Jan. 1851, MAM. PLP. 21–49–9.
[46] T. Roberts to J. Bunting, 15 June 1851, ibid. 90–21–9.

influence, such as his former college tutors. It is interesting to note that by the later years of the nineteenth century obituarists were laying much more emphasis on the fund raising abilities of their subjects, often at the expense of rather less worldly virtues. Small wonder that Savil Hatherton, a rather poor nonconformist novelist, suggested that among all the Free Churches there was 'too great an eagerness for men who seem likely to command merely material prosperity without regard to any other consideration'.[47] Stella Davies recalled that her brother Waller made his name in the Wesleyan ministry as a 'beggar'. He could, she wrote, 'make the most eloquent and heart rending appeals for subscriptions ... Hundreds of thousands of pounds passed through his hands.'[48] Even allowing for a certain amount of sisterly exaggeration the point is made. Financial acumen was a desirable ministerial virtue. Lack of it, or a wish to establish a different order of priorities, may again have been responsible for some decisions to leave the ministry altogether.

Obviously, much depended upon relationships between ministers and laymen. All the Methodist connexions relied very heavily upon the laity for the maintenance of their ministries and organization. Wesleyan lay preachers outnumbered the full-time ministers by seven to one in 1883. The ratio was even more striking among the Primitives, over ten thousand lay preachers swamping 541 ministers in 1859. Friction was endemic, especially in the first half of the nineteenth century, and while the origins of Methodism's major schisms were often extremely complex, most of them involved some disagreement about the degree of power which ministers should have and how much democratic rule should be permitted. Under Bunting, the position of the Wesleyan ministers was deemed supreme. Although they were subject to the oversights of district meetings and an individual could be called to account by an aggrieved party, the ministers tended to stick closely together. As they were moved so frequently their most stable and permanent

---

[47] *Manchester, Salford and District Congregational Magazine*, 9 (1887), 81.
[48] S. Davies, *North Country Bred* (1963), 78.

relationship was with the annual Conference, in which ministerial supremacy was enshrined. The general consensus was well put by one delegate in 1878 when he observed that 'many passages of Scripture render it abundantly clear that the governing power in the Church ... belongs exclusively to the clergy ... and that to the laity ... it belongs only to obey'.[49] It was such an attitude that had contributed in 1797 to the secession of the Kilhamite New Connexion in which the lay voice was stronger.

At the opposite extreme to the Wesleyans were the Primitives, whose connexional organization greatly circumscribed ministerial power at both national and local level. Primitive ministers were truly servants of the Church to the extent that the predominantly lay Conference issued very strict regulations in the early years of the century concerning ministerial duties and dress. The differing philosophies underlying the constitutional arrangements of the various Methodist connexions were well illustrated in the famous cartoon, 'Emblems of Methodist Polity', reproduced in Kendall's definitive history of the Primitives. Wesleyanism was represented as a fat priest on the back of a thin layman and described as 'priestly tyranny'. A layman and minister with linked arms illustrated the 'equal rights' of the New Connexion, while two laymen riding a minister and beating him with a stick pictured the 'lay despotism' of Primitive Methodism. Bible Christian ministers were given a certificate of approval each year at the behest of their local circuit. Thus John Barnwell's obituary noted that he had been dropped from the list of approved men in 1841 because 'his preaching did not satisfy the generality of his hearers'.[50] Free Methodism was equally restrictive of its ministers since, like the New Connexion, it had emerged largely as a reaction against what its adherents regarded as the excessive power of the full-time ministry within Wesleyanism. The general sentiments of Free Methodism were well expressed by one of the characters in Mrs Stovin's *Journals of a Methodist Farmer*. 'It was an exceptional platform by the absence of clericals. I would

---

[49] Quoted in R. Currie, *Methodism Divided* (1968), 167.
[50] Bible Christian Conference, *Minutes* (1892), 9.

to God that more laymen were called out to pulpit and platform labour.'[51]

In all of the Methodist connexions the potential for conflict and tension between the lay and ministerial elements was heightened by the operation of the itinerant system. Although a certain amount of local preference was allowed it was always possible that a circuit might be allocated a man whose temperament, practices, theological outlook, or ministerial style were unacceptable. By the time some mutual readjustments had occurred the chances were that the minister might be restationed in another circuit. The Methodist press frequently urged tolerance upon stations about to receive new men although such pleas did not always fall on particularly receptive ears. When F. W. Bourne preached his first sermon at Chatham in 1852 his words 'fell coldly upon my auditory. The attention of the people, in the entire absence of all responsive feeling, was ominous. It foreboded evil.'[52] 'Last Sabbath', noted Mrs Broadbelt in her diary, 'we had our new preacher. Our expectations were not very high, for we heard he was none of the brightest.'[53] New men, especially if they were young or fresh out of college, were always likely to clash with accepted practices or with vested interests since many people had strong emotional attachments to chapels, even if they did not attend regularly. In this situation, particularly in rural areas where congregations received only infrequent visits from the minister, most local initiatives and activities were orchestrated by laymen who found it relatively simple to build up positions of personal influence and power. The temptation to do so must have been almost irresistible to comparatively obscure men who for much of the century had little other opportunity to acquire recognition and status in the world. The Wesleyans tried to put some check on this tendency by decreeing that lay leaders and stewards should be appointed on an annual basis. This failed to solve the problem, however, since the annual appointment provision did not extend to

[51] J. Stovin (ed.), *Journals of a Methodist Farmer, 1871–1875* (1982), 80–1.
[52] W. Luke, *Memorials of Frederick William Bourne* (1906), 48.
[53] S. Thompson, *Memoir of Mrs Anne Broadbelt* (1838), 327.

the trustees, who were frequently the real powers in chapel society because they controlled the purse strings.

Lay officials could, and did, grow immensely powerful. Elijah Morgan wrote in some distress to Bunting in 1836 that in his circuit the local preachers 'seem to have thought they could do better *without* Travelling Preachers'.[54] Bunting received a similar complaint from the Revd H. Ransom at Yarmouth a few years later. Ransom's income had been reduced in order to pay off the circuit debt, and the stewards had further requested that neither of the two men currently serving the station should be invited back. 'You know how easy it is', he wrote, 'for men living at ease in their native soils thus to conspire against us, while we are comparatively strangers among them.' He was being asked to move, he went on, because his voice was judged to be too weak, his colleague because he was thought to be 'not sufficiently polite for the people'. The real reason, he added darkly, was that the circuit stewards wanted absolute control.[55] At about the same time T. R. Jones complained that the accommodation provided in his Glasgow circuit was damp, situated in a poor area of the city, and sited next to a brass foundry. He got short shrift from the stewards who took the view that it was good of them to provide him with anything at all.[56] Even the Wesleyans, it seems, despite their strongly entrenched position, were not always well treated by their lay officers. Amongst the Primitives the discipline which laymen exercised verged sometimes on the tyrannical. The Hull circuit suspended one unfortunate individual for 'being late at Easterington Chapel, lying late in the morning, speaking crossly at Preston to some children when taking breakfast, and finally, for eating the inside of some pie and leaving the crust'.[57] In similar fashion another preacher was suspended for 'not governing his house and family as a Christian preacher'.[58] Quite clearly, such harshness prevailed only in a

[54] E. Morgan to J. Bunting, 18 July 1836, Ward, *Victorian Methodism*, 150.

[55] H. Ransom to J. Bunting, 18 June 1845, MAM. PLP. 86–20–8.

[56] Quoted in A. J. Hayes and D. A. Gowland, *Scottish Methodism in the Early Victorian Period* (Edinburgh, 1981), 122.

[57] H. B. Kendall, *The Origins and History of the Primitive Methodist Church*, 2 vols. (1905), ii. 84.

[58] An event recalled in *Primitive Methodist Leader*, 21 Jan. 1915.

minority of cases and in some instances both parties must have been prepared to tolerate the perceived failings of the other side in the interests of preserving Christian unity; the more so because at the level of the individual chapel this dynamic of lay-ministerial tension could be contained simply because the preacher would normally be moved before too long. It does seem likely, however, that in some instances at least the burden was too great and men slipped out of the ministry and of the historical record. It is significant that the greatest number of losses appear to have occurred in the first four years of ministerial careers, when individuals were perhaps most vulnerable, and also among the Primitives where lay influence was strongest. Not, of course, that the casualties were always invariably ministerial. Thomas Cooper was one well-known lay preacher who was driven out of the Wesleyan Connexion by a tough-minded circuit superintendent, and doubtless there were others.

One of the most potent and longstanding sources of friction within Methodism concerned finance and there is some indication in Bunting's correspondence that this was sometimes used as a weapon by laymen against ministers in the constitutional disputes of the 1840s.[59] Even though pay scales were centrally determined, responsibility for raising and handing over the minister's salary lay with local lay officers. The levels of remuneration are set out in Table 4.4 but great care must be taken in their interpretation. Salaries could be supplemented by extras, such as baptismal fees, and—mainly in rural areas—by payments in kind. On the other hand, rural areas were often remote from circuit authority and for part of the century their inhabitants had also to pay tithes to the Church of England. Ministers were sometimes afraid to press for full payment for fear of offending lay officials and it seems likely, therefore, that less hard cash changed hands than is suggested by the figures in Table 4.4. In the early part of the nineteenth century the Wesleyans held that the cost of building and maintaining a chapel should be defrayed from pew rents, while preachers'

---

[59] For example, see J. Kendall to J. Bunting, 2 Jan. 1835, Ward, *Victorian Methodism*, 131; W. Binning to J. Bunting, 10 July 1851, ibid. 408–9.

TABLE 4.4. Methodist Pay Scales at Selected Dates

Connexion	Date	Payment (£)		Allowances (£)	
Wesleyan	1800	Married man	16.00	Food	26.00
				Wife	12.00
				Servant	6.00
				Child (to 19)	6.00
	1859	Married man	117.00		
		Single man	93.00		
Primitive	1820	Married man	36.00	Rent	10.00
		Single man	16.00		
	1853	Married man	50.00	Subsistence	5.20
		Single man	16.00	Child (to 16)	10.00
	1893	Superintendent	88.00	Subsistence	
		Ordained man	84.00		
		Probationer			
		(year 1)	42.00		
		(years 2–4)	44.30		
United Free	1844	Married man	80.00		
		Probationer	55.00		
	1871	Married man	90.00	Free House or rent	15.00
	1880	Married man		Child (2–16)	6.30
	1905	Married man			
		Maximum	300.00		
		Minimum	110.00		
		Probationer	65.00		

Denomination	Year	Category		Allowance	
New Connexion	1812	Married man	48.00	Board	36.00
				Servant	8.00
				Child	6.00
				(Boys up to 8)	
				(Girls up to 12)	
	1862	Married man	68.00	House or rent	36.00
				Child	
				(Up to 6)	4.00
				(6–12)	3.00
				(12–18)	12.00
		Single man			
		On trial	24.00		
		After 3 yrs	26.00		
		After 4 yrs	44.00		
	1905	Married man		Board	36.00
		Maximum	180.00		
		Minimum	120.00		
		Probationer	80–90.00		
Bible Christian	1837	Qualified	12.60		
		On trial	10.00		
	1861	Married man	36.00	Board/Furnished House	
		After 4 yrs	42.00		
		Single Man			
		On trial	14.00		
		Full Connexion	16.00		
	1905	Minimum	100.00		
		Maximum	150.00		

allowances came from special collections and class monies. If the income from pew rent was insufficient then the burden of chapel débt also fell on to the ordinary members of the local society. If they could not raise sufficient money then Conference could be petitioned for help. If Conference refused, or no appeal was made, then it was usually the preachers' salaries which suffered. In 1823, when his notional allowances should have given him £70 a year, Robert Halley received only £30 and he had to supplement his income, as did several of his colleagues, by taking on private teaching.

The financial burdens on chapel members increased with the great influx of married preachers in the early nineteenth century which pushed up the costs of providing housing and children's allowances. However, James Macdonald discovered that in his new circuit in 1817 'children of the preachers receive nothing' and by the following year some of the child allowances were being paid in the form of books.[60] Only the establishment of the Centenary Fund in 1839 brought any longer term financial security but it long remained the case among the Wesleyans, as in the other connexions, that ministerial income was subject to the vagaries of economic fluctuation, local circumstance, laymen's whims, and to the philosophy which Bunting espoused that over-generous payment would 'indispose us for laborious effort, would insulate us from the poor ... the Church cannot reasonably be expected to do more for its ministers than place them on the same pecuniary level with the *middle class* of its own members'.[61] Thus one man wrote in high dudgeon to the Wesleyan General Committee in 1851 to enquire if there was anything left in the Fund for the Relief of Distressed Ministers. Spalding circuit, he said, 'professes to give me 16/- per week, out of which I have to provide coal and doctoring bills; at the last Quarter Day in consequence of the stopping of supplies in many parts of the Circuit, I only received one half my allowance, the Circuit Steward refusing to advance anything ...'[62] At about the same time a less aggressive colleague, Timothy Moxon, was grateful to re-

[60] F. MacDonald (ed.), *The Letters of James MacDonald, 1816–1831* (n.d.), 40.
[61] J. Bunting to E. Grindrod, 2 Mar. 1831, Ward, *Victorian Methodism*, 8–9.
[62] T. Burrows to J. Bunting, 10 Jan. 1851, MAM. PLP. 21–11–5.

ceive a grant from the Contingency Fund: 'This I got immediately cashed and paid several bills. I highly disapprove
of Bills—and would not run them if not compelled—my
allowance not being paid when due, I am put into
difficulties.'[63] Fifty years later, by which time the whole
system had been placed on a much sounder financial and
organizational basis, Peter Mackenzie still received only
£100 a year (well under his entitlement as a married
preacher) and no child allowance.

Men in other connexions suffered similarly. In the middle
1840s the forerunners of the United Free Methodists tried to
avert a financial crisis by placing a levy of £5 on each of the
preachers. One of their most influential men, Richard Chew,
made ends meet in his early days by working on the principle of never thinking of 'what I wanted or what I liked, but
what I could do without'. Thus he ate meat but once a day,
relied on porridge for all his other meals, and always
travelled third class on the train.[64] A major financial crisis,
also in the mid-1840s, meant that New Connexion ministers
received no child allowances and only a part of their salaries. As late as 1898 the conference expressed some concern at
the failure of many circuits to provide housing for the ministers. The greatest degree of deprivation, however, was probably experienced by men in the Bible Christian and Primitive connexions. Both were relatively poor and paid their
men accordingly. William Clowes and his wife received so
little in their first Primitive pastorates that they dined 'when
by ourselves on a little suet and potatoes, or a piece of bread
and a drink of water'. Further stringencies forced them to
sell off their sole luxury—a feather bed—for 'it was a maxim
with us ... never to go into debt'.[65] Some of the early
Primitive preachers, including Hugh Bourne, were advocates
of free gospelism—living by faith rather than on a guaran-
teed salary—and traces of this lingered until the 1850s
among some members of the movement. Salaries were never
generous and in 1823 all Primitive itinerants were asked to
contribute £1 to enable some payment to be made to those

[63] MSS Journal of the Revd Timothy Moxon, 7 Jan. 1850, MAM. P5.
[64] E. Boaden, *Memoir of the Rev Richard Chew* (1896), 44.
[65] J. T. Wilkinson, *William Clowes, 1780–1851* (1951), 31.

who had received nothing at all during the year on account of the prevailing economic distress.

But even in better times preachers did not always receive their due rewards promptly, as Joseph Preston's surviving account books reveal all too eloquently.[66] Starting in his first circuit at Hepton in 1824, moving thence to Cwm, and on to Salisbury in 1832, he received full payments regularly until September 1834 when the first entry of 'part-payment' appears. Thereafter the Salisbury stewards, and those at Brinkworth, where Preston ministered with some success until 1842, were able to pay him on time and in full. His real difficulties began when he was moved to Redruth in 1842. In this circuit Preston received his full entitlement—£11. 1s. 0d. plus £3.18s. 0d. children's allowance—on only one occasion out of thirteen quarter-days. The nadir was reached in March 1844 when his quarterly payment amounted to just under 19s. Pontypool, where he was posted in 1845, was initially more promising, but by June 1847 his pay was in arrears and remained so until he left for Frome in 1849. Four relatively secure years followed but his first quarter-day at Bristol in March 1853 brought in only part of his salary, and the circuit never once managed to pay him his full salary on time until June 1855. It is hardly surprising, therefore, that at least one man claimed in his biography of 1894 that his father had resigned the Primitive ministry because he could not manage on the small, irregular stipend, and the movement's most recent historian has suggested that such parsimony may well have deterred the half-hearted from entering and also encouraged a high turnover of manpower, a suggestion fully borne out by the figures in Table 4.1.[67]

Sometimes—perhaps quite frequently in rural areas—a circuit was dependent on the financial support of one or two wealthy individuals. Not only did this place ministers to some extent at the mercy of such lay figures, as the Revd T. Roberts had discovered, but it also threatened the financial security of some circuits. Thus the removal of a Mr Hosegood to Bristol in 1878 posed considerable problems for the

[66] Joseph Preston's Account Books, MAM. MA 598.5.
[67] J. S. Werner, *The Primitive Methodist Connexion: Its Background and Early History* (Wisconsin, 1984), 141.

local Bible Christian circuit of Seavington, since his weekly
contribution was well in excess of the average halfpenny
provided by the majority of members who were rural
workers.[68] In some instances, too, it is apparent that stewards were prepared to pay not some centrally determined
scale, but a figure which bore some relationship to the price
of local labour. Thus Dorsetshire Bible Christians in 1837
paid an annual salary reckoned the equivalent of a farm
labourer's wage.

It seems likely, then, that men frequently received less
than their prescribed due. This in itself must have forced
some out of the ministry, however reluctantly, because they
could just not afford to live. It is significant, therefore, that
the loss rates for all denominations as illustrated in column
C of Table 4.1 are highest in the first half of the century
when incomes were relatively small and most liable to
fluctuation. Drop-out rates remained quite high during the
years of the mid-Victorian boom, although by then a somewhat different financial consideration was probably at work.
With the possible exception of some Baptists and some of
those men in the smaller Methodist connexions, most nonconformist ministers by this time were aspiring to middle-
class status. Like those of similar standing in society at
large—'men of moderate fixed incomes'—they suffered from
the effects of the higher price levels associated with the
boom.[69] Significantly lower loss rates appear later on, by
which time the downward secular trend of food prices in
particular was undergirding a general improvement in
Victorian living standards. Improvements in the size and
certainty of the financial rewards attached to the ministry
were also working in the same direction and the *Primitive
Methodist* echoed a general sentiment when it suggested in
1894 that improvements in material conditions had helped
to stem the outward flow from the Methodist ministry.[70]
Even so, discontent over salaries, if now less prominent,

[68] M. D. Costen (ed.), *Wesleyans and Bible Christians in South Somerset: Accounts and Minutes, 1808–1907* (Somerset Record Society, Taunton, 1984), 129.
[69] The description is W. R. Greg's in his 'Life at High Pressure', *Contemporary Review*, 25 (1875), 634.
[70] *Primitive Methodist*, 19 Apr. 1894.

must have remained as a cause of some ministerial losses. David Waller was among the best paid of all the Wesleyans when he got £260 plus allowances while serving at Southport in 1876 but the suggestion that the typical Wesleyan salary was then about £200 a year evoked a storm of scornful rebuttals.[71] Even in 1879 about a third of all Wesleyan circuits were paying less than the prescribed minimum salary of £150 a year for married men and £80 for a single man. By 1905 only twenty New Connexion ministers, 10 per cent of the total, were getting more than the connexion's recommended minimum. Furthermore, rising prices after 1900 must have begun to impose fresh strains on ministerial pockets. Possibly the main effect of this, however, was not so much in driving men from the ministry but in deterring them from entering in the first place, especially as the range of alternative employments was widening. This at least was the suggestion of a delegate at the Primitive Methodist Conference in 1914. The volume of applications for the ministry varied, he claimed, with the level of secular wages.[72]

It would clearly be invidious to suggest that material matters such as income were a major consideration with most Methodist ministers. Like men in secular employments, they could not be totally indifferent to such concerns but for the majority earthly rewards were as nothing compared with the high calling of the Christian ministry. But we are here seeking explanations for those who found the ministry too hard to sustain. Certainly when we turn to consider the Baptists and Congregationalists similar evidence emerges to indicate that material affairs were important in helping to account for the high drop-out rates described in Table 4.2. In ·the 1840s the *Congregational Magazine* was to be found suggesting that young ministers were increasingly coming forward 'not so much as labourers in the vineyard of Christ as inquirers for an easy place, a good salary and respectability'.[73] This certainly appears to have been true of the Revd T. Lamb, who turned down an opening at Market Rasen in 1827 on the grounds that 'the work to be done here

[71] *Methodist Recorder*, 16 Jan. 1874.
[72] Reported in *United Methodist*, 25 June 1914.
[73] *Congregational Magazine* (1844), 127.

is, I really fear, more than my constitution would allow me to undertake with comfort, or even with safety'. He did not feel able to serve two congregations by preaching three times on Sundays, travelling eight miles to preach twice at a midweek service, and taking a fortnightly meeting at another outlying situation. 'The exertion, mental and corporeal,' he suspected, 'for which these services call, I really stand in doubt of my ability to undergo for a continuance.' Besides, he continued, giving the game away completely, he doubted if the Church could afford to pay more than £50 a year.[74] John Clifford was complaining about Baptists in a similar vein later in the century, lamenting their 'overeagerness to obtain wealth and their want of love to souls'.[75]

In dealing with this aspect of ministerial life among Baptists and Congregationalists, the historian is on even less secure ground than with the Methodists, for there were no centrally determined salary scales to act as a benchmark. Much depended on the size and situation of the individual church as well as on the reputation of the particular minister. In mid-century the major figures in Congregationalism could command impressive salaries. James Sherman was paid £500 a year by the 3,000 members of the Surrey Chapel. Raffles drew £700 from his Liverpool congregation, while Thomas Binney's salary at the Weigh House was £600. But these were large chapels and big names. Pew rents in less wealthy situations could not produce such large salaries and the average salary in 1830 was reckoned to be £100 a year for Congregational ministers.[76] This was what Eliakim Shadrack earned at Dursley in 1844, although over four–fifths of it came from the pew rents paid by just five families. When depression in the local woollen industry pushed down business profits sufficiently to drive away one of the families, Shadrack's income fell. By 1855 he was down to just over £65 a year. At Flockton, Joseph Sowerby earned just £8 a year and worked as a weaver for most of the week. George McCree earned rather more, but only because he supplemented his income by giving public lectures: 'Let it

---

[74] T. Lamb to T. Wilson, 6 Dec. 1827, DWL. NCA. 331/2.
[75] *General Baptist Repository*, 74 (1872), 303.
[76] A figure given in A. Peel, *These Hundred Years, 1831–1931* (1931), 26–7.

be frankly stated at once that they were a source of income to him.'[77] Before the development of a national education system, teaching was a particularly favoured form of income supplementation among many ministers. The most able or famous took in pupils for the ministry. It was in this way that Alexander Stewart was able to treble his £100 a year at Barnet by taking on five pupils at £40 each per year.

Guest preaching was another widely used means of generating extra income and one which became more remunerative as transport facilities improved. In general, however, this practice rested on the Scriptural principle of giving to those who already had, since the biggest fees were commanded by the most famous and, hence, the best paid. Most church treasurers, wrote W. H. Mills, knew the great divines by their doctrines but John Ogden Green, chapel treasurer at Wycliffe, Ashton-on-the-Hill, knew them 'by their price'.[78] If men like Sowerby serve as a timely reminder that some Congregationalists were badly paid, it is also worth noting that the Congregational Union claimed in 1853 that only about 10 per cent of ministers got less than £70 a year and it is evident that, as a group, the Congregationalists were better off than men in other denominations. Even so, there was still a gap between income and expectation in this, the most socially elevated and aspiring of the nonconformist denominations. In the late 1820s the average income of an Anglican curate was £81 a year and the average salary of all incumbents a little short of £300 a year.[79] In 1870 the Congregational Union organized a special conference to consider stipends. It concluded that there was a large number of ministers for whom inadequate financial support was provided.

Yet they were always better paid than their Baptist counterparts. True, one can find examples of relatively highly paid Baptists. One Exeter chapel paid its pastor £200 in 1868, and J. F. Makepeace recalled that his father earned £300 a year.[80] R. F. Jeffrey settled at Belfast's Mountpottin-

---

[77] *George William McCree: His Life and Work. By His Elder Son* (1893), 166.

[78] W. H. Mills, *Grey Pastures* (1924), 7. Wycliffe was a fictional representation of Albion Chapel, Ashton-under-Lyne.

[79] J. A. Banks, *Prosperity and Parenthood. A Study of Family Planning Among the Victorian Middle Classes* (1954), 179.

[80] Makepeace, pp. 2 ff.

ger Baptist Tabernacle in 1897 only when a salary of £250 was agreed, his lowest previous income being £237 received during his first pastorate after he left college.[81] Bloomsbury Chapel paid William Brock £700 a year in 1861 while in Liverpool Stowell Brown's stipend rose to £900. Much earlier, Benjamin Evans had received £100 when he settled at Scarborough in 1825, a figure which had risen to £150 by 1862. Much more typical, however, was John Cragg's salary in rural Norfolk in the 1860s. He had a rent-free house, an income from rent on church property of £25 a year, and hoped to raise another £10 or so from subscriptions, giving him a projected annual income of about £65. This was slightly less than the average salary which, according to one Baptist Union official in 1873, was received by men in English churches—about £75 a year.[82] Small wonder that Spurgeon should consider Baptist congregations to be parsimonious in the extreme, even though he personally was the object of affections and generosity which sometimes bordered on the idolatrous. It was remarkable but true, he once observed, that 'ministers of the Gospel were not able to live on much less than other people. They cannot make a shilling go as far as other people make a sovereign. Some of them try very hard, but they do not succeed.'[83]

It was in Wales, probably, that the Baptists were worst off. The Principality did not have a fully monetarized economy in the first half of the century and the uncertainties of employment made many chapels reluctant to take on full-time ministers. As a result, many of them were part-timers, sustaining themselves in the main by farming or shopkeeping. In mid-century it was reckoned that only about twenty Baptist and Independent ministers received more than £100 a year and that the average income was about £50. In 1862, seventy-seven Welsh Baptist churches paid their settled ministers a total of £1905, an average of less than £25 each. In low paid pastorates and in Wales generally, it seems likely that men slipped in and out of the full-time ministry as circumstances dictated. Although Baptist leaders did not care for this practice, rightly viewing it as a distraction from

[81] G. Hibbert, *Mountpottinger Baptist Tabernacle* (Belfast, 1978), 19.
[82] *Baptist Handbook* (1873), 59.
[83] Quoted in the *Congregationalist*, 3 (1874).

the proper tasks of the ministry, little of practical or comprehensive utility was done until the very end of the century
to remove its underlying economic causes.[84]

It has already been noted with reference to the Methodists
that drop-out rates fell quite sharply in the second half of
the nineteenth century, a trend also apparent among the
Congregationalists, though not the Baptists. Food prices
declined rapidly after 1873 with the importation of cheap
foodstuffs into Britain. Even those on fixed incomes benefited in real terms. By the end of the century such complaints about salaries as were heard from ministers tended
to come from those who found themselves in one or other of
two particular situations. The development of suburbs left
many chapels isolated in the major city centres, especially
London, with falling and generally poorer memberships,
as the wealthier took advantage of improved transport and
suburban building to move to more salubrious surroundings. Such chapels, said the Baptist Union in 1884, 'are
languishing for want of attendance, and are frittering away
their strength and the property which they hold from their
fathers in the vain attempt to battle with circumstances too
strong for them . . .'.[85] Another contemporary report described such chapels as being in a desperate state, their
pastors 'fighting desperately for bread and butter'.[86] By 1900
over 60 per cent of provincial Congregational churches had
less than a hundred members and only about fifty had more
than five hundred. About one in ten of all the denomination's
churches could not afford to support a full-time minister.
The average membership of Baptist chapels was about 140
but over 60 per cent of English congregations and over two-
thirds of Welsh chapels had less than this. It was estimated
in 1884 that a church with between fifty and a hundred
members could support a pastor only if it got a subsidy of
twenty or thirty pounds a year.[87] Almost a half of English

---

[84] See, for instance, Baptist Noel's comments to the annual assembly in 1867,
reprinted as 'A Brief Review of the Churches Associated in the Union', in *Cardiff
Memorial*.
[85] *Baptist Handbook* (1884), 21.
[86] *Christian World*, 22 Jan. 1891.
[87] *Baptist Handbook* (1884), 24.

Baptist ministers and over two-thirds of those in Wales received less than £100 a year.[88]

But it was probably the rural chapels that suffered most of all, as was the case with the Methodists and, for that matter, the Anglicans, too.[89] In those parts of the country worst affected by agricultural depression, farm incomes tumbled. The exodus of rural population left chapel rolls either stagnating or diminishing, pew rents falling and, as a result, ministerial incomes declining. 'We are compelled', admitted the Bible Christian Conference *Minutes* in 1891, 'to recognise the fact that in our rural districts the difficulties are increasing . . .'[90] Even earlier, at the very beginning of the agricultural depression, Alexander Maclaren had told the Baptist Union in his presidential address that in the rural counties of Hereford, Cumberland, Dorset, Lincolnshire, Oxford, Shropshire, Stafford, Surrey, and Sussex, three-fifths of the churches had an average membership of twenty-seven. 'Village nonconformity', he concluded, 'is in a perilous condition . . .'[91] At about the same time the *Christian World* offered books at cut prices to country ministers. Within a fortnight it had received letters from more than 260 men unable, so they claimed, to afford books at all. In the last quarter of the century the nonconformist press was dominated by complaints about the continuing hardships of rural pastors in the face of agricultural decline. One Congregationalist's wife told a paper that her husband's income of £54 a year was totally inadequate.[92] Another had rather more but found it impossible to make ends meet on £75: 'I feel sometimes heartbroken, and with the dreadful strain of pinching and saving, of having to do the family washing, sewing, housework with not a soul to help, I am so tired at night that I just sit down and nearly sob my heart out.'[93]

[88] Figures from *Christian World*, 27 Apr. 1911.
[89] For the Anglicans see C. Linnell, *Some East Anglian Clergy* (1961), 170. For the rural problems of late nineteenth-century nonconformity see A. Rogers, 'When City Speaks for Country: The Emergence of the Town as a Focus for Religious Activity in the Nineteenth Century', *Studies in Church History*, 16 (1979); D. H. Thompson, 'The Churches and Society in Nineteenth Century England', ibid. 8 (1972).
[90] Bible Christian Conference, *Minutes* (1891), 26.
[91] *Baptist Handbook* (1876), 60.
[92] *Independent and Nonconformist*, 28 Aug. 1891.
[93] Ibid. 31 Jan. 1895.

Given the revelations that Charles Booth and Seebohm Rowntree were soon to make about the extent of poverty in urban Britain, her complaint may appear less than justified.

The point was, however, that ministers believed that they had particular social responsibilities to fulfil and a status to uphold, a belief which was generally shared by chapel members themselves. The real, practical burden may have fallen on the wives, but it *was* difficult, as a correspondent to the *Baptist* argued, to maintain a proper position of responsibility on £60 a year.[94] Ministers were regarded as being part of the professional middle class and while Spurgeon and a few others could perhaps afford the appropriate life-style, the vast majority could not. Spurgeon's Riviera holidays may have been necessitated by ill health, but he also kept a carriage and pair, and had a penchant for expensive cigars. A much lesser Baptist light complained that he had to live on £50, plus a small allowance from the local County Association which covered his rent. He cast an envious eye on the neighbouring Wesleyan who had £150 a year and a free manse. Yet, he went on, 'I am expected to dress as well as he, to move in the same society, to be able to put my hand into my pocket just as he does, to send my child to the same school, and what applies to me applies also to my wife.'[95] By the time he wrote, the problem of small salaries had once again become a matter of general concern as all ministers were affected when the cost of living turned upwards after 1900. 'Everything has gone up during the last ten years', commented the *Primitive Methodist Leader* in 1915, 'except ministers' salaries.'[96]

Clearly the answer to the problems of low morale and manpower loss arising from inadequate incomes lay in the establishment of schemes to permit some supplementation of the lowest salaries. A Society for Augmenting the Income of Our Pastors had been established by the Baptists as early as 1869, largely at the instance of Joseph Angus and Charles Spurgeon. But it was a voluntary scheme only. Each participating church paid in ten pounds a year and the proceeds of

[94] *Baptist*, 14 Feb. 1873.
[95] *Baptist Times and Freeman*, 4 Apr. 1914.
[96] *Primitive Methodist Leader*, 29 Apr. 1915.

the invested capital were distributed to those churches in the scheme whose ministers earned between £60 and £120. In its first year of operation the fund provided over £22 to each qualifying chapel.[97] The Congregationalists had a Church Aid Society which paid out small doles to those ministers who could satisfy the administrators that they were maintaining congregations and memberships. But the schedules which applicants had to complete were akin to those of the Charity Organisation Society and the scheme's impact was thus very slight. This, too, was a voluntary arrangement and herein lay the rub for the independent churches. In both denominations there was considerable resistance to any centrally organized and funded scheme of sustentation on the grounds that it would compromise the basic tenet of congregational autonomy. The Congregational Union rejected a sustentation scheme for this reason in 1872 and again in 1895. Not until 1909, by which time the problems were otherwise insoluble, were the political objections overcome and a target of £250,000 set for a fund which was to guarantee everyone a minimum salary of £150. The prodigious energies of J. H. Shakespeare galvanized the Baptists into adopting a similar sustentation programme. By 1914 he had helped to raise a quarter of a million pounds to underwrite minimum salaries of between £100 and £150 a year. Churches had to provide a set portion of the minister's salary and could then apply to the Baptist Union for a contribution to bring the stipend up to the recommended levels. As with the Congregationalists, this was an important step in the transmogrification of Baptist polity, as the petitioning chapel had to be supported by the local county association and had to belong to the Union, which had absolute discretion in making or withholding grants.

The level of salary that a particular individual could command depended to some extent on the sort of relationship he had with his flock, and this leads us to a second explanation of ministerial loss. It seems probable that, as with the Methodists, some men were driven from the ministry by the frictions which bad relationships could generate. It is true

[97] *Freeman*, 3 Feb. 1871.

that we are dealing with bonds that were usually cemented with Christian ideals of love, service, and submission. Ministers were generally acknowledged to possess an authority which derived from Christ himself, obviously not a source to be lightly disregarded by genuinely God-fearing people. Nevertheless, there is evidence that the practice was quite often less rosy than the theory. In both Baptist and Congregational traditions, a domineering minister facing a strong-willed congregation, a young man preaching new theological ideas in a conservative chapel, the power of the purse proud or the ambitious office holder—all could easily cause relationships to degenerate into sour confrontation, love replaced by virtual tyranny. 'Noone acquainted with the state of the Congregational churches', commented the *Christian World* in 1871, 'can candidly deny that it exists . . . Many a man well fitted to adorn the Christian ministry and do good work in the vineyard of Christ has turned away for ever from the Congregational Church.'[98] Thus when Robert Martin died in 1852 it was reported that he had been chronically depressed for two years as a result of differences between himself and his congregation. William Judson quit the Congregational cause at Saffron Walden because of 'the unhallowed proceedings of a party in his congregation, who, . . . loved to have the pre-eminence'.[99]

In both denominations ministers were called, usually by a vote of the members of what were in fact independent churches. Unlike their Methodist counterparts, neither the minister nor the church members were ultimately subject to any higher authority—at least, not any earthly one. Yet even the very process of selection could create problems for the minister concerned. In 1835 rival factions in the Tockholes Independent Chapel called two ministers simultaneously. On the next Sunday, both arrived at the chapel. One occupied the pulpit and announced a hymn, whereupon supporters of the second man gave out Psalm 119 and proceeded to take ninety minutes to sing through its 176 verses. Not surprisingly, perhaps, the congregation split and Tock-

[98] *Christian World*, 1 Sept. 1871.
[99] *Evangelical Magazine*, 30 (1852), 601.

holes found itself with two Independent churches for a while. One minister later recalled that in 1834 he had been involved in elections for pastorates at four different churches. Although he was defeated every time he had in each case a sizeable minority support which must have been a matter of some concern to the successful candidate.[100]

Some ministers expected to be given considerable powers by their churches. Thus Joseph Parker told the deacons of Manchester's Cavendish Street Chapel that he would accept the pastorate only 'if I have granted to me the presidentship of the church, and of the court of deacons, and I honourably submit to you ... that the pastor's position should be acknowledged as chairman of your meetings'.[101] Yet by any standards Parker was a denominational giant, and what was possible for a man already of high standing, a proven soul winner, an attractive preacher, a successful fund raiser and pew filler, was not possible for men of lesser reputations and statures. They must always have been much more vulnerable to congregational demands and pressures, especially if they were just starting their careers. The decorative hyperbole of William Best's comments should not be allowed to obscure their very substantial foundation of truth. Mulling over in his mind whether or not to accept a particular invitation, this young Baptist wrote: 'My preaching perhaps would not suit them. It might be too simple, or too elaborate; too intellectual, or not sufficiently so; too highly Calvinistic; not doctrinal enough; the tie of my cravat might not suit their taste, or the fashion of my whiskers. I might not be tall enough. Churches are very funny sometimes.'[102]

In such situations some men became virtual hostages to particular factions within their churches. Simon Binks found his new congregation at Lutterworth divided among Antinominians, infant and adult baptizers, and a family clique into which the previous minister had married and which, therefore, had been accustomed to exercising

[100] These episodes are described in B. Nightingale, *Lancashire Nonconformity*, 6 vols. (Manchester, 1890–1903), ii. 17, 276.
[101] W. Adamson, *The Life of the Rev Joseph Parker DD* (1902), 68.
[102] 'Selections from the Letters of the Late Rev William Best BA', *Baptist Magazine*, 69 (1877), 208–9.

considerable influence. It was in some despair that Binks wrote to his erstwhile mentor, Thomas Wilson, asking for advice on how to preserve unity and retain his own independence.[103] Wilson was involved for nearly half a century in placing students from Hoxton and Highbury into pastorates and his correspondence reveals just how exposed ministers could be to behind-the-scenes scheming on the part of their congregations. Thus a Mr Newland complained about the Revd Blackett at Harley: 'I fear he is not making much advance ... his delivery and even reading of the Scriptures is so very schoolboyish that he gains no reception of hearers and meets with but little attention when he goes in places adjacent.' Newland added that in his opinion and also that of his friends at Harley Blackett should be asked to leave at the end of the year if there was no improvement. He concluded: 'Mr B. is now in the North visiting his Fds. & knows not of this letter. If you write to him proposing any other place you had probably better not mention having heard from me.'[104] Small wonder that John Angell James should later reckon that in many Congregational and Baptist churches 'the pastor is depressed far below his just level ... his opinion is received with no deference, his person treated with no respect'.[105] By the end of the century things were even worse, at least for Congregationalists. In an attempt to bridge the gap between pastor and people, and also to counter the growing sacerdotalism of the Church of England, some ministerial prerogatives had been removed or diluted, prompting J. H. Rigg to claim that Congregational ministers, like Baptists, had 'the burden but not the power; office without prerogative and responsibility without authority'.[106]

If, as seems likely, problems of power, status, and salary were liable to unsettle men working in the Old Dissenting ministry, it is important to remember that such concerns may not always have driven them out of the ministry altogether. Unlike the centrally directed and regularly moved

---

[103] S. Binks to T. Wilson, 1 Jan. 1828, DWL. NCA. 331/6.
[104] R. Newland to T. Wilson, 2 Jan. 1828, ibid. 331/8.
[105] J. A. James, *Church Member's Guide* (1850), 60.
[106] J. H. Rigg, *A Comparative View of Church Government* (1887), 177. Identical sentiments were expressed in Lord Snell, *Men, Movements, and Myself* (1937), 117.

Methodists, they were free agents and if a particular situation became too unbearable then they were free to seek another. Some, as we have seen, went abroad in the quest for more congenial circumstances. Others preferred to move within Britain. Table 4.5 shows that consistently throughout the nineteenth century about three-quarters of all Congregational pastorates lasted for less than ten years. The experience of Henry Bevis, who left college in 1836, took his second church in 1838, and retained it until his death in 1893 is, therefore, quite exceptional. Pastorates of under five years remained at a fairly steady level, just short of 50 per cent for the whole period between 1861 and 1911, just over 50 per cent for the earlier period. Among the Baptists there were some signs of increased mobility. Pastorates of less than ten years accounted for about 70 per cent of the total until mid-century, and rose to over 80 per cent among men entering the ministry between 1891 and 1911. From about 1870 onwards the number of pastorates of less than five years also increased. The *Freeman* had no doubts as to the real origin of this trend: 'Among the causes of ministerial unsettlements the smallness of the stipend attached to the office of pastor occupies a prominent place.'[107] The paper reverted frequently to this theme during the next quarter-century, publishing a letter in 1893, for example, from an irate deacon who complained that his minister had just moved to a new church, a decision, he claimed, that had been prompted purely by 'money considerations'.[108]

Amongst both Baptists and Congregationalists there was growing disquiet by the end of the century about the whole problem of increasing ministerial movement, Baptists in particular expressing fears that the whole process was degenerating into an undignified scramble for places. This was a danger increased by the continued presence in the Baptist ministry of a substantial proportion of untrained men. Although Table 2.1 shows that only a quarter of new entrants between 1890 and 1919 lacked formal training, almost a half, 47 per cent, of those currently pastoring congregations

---

[107] *Freeman*, 14 July 1871.
[108] Ibid. 1 Sept. 1893.

TABLE 4.5. Length of Congregational and Baptist Pastorates (%)

Length (yrs)	Year of Entry											
	1841–61		1851–71		1861–81		1871–91		1881–1901		1891–1911	
	Bap	Cong	Bap	Cong	Bap	Cong	Bap	Cong	Bap	Cong	Bap	Cong
0–5	43.5	51.8	44.8	50.2	44.1	47.5	46.0	47.2	49.6	46.9	51.2	45.7
6–10	26.9	23.9	27.0	24.8	29.0	26.1	30.0	27.6	29.1	28.5	30.4	30.3
11–15	11.7	9.1	11.1	9.1	11.1	8.6	8.8	8.8	9.9	11.0	9.8	12.6
16–20	6.7	5.6	6.5	5.2	6.4	3.8	5.1	3.8	3.7	4.4	3.4	6.0
21–5	3.8	3.4	3.0	2.6	2.8	2.7	2.7	2.3	2.1	2.5	1.5	2.1
26–30	3.1	3.0	1.5	2.7	1.3	3.5	2.3	2.7	2.4	1.7	1.9	0.7
31–5	0.9	1.3	1.2	1.9	1.0	2.6	1.3	2.5	0.8	1.2	0.8	0.8
36–40	1.6	0.6	2.1	1.6	2.3	2.5	1.3	1.8	0.8	0.8	0.4	0.4
41–5		0.3		0.7		0.9	0.9	0.8	0.8	0.4	0.6	0.2
46+	1.4	0.7	1.2	0.7	1.4	1.1	1.0	1.1	0.8	0.6	0.4	0.1

in 1901 had not received a college education.[109] This acted
to keep down salaries because untrained men commanded
and probably expected to receive lower incomes, a feature
not without appeal in a relatively poor denomination.
But the ease with which untrained men could enter the
ministry exacerbated the Baptists' enduring problem of
oversupply to which Spurgeon's College was already making
a major contribution. In 1891 the President of the Baptist
Union, James Owen, acknowledged that 'the supply of
ministers is in excess of the demand'.[110] 'Mnason' took this
up in an article in the *British Weekly*, pointing out that over
half of the men listed in the current *Handbook* as unemployed had entered the ministry within the last thirty years
and could not, therefore, be regarded as retired on grounds
of age. Despite indignant rebuttals by the college, it was
further asserted that over three-quarters of the unemployed
were former Spurgeon's students.[111] But whatever its precise causes, there was clearly a problem of settlement and
removal among the Baptists by the later years of the century
and in 1887 the Baptist Union responded by establishing a
Board of Introduction and Consultation. It did not work well
and not until 1914 was a more effective scheme adopted as
part of Shakespeare's package to improve ministerial training, income, and career prospects.

The Congregational Union was under similar pressures
and also produced a scheme before the war. Again, the motive was partly to introduce some sense of order and dignity
to a very chaotic and apparently mercenary process. But the
new machinery was also designed in the widely shared—
but erroneous—belief that the Congregationalists, too, were
suffering from an oversupply of ministers. This was a claim
which had resurfaced regularly ever since Dr Hannay had
made it at the annual assembly in 1881. Thus 'Better Times'
reckoned on 'good authority' that in 1911 the denomination had a hundred empty churches but four hundred

[109] J. Munson, 'The Education of Baptist Ministers, 1870–1914', *Baptist Quarterly*, 26 (1876), 324.
[110] *Baptist Handbook* (1891), 37.
[111] *British Weekly*, 26 Mar. 1891. There was again considerable correspondence about the glut of ministers in *Baptist*, 4, 11, 18, 25 Jan. 1895.

unemployed ministers.[112] In 1914 J. H. Riddette estimated that there were currently 160 churches without pastors, 200 men looking for situations, and a further 60 students due out of college in the summer.[113] That he could produce such radically different figures within three years of 'Better Times' indicates just how unreliable and misleading the statistics could be. Many of the names listed in the *Congregational Yearbook* as being without pastoral charge were those of men already retired or engaged in education. In 1891 a *British Weekly* survey calculated that there were 572 unemployed ministers for 327 vacancies, but it went on to point out that rather more than 60 per cent of the unemployed had been in the ministry for more than thirty years and could probably be regarded as retired. This would appear to have been a well-founded assumption, for Table 4.1 indicates that the typical ministerial career for those entering in the 1860s was rather less than thirty years: over half of those beginning in the period 1861–81 had careers which lasted for less than twenty-four years. Supply and demand among the Congregationalists, in other words, would appear to have been in rough balance. Indeed, the Secretary of the Congregational Union suggested as much when he stated in 1895 that of 633 men listed in the *Yearbook* as being without pastoral charge, 310 were described as being either in education or retired. He reckoned that this was an underestimate and that 375 would be a more realistic total. This left 258—at a time when there were 271 vacant churches.[114]

But if oversupply did not push Congregationalists to frequent movement or even out of the ministry altogether, it is apparent that, as with Methodists and Baptists, secular considerations such as salary, working relationships, and material conditions often did so. Certainly the majority soldiered on, as the *Methodist Recorder* had it, in 'obscurity. Quietly and unobtrusively ... amid discouragement and privation, and under a multitude of depressing influences'.[115] But

[112] *Christian World*, 24 Aug. 1911.
[113] Ibid. 5 Feb. 1914.
[114] *Independent and Nonconformist*, 3 Jan. 1895. In London in 1891 it was reckoned that only 38 out of 421 ministers were genuinely unemployed at a time when 19 metropolitan chapels were without pastors, *Congregational Yearbook* (1891), 453.
[115] *Methodist Recorder*, 8 Aug. 1873.

against this background has to be set the evidence of this chapter that, despite its aura of apparent immutability, the manpower of the Victorian ministry was subject to a ceaseless ebb and flow. This was, furthermore, a tendency less marginal than some might care to believe.

5

Private Lives

ONE day in August 1818 Ben Carvosso, a young Wesleyan preacher, found his daily devotions powerfully interrupted by thoughts of marriage. With some perplexity he noted that 'the season of my life is come ... for entering on that state; but, if I am ever permitted to take the step, I know not as yet on what object to fix'. A few days later, at prayer once more, the name of a female acquaintance came into his mind: 'Ever since, my mind has been drawn towards her as the only fit person I know.'[1] Shortly, he put pen to paper and approached the young lady who, after expressing some suitably decorous surprise at Carvosso's proposal, which had come very much out of the blue, accepted his offer of marriage. Within a month a few minor technical problems had been overcome and Carvosso was noting happily in his private journal that there were no obstacles 'to our union arising from want of natural affection'.[2] Andrew Lynn's consultations with the Almighty on the same subject, however, produced a rather different outcome. One night, he recalled, it seemed as if God was speaking directly to him: 'If thou get married, thou wilt shut up thy way into the ministry and I will flog thee.'[3] Lynn took the hint and deferred his plans. Jabez Bunting was another to whom this whole subject was a matter of no little soul searching. He was, he admitted, much attracted to Sarah Maclardie, but he had some doubts as to whether it was consistent with his duty as a minister 'to engage in such a relation at all'. The object of his affections was, he believed, sincerely and truly, 'but not eminently', pious, and the influence of her early Calvinistic upbringing

[1] G. Blencowe, *The Faithful Pastor. A Memoir of Rev Benjamin Carvosso* (1857), 50–1.
[2] Ibid. 58.
[3] A. Lynn, *Methodist Records* (1858), 98.

had not yet been entirely eradicated. Furthermore, he feared that her vivacious and cheerful temperament might 'easily affect a mind like mine with similar levity, the bane of all spiritual religion'. On reflection, however, he decided that she could probably overcome this by prayer and an increase in vital religion. This left only the matter of her dress, 'at present far too gay and costly and worldly'. Still, he concluded, with an arrogance at once breathtaking and eloquent of the nature of contemporary marriage relationships, 'she would probably promise to make the necessary amendments, on proper representation'.[4] Nor were his hopes misplaced, for Miss Maclardie did become his wife. After her relatively early death, Bunting remarried but it was a step which he took in a no less calculating manner, asking his friend, W. B. Stephenson, to ascertain whether Mrs Martin was *'judicious, sensible . . . companionable . . . cheerful . . . conversational'*.[5]

It is impossible to know whether all Methodist ministers, still less all nonconformists, so took to heart Wesley's admonitions in *Twelve Rules of An Helper* to engage in wide consultation and solemn prayer before marrying, but it is clear that the majority of them did marry. The national censuses taken decennially between 1871 and 1921 showed that between 10 and 12 per cent of men in the population never married. Table 5.1 indicates that throughout the whole of the nineteenth century the proportion of unmarried ministers was consistently much smaller than this. Two explanations seem likely. For one thing, celibacy was associated particularly with Catholicism. Protestants did not share the Catholics' sacerdotalism which sought to separate the priest off from the lives of ordinary people, both by education and marital status. One contributory element to the persistent popular anti-Catholicism of Victorian England was the belief that this practice of celibacy by priests was in some way less than manly and the Wesleyan J. H. Rigg merely echoed Charles Kingsley's earlier innuendo when he suggested that the Oxford Movement had in it a strong

---

[4] T. P. Bunting, *The Life of Jabez Bunting* (1859), 150–5.
[5] J. Bunting to W. B. Stephenson, 24 Dec. 1836, Ward, *Early Victorian Methodism. The Correspondence of Jabez Bunting, 1830–1858* (Oxford, 1976), 172.

TABLE 5.1. Percentages of Nonconformist Ministers Marrying

Yr of Entry to Ministry	Wesleyan (times married)				Primitive (times married)			United (times married)			Baptist (times married)				Congregational (times married)		
	0	1	2	3	0	1	2	0	1	2	0	1	2	3	0	1	2
1840–69	1.0	77.3	18.5	3.0							2.0	78.5	18.3	1.0	0.9	87.7	11.4
1850–79	1.7	79.3	16.3	2.5				3.0	88.7	8.2	3.4	81.2	15.3		0.7	91.3	8.0
1860–89	1.9	83.4	13.5	0.9	6.8	81.5	11.6	4.6	88.5	6.7	2.6	87.3	10.0		1.3	91.8	6.7
1870–99	3.8	82.5	12.6	0.9	7.2	83.2	9.6	4.1	86.1	9.7	1.7	89.6	8.0	0.5	2.0	95.2	2.7
1880–1909	4.3	86.9	8.7		7.2	84.7	7.9	5.8	84.1	10.0	3.2	88.0	7.6	1.0	3.1	87.8	8.9
1890–1919	3.7	89.5	6.7		3.7	90.1	6.0	3.3	85.5	11.1	4.6	83.0	11.1		3.3	89.1	9.4
1900–29	1.7	93.0	5.2		6.0	89.5	4.3				5.9	80.5	12.6	0.7	2.2	85.0	12.6

homoerotic impulse.[6] Yet over and above any wish which nonconformist ministers may have had to distance themselves from any similar suspicions there was another, arguably more powerful if more mundane reason for a high incidence of marriage among them: social propriety. Ministers perforce had to deal with a range of social and personal matters which might more suitably—in the tightly circumscribed moral world of the Victorian nonconformist—be dealt with by women or by married men. It would not have been deemed seemly, for example, for a bachelor to attend alone to a young woman.[7]

Similar explanations must lie behind the relatively high rates of remarriage apparent in Table 5.1. Death-rates showed no sustained downturn until the early 1870s and remarriage was, therefore, quite common. It has been estimated that 11.27 per cent of all people marrying in the mid-nineteenth century were doing so for the second or subsequent time.[8] Yet among Baptists and Wesleyans entering the ministry at roughly this time, 1840–69, about a fifth were married more than once. Initially, the Congregational ministers' pattern was more in line with national trends, perhaps because their conditions of service were generally less onerous than those in other denominations. Congregationalists' remarriage rates increased after 1870 but few ministers could stand comparison with John Stephenson, a Primitive, who married for the fourth time in 1870 at a fairly advanced age. A few weeks later he was reported to be 'completely prostrated both in body and mind'. A brief spell in a county asylum helped to restore his mental equilibrium somewhat, but he remained 'very weak in body'.[9]

Although it cannot be statistically verified from the available evidence, it appears to be the case that the ministers tended to marry within their own denominations.[10] The

[6] On this see G. Best, 'Popular Protestantism in Victorian Britain', in R. Robson (ed.), *Ideas and Institutions in Victorian Britain* (1967), 124; D. Hilliard, 'UnEnglish and Unmanly: Anglo-Catholicism and Homosexuality', *Victorian Studies*, 25 (1982).

[7] For similar considerations in an Anglican context see O. Chadwick, *Victorian Miniature* (1960), 25–6; H. B. Thompson, *The Choice of a Profession* (1857), 70.

[8] E. A. Wrigley and R. Schofield, *The Population History of England, 1541–1871: A Reconstruction* (Cambridge, 1981), 259.

[9] *Primitive Methodist Magazine* (1874), 239–40.

[10] This was true of other denominations as well. See, for example, A. W. Ferguson, *Sons of the Manse* (Dundee, 1923), 123, a study of Scottish Presbyterianism.

Methodists indeed put pressure on their men to do so. Bible
Christian rules 'recommended' that their preachers should
choose partners from among the sisters, while in 1823 the
Wesleyan Conference decreed that a ministerial marriage
outside the connexion was 'an instance of culpable impu-
dence'.[11] Even if they relaxed this somewhat dictatorial attitude later on, the Wesleyan authorities still took a very
serious view of the whole matter and the records show that a
number of Didsbury and Headingley students suffered loss
of seniority in the late nineteenth and early twentieth centuries because they had broken off engagements.[12] Propriety
was still important, even though its form had been changed.
According to Joseph Preston's journal, the preachers expelled by the Primitive Conference in 1847 included one 'for
courting several women at the same time' and another who
had married 'before his time'.[13]

   No such central controls could be exerted by either the
Baptist or the Congregational Union but the trend was still
towards marriage within the appropriate denomination. Indeed, this was only to be expected, given the rather closed
world of the nonconformist, especially in the first half of the
century, but it does not appear to have diminished over-
much even when social horizons and spatial mobility expanded later on. Many a surviving late nineteenth-century
testimony indicates quite clearly that the chapel was still a
major focus for romantic activities.[14] As the major figures in
complex networks of social relationships, ministers were the
natural focus of attention within chapel communities. Every
one of them, commented an anonymous observer in 1903,
was 'destined from the earliest period of his studies to be a
great man in a little world'.[15] Such hero-worship frequently
began in childhood, as the anthropologist A. D. Rees noted

---

[11] J. M. Turner, 'Methodist Religion, 1791–1849', in R. Davies, A. George, and
G. Rupp (eds.), *A History of the Methodist Church in Great Britain*, 3 vols. (1965–83),
ii. 111.
[12] Didsbury Management Committee Executive Minutes, 9 Mar. 1905, Didsbury
College Archives, A1/3/1, Wesley College, Bristol.
[13] Journals and Notebooks of Joseph Preston, p. 29, MAM. MAW MS 296A.
[14] For example, W. R. Kent, *Testament of a Victorian Youth* (1938), 126. At a chapel
social 'boys followed seniors' disgraceful example and conducted girls to seclusion of
library corner and, curtains drawn and lights out, did certain business'.
[15] Anon., *The Nonconformist Conscience Considered as a Social Evil and a Mischief-
Monger by One Who Has Had It* (1903), 24–5.

in his study of rural Montgomeryshire. Almost every child, he claimed, was acquainted with the local ministers. 'As often as not a Gallery of the most distinguished of them has looked down on him from the walls of his father's house as he grew up . . .'[16] Similarly, Lax of Poplar recalled that as a child he 'watched every movement, drank in every word, and regarded the man as a kind of demigod'.[17]

But it was adolescent girls who were most prone to respond in this way as one Wesleyan preacher's daughter noted when she returned home from boarding-school one summer to find all her peers speculating wildly about the amorous intentions of the new young preacher who had just joined her father's circuit.[18] Doubtless it was behaviour of this sort which had prompted one writer to warn in 1847 that 'some ministers were exceedingly popular when considered as "fine tall handsome young men, and unmarried," though their sermons were then meager [*sic*] and superficial to an almost extreme degree'.[19] Yet the magnetism was by no means in one direction only. In 1846 J. W. Greeves wrote to his friend in terms which, as he himself acknowledged, would not have found him much favour in the eyes of the Wesleyan hierarchy:

Between you and I, I am getting on especially, pre-eminently well among the young ladies. O the darling creatures Luke. They steal my poor heart every day and leave me to moan my solitary lot. . . . I preached at the Buxton Road Chapel on Monday night and O Luke had you seen what a flock of the dear creatures were gathered together it would have enraptured your very soul. But there's one oh! She is a beauty and I verily believe I am in love with her. . . . But I am obliged to be very quick and have only seen her once a day since Richmond, and walked with her twice—for Billy Bunting is visiting here and I have no wish for him to hear of my gallantry. It would you know be very dangerous . . . I wish you a very happy vacation, a first rate circuit, and a pretty, good tempered wife with some money . . .[20]

[16] A. D. Rees, *Life in a Welsh Countryside* (Cardiff, 1975), 114. Cf. W. J. Edwards, *From the Valley I Came* (1956), 89.
[17] W. H. Lax, *Lax His Book* (1937), 103.
[18] K. Crawford, *The Autobiography of a Methodist Preacher's Daughter* (Isle of Man, 1880), 208.
[19] J. Kendall, *Ministerial Popularity* (1847), 25.
[20] J. W. Greeves to Luke, 9 July 1845, MAM, PLP. 46–28–5.

Similarly, R. J. Campbell positively revelled in the attention he received—and encouraged—from rich, adoring young women. He cultivated something of a personality cult, launching his own journal, the *Christian Commonwealth*, and selling signed photographs of himself.

Such pictures were doubtless more aesthetically appealing than the rather dry prose which characterized the Methodist minister Joseph Bush's mid-century pamphlet, *Courtship and Marriage* (1847). This manual contained over fifty pages of advice to young people on marriage and covered almost every conceivable aspect (except the physical), from the qualities desirable in a potential partner to the best day of the week for the actual ceremony. Bush began his advice to young men by raising the question of the best time to marry. His answer was pointed and unequivocal—'as soon as you have a fair prospect of being able to support a wife'.[21] It was advice apparently well heeded. Table 5.2 shows that the average age of first marriage among men entering the Congregational ministry between 1830 and 1899 was 29.13 years. This compares with the average age of men of comparable social status—clergy, merchants, doctors, and lawyers—which was 29.93 years between 1840 and 1870.[22] Such high marriage ages reflect the fact that the Old Dissenting colleges would not generally accept married men for training and most of the surviving minute books contain references to individuals expelled for marrying during their courses. Obituarists did not generally supply sufficient information for the Methodists to be included in Table 5.2, but there is little reason to think that they were at all out of line with the averages shown for the Old Dissenting ministry. Even in the earlier years of the century when only a relatively small proportion of men attended formal training institutions for one or two years at most, Methodist preachers were generally barred from marrying during their probationary service, although it was sometimes possible, as Robert Newton did, to get special dispensation from Conference to marry early. Otherwise, Joseph Preston's experience was

[21] J. Bush, *Courtship and Marriage* (1847), 5.
[22] J. A. Banks, *Prosperity and Parenthood. A Study of Family Planning Among the Victorian Middle Classes* (1954), 48.

5. Private Lives

TABLE 5.2. Marriage Ages of Baptist and Congregational Ministers

	Years of Entry to Ministry		
	1830–99	1850–1919	1870–1929
Baptist	26.80	28.18	28.60
n	100	100	94
Congregational	29.13	28.90	28.60
n	108	125	109

probably more typical. He began as a regular travelling preacher in 1824 when he was twenty-one years old and married at the beginning of 1832, aged about twenty-nine. The rather lower marriage age among Baptists in the first period covered by Table 5.2 is probably a reflection of the fact that many more of them were part-time men whose prospects for early marriage were enhanced because they had some form of supplementary income. As the proportion of trained Baptists increased, so did the average age at first marriage until by the last third of the century it was identical with that of the Congregationalists.

This long wait for marriage was clearly worth while, however. As one observer noted wryly in the *Primitive Methodist Leader*, 'a special providence seems to have watched over their selection of wives ... according to the [Aldersgate] magazine (in which appears nothing but what is true) they were all noble women and model wives'.[23] But if decorum thus dictated that they were all perfect the cracks in the veneer of Victorian respectability were sometimes visible. A Wesleyan, Mr Poole, had publicly to repudiate the enormous debts run up by his alcoholic wife and subsequently he felt compelled to abandon the ministry. John Pye Smith, Principal of Homerton College, married an older woman within seven months of meeting her but regretted his haste for the rest of his life. 'If blame attached to him for the suddenness of such weighty movements, his strength of nature and state of feeling held him up to the very spirit of

[23] *Primitive Methodist Leader*, 7 Dec. 1911.

his marriage vows for thirty years of toil and sorrow ... '[24]
John Warburton's wife was driven almost to distraction by
his commitment to the Baptist ministry. Leaving home one
Saturday to walk to his Sabbath day preaching engagement,
Warburton was in a miserable frame of mind, for 'not one
penny of money, or one sixpenny worth of provision did I
leave in the house ... My wife declared that she believed I
should go on preaching until they were all starved to death.
But go I must ... '[25]

It was a common enough situation. It was also one which
highlights again the fact that it was often the wives who had
to pay the heaviest physical and emotional price for their
husbands' vocations, a price more expensive perhaps than
that paid by most women of comparable status in Victorian
society. It was with good reason, therefore, that Andrew
Lynn suggested that a minister's wife 'must not be a woman
with a woman's wants and weaknesses, but an angel with an
angel's energies and excellencies'.[26] One Primitive was so
sensible of the burden borne by the wives that he wondered
whether God had ever intended ministers to marry at all.[27]
Over and above the financial hardships and emotional deprivations discussed in the previous chapter were the expectations of chapel members and the perceived needs of the
wider community. Mrs Bickerdike, for example, used to visit
members of her husband's flock regularly but she also made
it her business to confront 'some of the most irreligious
persons in their respective localities. A short time before her
death she visited a family ... whose shop was open on the
Lord's Day, to whom she gave advice and warning ... '[28]
Even those who did not thus aspire to the role of moral
watchdog still found plenty to do within the framework of
regular chapel life. Mrs Mitchell collected money for the
poor, ran a weekly class, and in addition found that 'many of
the old men come and tell me their troubles, and the young

---

[24] J. Medway, *Memoirs of the Life and Writings of John Pye Smith DD., LLD., FRS., FGS* (1853), 94.
[25] J. Warburton, *Mercies of a Covenant God* (Manchester, 1838), 81.
[26] Lynn, p. 227.
[27] G. Herod, *Historical and Biographical Sketches Forming a Compendium of the History of the Primitive Methodist Connexion to 1823* (1857), 360.
[28] *Primitive Methodist Magazine* (1857), 570.

lassies seek to tell their tales when the Minister is likely to be engaged'.[29] It was therefore quite understandable that one mother should object to her daughter's proposed alliance with the Revd Robert Eaglen because she feared the hardships which her daughter would have to bear 'in so arduous a calling', although she added that she thought Eaglen's countenance was already such as to mark him for an early grave.[30] Above all, in the first half of the nineteenth century when circuits were generally large, there was the constant strain of repeated separation for Methodist wives. William Clowes's partner died while he was away at the furthest end of his circuit. On his return he was relieved to learn from colleagues that there had been no doubts as to his wife's final eternal safety but he confessed that her demise had been hastened by the effects of his frequent travelling. She 'felt her loneliness and deprivations with strong sensibility. When I was called to leave her for long periods ... her distress was often extreme ...'[31]

On top of these pressures, which were peculiarly associated with the demands of the ministerial calling, went the ordinary domestic commitments of running a home and raising a family, often on a low income and in less than ideal surroundings. Given the minister's unspecified hours of work and the wide-ranging tasks to which most of them felt called, it is not surprising that these burdens fell frequently on the wives. Later memoirs are certainly full of fond acknowledgements of this maternal input into childish lives but it is again necessary to set these tributes to the successful against the experience of the less well known: those referred to in the previous chapter whose only outlet for frustration was a bitter letter to the press; those like the Methodist minister's wife who wrote in some despair to the *Christian World* in 1893 about her unhappy lot—too little money, too little time to herself, too many children, and constant physical exhaustion caused by repeated childbearing. These last two points evoked a very sympathetic response from the editor. 'The conditions are assuredly wrong', he wrote, 'which bring one

---

[29] J. Mitchell, *Memoir of Mrs E. K. Mitchell* (1844), 233.
[30] *Primitive Methodist Magazine* (1896), 147.
[31] J. Davison, *The Life of the Venerable William Clowes* (1854), 200–1.

member of the marriage partnership into a bondage so cruel.' He went on as boldly as was possible in the context of contemporary mores to advocate birth-control. It was, he said, too delicate a matter to discuss intimately in print, but 'apart from certain methods of limitation, the morality of which is gravely questioned by many, there are certain easily understood physiological laws of the subject, the failure to know and observe which is inexcusable on the part of either men or women in these circumstances'.[32]

In fact, the evidence suggests that by the time he wrote many ministers had already opted for some form of family limitation, although it is difficult to write with accuracy on this subject since the types of evidence used in this study do not always distinguish clearly between living and dead offspring. With high infant mortality for virtually the whole of the nineteenth century, almost every biography contains some record of an infant death, for which one single example may stand proxy. When Mrs Timms's daughter died at seven months her reaction was a fairly typical mixture of grief and acceptance. 'O how painful to nature! My heart bleeds. I am jealous of the worms ... This consoles me, *it is the will of my heavenly Father.* I know it is my duty to submit and to be resigned. Perhaps she is taken from some impending storm.' [33] Even when infant mortality turned down after 1900 the high casualty rates of the First World War took a toll in ministerial families as elsewhere. Both Francis Marrs, a United Methodist, and Sam Newling, a Baptist, had large families decimated by the loss of three sons in the fighting. The existence of such children, already dead by the time of their father's own decease, might well have been missed in obituaries which usually, although not invariably, provided a count only of those children still alive at the time of their father's death.

But if the figures contained in Tables 5.3 and 5.4 are thus lacking in strict accuracy and may be something of an underestimate, the underlying trends are clear. In all denominations the mean family size fell from about three for

[32] *Christian World*, 15 June 1893.
[33] E. Morgan, *Memoir of the Late Mrs Mary Timms* (Watchett, 1835), 85–6.

TABLE 5.3.   Mean Number of Children Per Ministerial Marriage at Specified
Periods

Period of Marriage	Wesleyan	Primitive	United	Baptist	Congregational
1860–89			3.1	3.5	3.0
SD			2.1	2.3	1.9
1870–99	2.8		2.8	3.1	2.8
SD	1.8		1.9	2.0	1.9
1880–1909	2.4	2.2	2.4	2.8	2.4
SD	1.6	1.7	1.5	1.8	1.7
1890–1919	2.2	2.0		2.3	2.2
SD	1.5	1.5		1.6	1.6
1900–29	1.9	1.8		1.9	1.8
SD	1.2	1.2		1.4	1.3

SD = Standard Deviation

marriages contracted before 1880 to less than two for those married after 1900, a decline illustrated in a different format in Table 5.4. By the period 1900–29 ministerial family size was very much in line with general trends in the population as a whole. Calculations based on the Registrar-General's returns indicate that 17 per cent of marriages taking place about 1925 remained childless while about half produced one or two children.[34] Unless one is to posit some unexplained decline in ministerial fertility towards the end of the century the only logical explanation for the patterns evident in Tables 5.3 and 5.4 is that the ministry as a group was practising birth-control. It has long been recognized that family limitation first began among the higher social groups, and while nonconformist ministers may not be so defined in terms of income, they were accorded a high place in contemporary society and men of all denominations shared in the general middle-class alarm about rising costs of living and schooling in the third quarter of the century, concerns which are thought by some to have inspired the trend to smaller families.[35]

Although the precarious nature of the statistical record

[34] D. C. Marsh, *The Changing Social Structure of England and Wales, 1871–1961* (1965), 43.

[35] Banks, pp. 132 ff. See also R. Mitchison, *British Population Change Since 1860* (1977).

TABLE 5.4. Percentage of Ministerial Families with Given Number of Children

Dates of Marriage	Number of Children										
	0	1	2	3	4	5	6	7	8	9	10+
1860–89											
•Wesleyan											
Primitive	8.5	14.8	12.7	18.0	12.7	7.4	9.5	2.1	3.2		
United	11.4	14.9	14.0	20.1	11.4	17.4	2.6	5.2	0.8	1.7	
Baptist	`7.5	11.7	19.3	18.4	12.6	13.4	4.2	7.5		3.3	1.6
Congregational	5.0	16.1	28.2	20.2	12.1	9.0	3.0	7.0			1.0
1870–99											
Wesleyan	9.5	16.1	22.8	16.1	18.0	7.6	6.6	2.8			
Primitive	12.3	16.4	18.5	15.4	12.3	6.1	10.3	1.0			
United	12.5	16.0	21.6	18.3	12.5	12.5	2.5	4.1	0.8		
Baptist	4.2	16.9	21.8	22.5	12.6	11.2	3.5	3.5	1.4	1.4	0.7
Congregational	8.1	19.0	25.4	16.3	10.0	13.6	2.7	3.6			0.9
1880–1909											
Wesleyan	10.1	23.7	24.5	17.7	16.1	2.5	2.5	2.5			
Primitive	13.2	22.4	28.9	10.2	9.3	3.7	7.4				
United	19.6	33.3	18.6	10.7	3.9	2.9	1.9				
Baptist	6.0	19.5	25.6	19.5	12.8	10.1	2.0	1.3	1.3	0.6	0.6
Congregational	13.5	22.5	21.0	20.3	9.7	9.0	0.7	5.2			
1890–1919											
Wesleyan	10.2	24.7	29.9	18.8	11.1	1.7	1.7	1.7			
Primitive	14.9	22.0	32.2	14.1	7.0	3.1	3.1				
United											
Baptist	10.7	23.0	25.1	20.8	10.7	5.7	2.1		1.4		
Congregational	15.7	24.4	17.3	24.4	7.8	7.8	0.7	1.5			
1900–29											
Wesleyan	11.4	30.2	30.2	16.6	9.3	1.0		1.0			
Primitive											
United											
Baptist	16.0	26.4	23.5	20.7	9.4	2.8	0.9				
Congregational	16.0	30.7	22.8	22.8	5.2	0.8		0.8			

must not be forgotten the evidence of Table 5.3 suggests that ministers had been practising family limitation since at least mid-century. The mean size of ministerial families started in the period 1860–89 appears to have been slightly over 3. Nationally, the mean size of completed families born to marriages contracted in the 1860s was 6.2 children, falling to 5.3 for marriages taking place in the 1870s.[36] True,

[36] N. Tranter, *Population and Society, 1750–1940: Contrasts in Population Growth* (1985), 60.

there were disagreements among nonconformists about the actual mechanisms of control that were permissible, and it was suggested in 1916 that the majority 'would unhesitatingly condemn' artificial methods, but their more liberal theological stance, emphasis on the individual conscience, and wider representation among those classes most desirous of restricting family size, perhaps helped to ensure that control was more common among nonconformists than among the members of other churches.[37] In this, as in other aspects of nonconformist life, the ministers apparently led the way. Yet we should notice also the implications of Table 5.3. If the typical ministerial family was getting smaller and, at the same time, a growing proportion of new ministers were being drawn from ministerial homes, then the long-term outlook for ministerial recruitment was bleak indeed. For a while, perhaps, the problem was held at bay by another trend which is plotted in Table 5.5—the diminishing loss to the ministry accruing through early retirement and premature death. In all denominations, except the Baptists, between 2 and 4 per cent of the men entering the ministry between 1881 and 1901 had retired or died within fourteen years of beginning. The somewhat higher Baptist figure, 7 per cent, was produced by the oversupply of candidates which encouraged others into early retirement.

Earlier in the century, however, such losses had been substantially higher. Of ministers who began their work between 1841 and 1861, for example, rather more than a tenth of Wesleyans, about 8 per cent of United Methodists, 16 per cent of Baptists, and 14 per cent of Congregationalists had either died or retired within fourteen years of entering their ministries. Given a normal entry age somewhere in the early to mid-twenties, these men were lost by their early forties. Only the Primitives appear to have avoided these high losses and this is probably an aberration caused by the presentation of the statistics. It will be remembered that they had very much higher rates of men failing to complete their

[37] J. Marchant (ed.), *The Declining Birth Rate* (1916), 66. On this subject generally see P. Campbell, 'Birth Control and the Christian Churches', *Population Studies*, 14 (1960). There are some interesting comments also in P. Branca, *Silent Sisterhood: Middle Class Women in the Victorian Home* (1975), 114–29.

probation, and some of these losses may in fact have been caused by premature death or retirement. (See Chapter 4, above.) All professional men, W. R. Greg told the Royal Institution in 1875, were having to work harder than their grandfathers. The pressures of modern life were such as to force 'one after another of them to break off (or to break down) in mid-career, shattered, paralysed, reduced to premature inaction or senility'.[38]

The evidence of Table 5.5 would appear to offer support for the widespread contemporary belief that physical collapse and premature death were frequent concomitants of dedicated ministerial work. It also lends further support to the arguments advanced in Chapter 4 about the heavy demands made on individuals in the ministry. The results of this are plotted in Table 5.6, which shows that, taking the whole period from 1820 to 1929, about a third of Congregationalists, a quarter of all Methodists, and between a third and a half of Baptists died while still engaged in the active ministry. Spurgeon actually included in his lectures one on fainting fits on the grounds that 'most of us are in some way or other unsound physically'.[39] 'How painful', commented an observer in the *General Baptist Repository*, 'to see a noble spirit stirred with holy and benevolent designs held back or tied down by a sickly body. Such instances are frequent.'[40] Indeed they were, as Table 5.7, which shows the proportion of retirements prompted by ill health, confirms. Thus John Bumstead became a Wesleyan supernumary at the age of fifty-seven in 1851 'by reason of age and growing infirmities'.[41] Isaac Page broke down at Greenwich and for many months 'could not read the Bible or pray, or speak on religious matters without the warning sensation in my head ... Spiritually, I was as a man carried through a dark tunnel.'[42] The Baptist Charles Baines Williams retired early after a series of physical collapses, dying after the third one in 1912.

[38] W. R. Greg, 'Life at High Pressure', *Contemporary Review*, 25 (1875), 629.
[39] C. Spurgeon, *Lectures to My Students* (1976 edn.), 155.
[40] *General Baptist Repository*, 13 (1851), 121.
[41] Wesleyan Conference, *Minutes* (1851), 578.
[42] I. E. Page, *A Long Pilgrimage* (1914), 188.

Diagnostic technique in the nineteenth century was notoriously suspect but apart from such obviously disqualifying and identifiable disabilities as blindness and deafness, the evidence, such as it is, suggests three main medical conditions to which ministers were especially prone. The cause of death can be established with some accuracy in the case of 223 of the men used in this study who served in the ministry after 1790 and who died, in the main, before 1914. It seems reasonable to suggest that similar causes contributed to the high rate of premature retirements as well. Tuberculosis accounted for 9.8 per cent of the deaths, an eloquent comment on the low incomes, poor diet, and inadequate housing with which many men had to contend.[43] Heart-related diseases accounted for another 17.9 per cent of the deaths, while the biggest single killer of all, judging from the description of the classic symptoms of paralysis and loss of speech, was strokes, which carried off about a quarter of the deceased. It is perhaps strange that stress related disease should have killed so many men in a profession which, in theory at least, provided a natural outlet for tensions in the form of prayer. In practice, however, those same beliefs which ought to have provided a safety valve may well have contributed to the stress, such was the compulsion which many ministers had to see individuals saved. Thus one New Connexion man wrote in 1845 that 'I cannot live in the ministry except I am useful. I would become a fool to save souls.'[44] Thomas Nightingale, the Wesleyan, was equally fervent. 'I must have souls, *souls*, SOULS, or retire from the work of the ministry.'[45] Joshua Dyson did not allow a fatal illness to deter him from visiting an average of fifty families a week during his last year of life. It was, remarked his obituarist, 'his intense zeal for the cause of Christ which impelled him

---

[43] R. Dudfield, in his 'Note on the Mortality from Tuberculosis from 1851–1905', *Journal of the Royal Statistical Society*, 70 (1907), 456–8, calculated that 15.71 per cent of all deaths in England and Wales between 1851 and 1860 and 9.23 per cent of all deaths between 1891 and 1900 were caused by tuberculosis. Most of the reduction, he believed, was in deaths among those aged under fifteen. Ministerial death rates from the disease, therefore, seem to have been very much in line with those of the adult population at large.

[44] J. Stacey, 'Memoir of Rev J. Hilton', *Methodist New Connexion Magazine* (1852), 457.

[45] T. Nightingale, *Some of the Reminiscences and Experiences of my Life* (1891), 56.

TABLE 5.5. Percentage of Ministers Dying (Dec.) and Retiring (Ret.) at Selected Intervals since Career Commencement

	Period of Commencement													
	1831–51		1841–61		1851–71		1861–81		1871–91		1881–1901		1891–1911	
	Dec.	Ret.	Dec.	Ret.	Dec.	Ret.	Dec.	Ret.	Dec.	Ret.	Dec.	Ret.	Dec.	Ret.
Wesleyan														
By 4 yrs	4.8		5.8		5.2		3.0		0.8		0.5		0.6	
By 14 yrs	7.2	0.8	9.0	1.2	8.7	1.7	5.3	2.2	3.3	1.6	2.1	2.1	1.8	1.8
By 24 yrs	8.8	2.4	9.6	3.8	9.6	4.3	6.8	6.1	4.9	4.1	3.7	4.2	4.4	3.1
By 34 yrs	16.1	16.1	16.7	15.4	13.1	17.5	12.2	17.5	9.9	14.0	7.4	17.4	6.9	15.7
By 44 yrs	25.8	35.4	24.5	40.6	22.8	46.4	20.6	48.0	19.0	48.7	12.6	56.6	11.3	59.7
Primitive														
By 4 yrs	0.9		2.3		0.9		0.8		2.2		1.1		1.2	
By 14 yrs	2.9	0.9	3.9	0.7	0.9		2.5		2.2		2.3	1.1	2.5	1.2
By 24 yrs	5.8	2.9	7.8	2.3	5.5	0.9	5.1	0.8	4.4		3.5		3.8	3.8
By 34 yrs	6.8	13.7	11.0	9.4	11.0	5.5	9.4	6.8	12.2	1.1	14.1	7.0	17.9	5.1
By 44 yrs		23.5		19.6	14.6	22.9	17.2	26.7		8.8	Not statistically valid			

	1831-56	1831-51	1841-66	1841-61	1851-76	1851-71	1861-86	1861-81	1871-96	1871-91	1881-1906	1881-1901	1891-1916	1891-1911
United														
By 4 yrs	2.0		2.2	0.5	1.3	0.4	1.1	0.3	0.4	0.9		0.9	0.5	1.1
By 14 yrs	4.0	4.0	3.4	4.5	3.9	4.8	3.4	4.1	3.1	3.6	0.9	1.8	1.6	2.2
By 24 yrs	6.1	8.1	5.1	8.0	6.9	7.8	5.7	7.6	5.9	5.9	3.7	2.7	6.1	2.2
By 34 yrs	9.1	16.3	8.6	13.7	9.1	12.6	9.1	11.7	10.0	8.6	9.2	6.0	10.6	6.1
By 44 yrs	14.2	34.6	15.5	32.1	14.8	34.4	14.4	22.4	14.1	42.5	14.3	45.8	16.7	49.7
Baptist	1831-51		1841-61		1851-71		1861-81		1871-91		1881-1901		1891-1911	
By 4 yrs			2.3	0.7	2.1	0.7	0.8		0.8	0.8	0.7	0.7	1.1	0.5
By 14 yrs			12.3	3.8	9.1	3.5	7.8	3.5	5.3	3.5	1.4	5.7	2.3	4.7
By 24 yrs			15.3	5.3	13.3	5.6	11.4	6.1	10.7	8.0	4.3	11.5	5.9	9.4
By 34 yrs			19.2	17.6	15.4	14.7	14.0	17.5		14.2	9.3	16.5	11.2	13.0
By 44 yrs			23.0	24.6	17.6	26.0	16.6	30.7	18.7	31.2	23.0	31.6	23.6	28.9
Congregational														
By 4 yrs	6.6		4.5	1.0	2.8	1.1	0.5		0.9		0.4	0.4		
By 14 yrs	12.5	1.4	9.0	2.0	5.6	1.6	2.5	0.5	2.3	0.9	2.4	1.4		
By 24 yrs	17.6	5.1	13.1	4.0	7.3	5.6	4.0	3.0	4.2	3.7	4.9			
By 34 yrs	23.5	12.5	18.1	9.0	10.1	11.2	9.0	10.1	9.0	12.3	11.4	9.4		
By 44 yrs	27.2	21.3	22.2	20.7	14.6	25.8	13.1	27.2	14.2	35.5	17.9	34.3		

Table 5.6. Percentage of Ministers Dying in the Ministry

	Year of Starting								
	1820–49	1830–59	1840–69	1850–79	1860–89	1870–99	1880–1909	1890–1919	1900–29
Wesleyan		32.7	25.8	25.9	27.8	28.5	24.4	23.7	25.9
Primitive		21.5	28.0	27.1	30.6	29.2	28.8	22.8	21.8
United			31.5	26.0	25.8	24.2	28.2		
Baptist	50.4	54.3	53.3	49.6	42.4	39.0	34.7	34.4	30.0
Congregational	35.9	35.3	32.3	32.6	36.4	39.4	35.2	31.1	30.6

TABLE 5.7. Percentage of Ministers Retiring for Health Reasons (% of All Retirements)

Year of Starting

	1840–69	1850–79	1860–89	1870–99	1880–1909	1890–1919
Wesleyan		17.0	16.6	15.9	11.9	13.4
Baptist		20.7	18.8	20.6	12.5	16.3
Congregational	24.7		17.5	14.8	14.9	14.1

to sacrifice his own health and even life, that he might save those for whom the Saviour died.'[46] Charles New expressed well the sense of burden which the ministry carried for many of its practitioners. He was, he wrote, 'responsible for the eternal welfare of hundreds of souls who must either be lost or saved according to the efforts I make to save them, by my example, my prayers, my faithfulness in and out of the pulpit. Good God! Who can bear this terrible pressure?'[47] Combined with the material deprivations and personal pressures discussed in the last chapter, such drives may well have contributed to significant tensions which resulted ultimately in physical symptoms, forcing men to retirement and—sometimes—to the grave. Certainly both Spurgeon and Clifford were prompted to make such connections by the spate of deaths among young Baptist ministers which occurred in 1875.[48] Perhaps the late century diminution in evangelistic fervour, coupled with a growing .tendency among mainstream nonconformists to reinterpret the doctrines of hell and everlasting punishment into a less disconcerting format, reduced this type of pressure on individual ministers. More certainly, material conditions had generally improved by the end of the century and Table 5.5 does indicate a drop in the proportions of those lost by premature death and retirement among the cohorts entering the ministry after 1881.

Care must be taken in any case to keep these losses in proper perspective. The very weakest succumbed, either physically or emotionally, to the pressures of ministerial life but, somewhat paradoxically perhaps, the generality of ministers could look forward to relatively long lives. It was widely believed in Christian circles that godliness and long life went together, Joseph Bush arguing, for example, that 'you will live longer for attending a place of worship ... your body will wear longer if you keep His laws than if you break them'.[49] Calculations made by one contemporary with

[46] *Primitive Methodist Magazine* (1874), 303.
[47] S. S. Barton, *Life of Charles New* (1889), 18–19.
[48] Clifford's remarks were on the theme of 'Ministerial High Pressure', *General Baptist Repository*, 77 (1875); Spurgeon's comments appeared in *Sword and Trowel*, Aug. 1875.
[49] J. Bush, *Six Reasons for Going to Chapel* (1858), 12.

reference to the period 1758–1843 suggested that Anglican clergy had the longest life expectancy of all the professions. Those who died after their fifty-first birthday attained an average of 74.04 years.[50] As Table 5.8 shows, the average age of nonconformist ministers dying after the age of fifty-one was somewhat lower, about seventy-one, although the time periods are not strictly comparable. It is clear, however, that the ministers enjoyed longer lives than the general population. It has been estimated that for most of the period between Elizabethan and Victorian times a man of twenty could expect to live for a further 35 to 40 years.[51] Estimates made by the Equitable Life Assurance Society suggest a life expectancy of 41.5 years for a male aged twenty in 1840, rising to 43.2 years for a similar individual in 1900.[52] The average life span of ministers, who usually began their careers in their early to mid-twenties, was rather higher than this. Depending on the denomination, it was between 65 and 68 in the 1840s, and between 71 and 74 by the turn of the century. By this time ministers were on average well behind other professional groups in terms of income but as a group they tended to be abstemious, and technical improvements, especially in transport, served to reduce somewhat the physical demands on a ministry whose duties were in any case increasingly a matter of maintaining the existing establishment rather than of extending it in any sustained and vigorous fashion.

It is also important to remember that for much of the century retirement was hindered by the fact that few men were able to save enough to keep themselves in their declining years. Methodists' retirements were ultimately a matter for Conference but all the connexions had some sort of pension arrangements. The New Connexion established a Beneficent Fund quite early in its history, the Free Methodists had a retirement arrangement by 1862, while by 1875 a retiring Primitive minister could expect to receive about a pound a year for each year of service completed before his

---

[50] W. A. Guy, 'On the Duration of Life in the Members of the Several Professions', *Journal of the Statistical Society*, 9 (1846), 350 ff.
[51] Wrigley and Schofield, p. 453.
[52] M. Davies, 'A Survey of British Scientists', *Science Progress*, 68 (1982), 8.

TABLE 5.8. Death Ages of Nonconformist Ministers

	Years of Starting Ministry							
	1830–59	1840–69	1850–79	1860–89	1870–99	1880–1909	1890–1919	1900–29
Wesleyan								
Average Age at Death	67.8	67.9	68.4	69.2	71.1	73.3	73.7	72.9
Modal Band	75–9	70–4	70–4	70–4	80–4	70–4	80–4	70–4
Average Age of those dying at 51+ years	71.4	73.3	72.7	73.6	74.2	73.4	74.1	75.2
Primitive								
Average Age at Death		66.2	67.3	66.0	69.0	72.1	74.9	74.6
Modal Band		70–4	70–4	70–4	80–4	75–9	75–84	70–9
Average Age of those dying at 51+ years			71.5	71.5	74.7	76.0	76.8	75.6

United								
Average Age at Death Modal Band	65.2 65–9	65.1 75–9	66.7 75–9	66.8 75–9	70.5 80–4	71.8 70–4	72.0 85–9	
Average Age of those dying at 51+ years	70.2		72.4	72.6	74.0	73.4	73.8	
Baptist								
Average Age at Death Modal Band		64.5 70–4	66.5 70–4	68.2 70–4	69.2 70–4	69.8 75–9	71.3 75–84	71.8 75–9
Average Age of those dying at 51+ years		70.2	69.8	71.7	72.3	73.3	74.2	74.1
Congregational								
Average Age at Death Modal Band	66.0 70–4	68.1 70–4	68.1 65–9	68.3 70–4	68.4 70–4	71.6 75–9	73.1 75–9	72.5 75–9
Average Age of those dying at 51+ years	71.0	72.5	72.3	71.6	72.1	73.5	75.0	73.9

retirement. The main source of funding for this came from the proceeds of Book Room sales, although there were also grants from Conference, and contributions from circuits and annuitants. The Wesleyans had an Auxiliary Fund by 1813 and donations to it were used to supplement the provisions preachers made for their old age through their Annuitant Society. A proposal to use the Centenary Fund to support the many for whom this provision was inadequate was rejected for fear that it would require the whole of the sum raised for the Centenary Fund. In the end, the Wesleyans established a new Auxiliary Fund to provide for supernumeraries and the widows of deceased preachers, although even then there was opposition from poorer circuits objecting to the per capita levy made to finance the scheme. By the turn of the century a Wesleyan who retired after forty years' service could expect to receive a furniture grant of about £40 and a pension of £54 a year. It was not much since no accommodation was provided but retired Wesleyans were better off than men in other denominations for whom centralized arrangements were a long time in appearing.

Prior to 1852 the Crown had put aside a small sum (£1,695 in 1851) to relieve aged dissenting ministers and their widows. It was administered by a committee comprising three Baptists, three Congregationalists, and three Presbyterians. Most of the money went to Wales where nonconformist ministers were notoriously poor, but the typical grant was a paltry £5. This scheme was abandoned in the early 1850s, partly because the sums allowed were so small, and partly because the growth of disestablishment sentiment among nonconformists further nurtured their reluctance to accept state subsidies of this sort. Only those fortunate few who commanded large salaries could contemplate the prospect of retirement with any equanimity. For the rest the outlook was bleak. True, there were some resources available but they were usually small, privately administered, and sometimes regionally based funds. Thus fifty-five beneficiaries received £520 among them in 1850 from the Society for the Relief of Aged and Infirm Protestant Dissenting Ministers (founded 1818). At about the same time another thirty-two individuals were financially supported by the Protestant Union (founded 1798). In Essex, Watkinson's Trust funded small pensions for dissenting ministers or their widows, and there were similar organizations in Suffolk, dating from 1790, and in Gloucester, dating from 1799. The *Christian Witness* newspaper, founded in 1844, devoted its profits to a fund for aged ministers and paid out over £400 in 1846.

For those unable to tap such sources, the only capital which they were able to accumulate during their working lives was that presented to them by congregations as retiring gifts. Once again, however, it was usually the case that the best paid received the biggest rewards. John Stoughton's retirement years were fortified by the £3,000 presented to him when he left Kensington Chapel after a ministry of over thirty years. Camden Town Park Chapel members raised a similar amount for their retiring pastor. Yet such sums were by no means as common as casual perusal of autobiographical evidence might suggest. The *Patriot* cast a more penetrating light on the reality in 1854. 'We have sometimes been blamed for affording publicity to the small bounties which the churches occasionally offer to their ministers: and, to tell the truth, the sum has not infrequently been *so* small that we have thought it fit to cloak the infinitesimal display of liberality under the convenient generality of "a purse of gold".'[53] Thus one Baptist, Thomas Turner, took just £9 when he left Foulsham, while Robert Bowles left Hertford with sixteen guineas in his pocket. Within a year of leaving Soothill in 1887 John Warburton (whose farewell gifts had included handkerchiefs, an inkstand, an illuminated address, and seventy guineas) was appearing in a bankruptcy court, writing to a friend that 'I am insolvent, I am broken, I have failed ... I suppose it is no use asking a loan of thee ...'[54] Rather earlier, in the mid-1850s, the Congregational Union had appointed a special committee to investigate the affairs of a minister whose efforts to provide for his family against his retirement or death had gone disastrously wrong and taken him into the bankruptcy court.

---

[53] *Patriot*, 23 Jan. 1854.
[54] C. Hemington (ed.), *Memorials of John Warburton* (1892), 193.

In such circumstances it was not surprising that men were sometimes tempted to hold on to office when their usefulness was really over. They had, as one contemporary put it, 'too great an anxiety to retain the emoluments arising from the discharge of pastoral duties, and have found them a temptation sufficiently powerful to prevent them quitting the pulpit'.[55] Another result of this lack of adequate provision for old age and widowhood was that the Baptist and Congregational press was frequently swamped with begging letters from the families or friends of incapacitated ministers, a phenomenon which did not speak well of the nonconformist community.[56] In 1855 J. A. James, mindful of the plight of his less eminent brethren, offered the £700 with which a grateful congregation had sought to furnish his retirement as the basis of an annuity fund for which all retired Congregational ministers might be eligible. But much depended on the ability of the individual to find the initial subscription of £10 and by 1872 only 170 men were receiving pensions of £35 a year. Not until 1903, as part of its general review of ministerial conditions of service, did the Congregational Union accept a scheme whereby the minister and his congregation might jointly purchase the annuity, an arrangement which brought many more individuals into the system. The Baptists had also established a national annuity scheme in the mid-1870s, inspired by the pathetic press appeals made for the widow and seven children of the recently deceased Revd J. Wilshire. Once again, however, the plan was very much dependent upon individual initiative and resources. By 1875 about 615 men had contributed to a capital fund of £54,000 and a participant could expect an annual pension of about £45, although the scheme's finances were not put on to any really firm foundation until Sir George W. Macalpine made a generous gift to the capital fund in 1911. Welsh Baptists made their own arrangements in the form of a friendly society, Y Cym-

---

[55] I. Mann to J. Upton, 30 Oct. 1830. Quoted in J. Upton, 'Ministerial Problems, 1830', *Baptist Quarterly*, 10 (1940–1), 178–9.
[56] See, for example, *Baptist*, 16 Sept. 1892, which contained an appeal for contributions for the nine children of the Revd G. R. Jones, incapacitated by a stroke at the beginning of the year.

deithas Ddarbodol, although its coverage was also fairly patchy. Less than a fifth of eligible ministers belonged to it by 1915.[57] Even in retirement, it seems, the lot of the typical nonconformist minister was little more attractive than his working life had often been.

[57] T. M. Bassett, *The Welsh Baptists* (Swansea, 1977), 289.

6

Public Lives

IN the century before the outbreak of the First World War it was, as Professor Harrison has remarked, 'from the pulpit, whether in church or camp meeting, that public opinion was largely educated'.[1] The primacy of the sermon in nonconformist worship, symbolized by the central siting of the pulpit in most chapels, gave it a distinct advantage in this respect over the Established Church. Preaching provided nonconformity with one of its main channels of influence in contemporary society and it was probably this aspect of ministerial work that most distinguished the nonconformists from their Anglican counterparts. Any individual with a talent for public speaking was assured of a rapid rise to denominational and even national eminence. In an age when mass communication was for the most part a matter of the unmediated human voice, the great preachers were the star performers, their names often household words. Sooner or later, most of the better known gravitated to one or other of the leading metropolitan chapels, but even in provincial towns and rural areas relatively unknown visitors could usually be counted on to swell attendances. Such was the appeal of a guest preacher that some Anglicans even accused the nonconformists of arranging wholesale pulpit exchanges in order to bolster congregations on census Sunday in 1851.[2]

While this was evidently a gross exaggeration, it is true that for those who could combine a gift for words with a pulpit presence and an imponderable but vital charismatic quality, the crowds poured in. One popular preacher was booked at the age of seventy-one to supply pulpits at Luton

[1] J. F. C. Harrison, *The Early Victorians, 1832–51* (1971), 133.
[2] H. Mann, 'On the Statistical Position of Religious Bodies in England and Wales', *Journal of the Statistical Society*, 18 (1855), 145.

and Kettering, a programme he did not appear to relish. 'They published for me to preach eight times in the week; and at Kettering six times; and mostly in small chapels crowded to excess, and packed half an hour before I could begin, so that often when I was done, my coat was wet through with perspiration; and I got cold and my cough has been very troublesome.'[3] In the three months following his retirement Peter Mackenzie preached eighty-four times. Morley Punshon was so fiery that he could, it was claimed, 'lift all his hearers to their feet surging with the emotion roused by his eloquence and cheering wildly'.[4] So great was his talent that members of the London theatrical profession were alleged to attend his services in search, not of spiritual guidance, but of tips on presentation and vocal delivery. Spurgeon was another well able to fill chapels by his magnetic oratory. Describing a visit made to London by some of his rural relatives, the historian A. L. Rowse notes that it included the 'obligatory' trip to hear Spurgeon at the Metropolitan Tabernacle.[5] The Baptist giant was not unaware of his personal drawing power. Refusing an invitation to preach for Henry Allon in 1868 he explained that he had already been absent from his pulpit more than he liked 'at this season, when so many country people come or are brought by my people to "hear Spurgeon" '.[6] Isaac Foot recalled the difficulty he had in getting to hear an equally celebrated if less orthodox man, R. J. Campbell. Unable to gain admission at all to the morning service at the City Temple because it was full, he and his friends returned for the evening service, queued for an hour and then only just got seats, having had to 'fight and struggle like footballers'.[7]

If preaching was the main channel, it was by no means the only one through which nonconformist influence was disseminated, as the Revd J. Corbin's letter to the *Patriot* in 1852 recognized. 'There are in all places now, questions of local interest to be discussed, local societies to be patronised

[3] J. E. Coulson, *The Peasant Preacher: Memorials of Mr Charles Richardson* (1865), 339.
[4] W. Wakinshaw, *Gleanings from My Life* (1931), 96.
[5] A. L. Rowse, *A Cornish Childhood* (1942), 58.
[6] C. H. Spurgeon to H. Allon, 1 May 1868, DWL MS 24/110/313. Letters to Henry Allon.
[7] Quoted in S. Koss, *Nonconformity in Modern British Politics* (1974), 50.

and managed, local influence to be wielded, public positions
to be occupied. . . . In these things the minister should have
a place, a hand, a voice. His power should be felt in the town
as well as in the chapel . . .'[8] In some senses it was easier for
an Anglican incumbent to influence the general population
because churches tended to be sited in the centre of parishes,
whereas urban nonconformist congregations tended to be
drawn from a much wider catchment area. Nevertheless, it
is clear that many nonconformist ministers took Corbin's
advice very much to heart. Thus as A. J. Davies prepared to
leave Reading after a seven year ministry, one local paper
reported that his impending departure was a matter of regret not only to his congregation but in the whole town
because he had so established himself 'in the affections of his
church, . . . also in the warmest regard of all sorts and
conditions of people in the town that the rumour of his
approaching departure is causing widespread regret . . .
among political and social movements . . . and any cause
which would tend to the betterment of the people'.[9] Quite
clearly, Davies represented that brand of minister who had
not been content to confine his ministerial work to the
chapel community alone but had believed it legitimate and
necessary to be involved in the wider public life of the society in which he lived. Such involvement was widely thought
to have been fairly typical. W. H. Harwood's biography of
Henry Allon, published in 1894, commented that 'many
names might be mentioned of Nonconformist ministers
whose activity has been closely interwoven with all the best
life of the community'.[10] Similarly, the *Spectator* suggested
that the public profile of ministers was generally so high
that a dozen of them would 'stir a whole city district besides
directly influencing or even controlling their own congregations'.[11]

Yet once again it is legitimate to ask how far these suggestions were founded on anything more than general impres-

[8] *Patriot*, 11 Mar. 1852.
[9] *Reading Standard*, 11 Jan. 1908. Quoted in S. Yeo, *Religious and Voluntary Organisations in Crisis* (1976), 87.
[10] W. H. Harwood, *Henry Allon D. D. Pastor and Teacher: The Story of His Ministry* (1894), 3.
[11] *Spectator*, 24 Mar. 1874.

sions, culled perhaps from one or two unrepresentative
examples? Certainly, some individuals may have been inspired both in their private behaviour and public action by
ministerial example but it is impossible now to know the
extent of such influences. Some evidence points in exactly
the opposite direction. William Kent reckoned from his personal acquaintance of Victorian chapel life that 'Jack Jones
goes to Chapel to have a talk with Bill Smith. Mrs Robinson
goes not to meet her God, but to meet Mrs Brown.'[12] When
William Dawson quit the Wesleyan ministry it was because
of his growing conviction of 'the futility of speech to influence conduct'. He went on to admit that 'for years I had
spoken to the same people, and they remained the same
people. Nothing in their attitude to life was really altered.'[13]

In many of the burgeoning industrial communities of the
early nineteenth century nonconformist ministers were often
welcomed as the only men of education or social standing
and as such, they did acquire considerable influence. To
some extent this remained the case in growing towns and in
rural areas throughout the nineteenth century. It also remained true in Wales where the ministers were more closely
integrated by life style with the ordinary chapel-goer (full-
time ministers were not common until well after 1850) and
where they were closely identified with national aspirations
and anti-Anglicanism. A witness to the Royal Commission
on Trade Unions (1867–9) claimed that in South Wales the
nonconformist minister had 'more influence ... than any
man living'.[14] In the larger, more settled urban areas of
England, however, influence came ultimately to depend
much more on the individual's personality than on his office.
Characters like Spurgeon, Hughes, and Dale all had the
vitality and charisma that would have ensured their eminence, whatever occupation they had undertaken, but for
lesser men it was increasingly impossible, in urban areas at
least, to rely on the office alone to guarantee respect and
influence. One speaker told the Wesleyan Conference in the

[12] W. R. Kent, *Testament of a Victorian Youth* (1938), 272.
[13] W. J. Dawson, *Autobiography of a Mind* (1925), 314.
[14] Quoted in E. T. Davies, *Religion in the Industrial Revolution in South Wales* (Cardiff, 1965), 65.

Table 6.1. Communal Activities of Nonconformist Ministers (%)

	Type of Activity						
	1 Education	2 Philanthropy	3 Political	4 Learned	5 Theological Publication	6 Miscellaneous Literature	7 Nothing Recorded
Wesleyan							
1830–59		7.9	3.9	0.9	4.9	1.9	79.2
1840–69		5.8	4.2	1.6	4.1	0.8	77.5
1850–79		5.2	2.9	1.5	3.7	2.2	82.2
1860–89		6.3	2.5	1.9	6.9	3.8	72.1
1870–99		6.9	3.2	1.9	10.1	6.3	63.9
1880–1909		14.1	6.4	1.9	13.4	5.8	50.0
1890–1919		17.3	6.4	1.9	10.8	4.5	52.5
1900–29		19.8	5.3	1.5	8.3	1.5	57.2
Primitive							
1830–59		11.8	6.9	0.9	7.8	3.9	73.5
1840–69		13.2	12.3		7.0	1.8	71.9
1850–79		13.9	16.3		8.5	1.6	68.9
1860–89		14.4	15.3		9.9	3.6	66.6
1870–99		20.8	13.2	0.9	13.2	3.8	55.6
1880–1909		21.2	10.2	0.8	9.3	4.2	56.7
1890–1919		17.7	9.6	2.2	6.6	1.5	61.0
1900–29		13.5	8.4	1.7	4.2	3.4	69.7

Table header (spanning): **Not statistically valid**

United							
1840–69		19.4	9.2	0.9	12.0	4.6	59.2
1850–79		18.0	14.0	1.3	12.0	2.6	56.6
1860–89		13.2	13.8	1.2	10.6	2.5	62.2
1870–99		13.1	13.1	3.9	11.1	3.9	58.1
1880–1909		12.2	8.4	3.8	9.9	4.6	62.5
1890–1919	}						
1900–29							
Baptist							
1820–49	3.4	12.8	25.7	2.8	16.2	5.5	58.9
1830–59	3.1	18.2	26.4	2.5	14.9	7.4	53.5
1840–69	2.6	20.0	22.2	3.4	8.6	4.1	56.6
1850–79	1.2	22.2	21.0	3.7	6.6	3.1	55.1
1860–89	0.5	20.3	18.3	4.9	8.8	2.5	59.1
1870–99		17.2	18.1	4.7	9.3	2.3	57.2
1880–1909	0.4	14.3	13.0	3.2	7.4	1.9	64.3
1890–1919	0.5	14.5	13.4	1.6	5.3	1.1	62.3
1900–29		18.6	11.4	0.7	6.4	0.7	62.1
Congregational							
1810–39	9.3	12.1	28.0	0.8	15.8	1.8	42.0
1820–49	3.8	13.7	22.8	0.7	16.7	3.8	48.8
1830–59	5.9	12.5	17.6	1.2	12.5	5.1	65.6
1840–69	6.2	16.1	17.3	4.1	9.9	3.7	65.8
1850–79	3.6	18.6	20.7	5.3	5.1	3.1	62.6
1860–89	1.9	21.8	24.7	6.4	7.7	3.9	58.6
1870–99		19.7	25.1	4.1	6.8	7.4	52.7
1880–1909		16.3	19.3	4.1	8.6	7.1	54.0
1890–1919		17.1	16.5	3.4	6.2	5.7	50.8
1900–29		17.2	11.2	2.6	6.0	0.7	56.0

1880s that the people of Spitalfields 'care next to nothing for the ministerial office—their regard is almost purely personal'.[15] R. J. Campbell made the very same point in his autobiography, remarking that if a minister was 'a strong man, the possessor of popular gifts, he will be treated with plenty of consideration; but the consideration is not due to his office so much as to his personal qualities'.[16] Again, the chairman of the Hackney College Committee stressed the importance of better ministerial education in 1895 on the grounds that people would no longer listen to a man just because he was a minister. Respect for the actual office, he averred, was much diminished.[17] None of this is in any way incompatible with the fact that all but one of the two dozen or so Methodist ministers interviewed as part of an oral history project reckoned that when they began work in the 1920s some sort of regard for their office was still in evidence. They were, it must be emphasized, viewing things from the very different perspective of the 1970s.[18]

In seeking to establish some idea of the dimension of ministerial involvement in communal life, the historian is on much less sure statistical ground than in the previous chapters. Most obituaries record certain basic and usually verifiable facts about birthplace, details of career, marriage, retirement, and death. The inclusion of other information about broader activities was much more random. It is possible, for example, although it seems to have occurred infrequently, that a writer did not know his subject very intimately. He may not have approved of a particular activity or, more likely, might have belonged to a denomination which regarded extra-curricular activities with disfavour. In all such cases, information relevant to a particular minister's public life might have been often deliberately omitted. Alternatively, such activities might have been so encouraged and expected by denominational authority that an obituarist may have taken their existence for granted or contented

---

[15] Quoted in K. S. Inglis, *The Churches and The Working Classes in Victorian England* (1963), 90.

[16] R. J. Campbell, *A Spiritual Pilgrimage* (1916), 37.

[17] *Independent and Nonconformist*, 20 June 1895.

[18] C. Field, 'A Sociological Profile of English Methodism, 1900–1932', *Oral History*, 4 (1976), 91 n. 82.

himself with a bland generalization, such as 'active in public life'. The precise meaning of such statements is now impossible to recapture, except perhaps after considerable, highly detailed, local research. Finally, some public work or publishing activity might have appeared to a writer as too insignificant or ephemeral to merit discussion, although it might well have had some particular local importance.

On a more positive note, however, it is possible to supplement obituarial information with other material, much of it derived from the 'coming men' type of article which formed a staple element in Victorian denominational periodical literature. Although many of these features were often quite short they were more than simple character assessments and frequently included a wide range of information about their subjects. Even so, the figures in Table 6.1 cannot be taken in any sense as precise measures. They do not and cannot begin to explore the more subtle ways in which ministerial influences were exerted. Only the study of specific churches and individuals can reveal those. All Table 6.1 does, therefore, is to quantify minimum recorded levels of particular types of public activity, levels which might be increased in the light of further local researches. The figures can be used to indicate only very general trends over time in the scale and nature of some aspects of ministers' wider public life.

For the sake of analysis, activity has been divided into six broad categories in Table 6.1. Column 1 indicates the proportion known to have kept schools in conjunction with their ministries. 'Philanthropy' in column 2 embraces those who wrote about or who were activists in welfare movements—temperance, hospitals, libraries, welfare and improvement societies, school governors, Rotary, Toc H, and the like. 'Politics' in column 3 refers to membership of political parties and of overtly political pressure groups such as the International Arbitration League or, later, the League of Nations Union. It also includes men who served on elected bodies such as councils, boards of guardians, or education and school boards. Of course, the division between categories 2 and 3 is to a large extent quite arbitrary and a matter of personal interpretation. It is a moot point, for example, as to whether a temperance campaigner should be classified as a philanthropic or a political activist, although this same ambiguity was also apparent in the thinking of those numerous Victorian Christians who believed that the gospel had social and moral dimensions but who eschewed party politics as essentially worldly.[19] Activities included under 'Learned' in column 4 include writing on the arts and sciences, as well as membership of societies which might be generally defined as academic, cultural, or intellectual in scope—the Royal Geographical Society or the Dickens Fellowship, for example, as well as similar local societies. 'Theological Publication' in column 5 is self-explanatory, except to add that it includes hymn writing. The miscellaneous literature listed in column 6 covers works of poetry, as well as historical, fictional, and biographical writing. Finally, column 7 records those for whom no activity of any sort has been traced. It should be noted that each individual minister's activities have been classified under all the appropriate headings. Thus George Lane, who entered the Primitive ministry in 1892, appears in column 4 as a member of the Royal Geographical Society, in column 2 as a founder of the Stockton Rotary Club, and column 3 as a member of the Durham County Council. Ben Evans, a Baptist, was even busier. Active in the Anti-Corn Law League and Liberation Society, President of the Scarborough Temperance Society and founder of the town's Mechanics' Society, member of a local archaeological club, and the author of numerous works on history and theology, he appears in every column save the first and the last.

Educating the young was quite evidently a potent source of both influence and status reinforcement for ministers. It also had the added attraction that it involved the two tasks of instruction and pastoral care which were most akin to the central functions of the ministry itself. 'If a pastor finds it absolutely necessary for the support of his family to engage in any secular calling', wrote J. A. James in 1854, 'nothing is

---

[19] 'It is nevertheless our duty to go as far at least as to give our signature to every public measure which tends to ameliorate the condition of our countrymen, and to diffuse liberty and peace throughout the world. As it respects our Ministers, we presume they never take a public part in political discussions . . .', Methodist New Connexion, *Minutes* (1831), 52.

so nearly related to his own duties as that of educating youth.'[20] Yet as column 1 suggests, it was ever only a small proportion of Baptists and Congregationalists who doubled as schoolmasters (being employed by Conference and not free agents, Methodists were not technically permitted to take up supplementary occupations, although there is evidence to suggest that economic necessity forced some of them to ignore the rules). It seems unlikely that the figures would be much increased by further research or even by adding in those who provided private tuition for ministerial candidates. In some areas, mainly rural ones but also in rapidly expanding industrial communities, ministers were often the only people capable of offering anything more than rudimentary instruction in reading and writing. Apart from any desire to indoctrinate the young in the tenets of a particular denominational creed, the main ministerial incentive behind such activity was certainly financial, as James had recognized. Consequently, as ministers' conditions and pay improved somewhat, and as more adequate provision for education was made available by national and local government, so ministerial involvement in teaching tended to diminish, as Table 6.1 indicates. Even in 1854 James had been able to refer to the keeping of schools by ministers as a practice 'once so common' but 'now happily so rare'.[21]

Baptist and Congregationalist involvement in education was undoubtedly a reflection of their long traditions of scholarship and ministerial training, and also of their need to provide their own higher education in view of their exclusion from the English universities. The same reasons may be adduced for the greater contribution which the Old Dissenters made to what may be termed intellectual life as defined by columns 4 to 6 of Table 6.1. At least one in six of those men who entered the Old Dissenting ministry before 1849 turned a hand to publishing some theological work, although in many cases it was probably nothing more ambitious than a sermon or two. The late-century decline of the

---

[20] *Evangelical Magazine*, 32 (1854), 2.
[21] Ibid.

Baptist contribution in this area may perhaps be related to the growing preponderance in their ranks of men trained by Spurgeon, who did not place much emphasis on either the educational attainments of his students, or on scholarship for its own sake. With the exception of theological scholarship, the Methodists in general do not seem to have made much of an intellectual contribution at all, although it must be stressed that the table offers no guide whatsoever to the actual quality or significance of what was being produced. There was a deep-seated and long-standing suspicion of intellectual activity among the Wesleyans anyway which surfaced intermittently during the nineteenth century, most noticeably when the idea of establishing the Theological Institution was first raised. The Primitives' contribution to literature was meanest of all, the combined outcome of their generally poor educational backgrounds, humble social status, and, in the early part of the century at least, the connexion's emphasis on evangelism rather than on the pastoral aspects of the ministry. Growth was the all-absorbing priority and little time was left for reflection and other, less immediate involvements. Similarly, the relatively lowly origins of the Bible Christian component in United Methodism may have restricted their contribution to general literary activity, though this was more than compensated for by the connexion's high output of theological publication which in mid-century exceeded that of the other Methodists and of the Old Dissent as well. The explanation for this is to be found in the circumstances in which the Free Methodist connexion was established. It appeared in the 1850s as an amalgam of several small groups which had broken away from the parent Wesleyan body. In almost every case, the cause of the rupture had been disagreements about the forms and orders of Methodist church government and the disputes had been fought out not only on conference floors but also across many pages of polemical, doctrinal pamphlets.

Turning next to philanthropy and politics it again appears that in the first half of the century it was the Baptists and Congregationalists who were more deeply and persistently involved than the Methodists. True, there always existed an underlying unease among some Old Dissenting ministers about the validity of political activity and one of the most powerful and influential Independents in the first half of the century, William Jay, quoted with obvious approval Dr Chalmers's warning that men who became political activists were often 'sadly drawn off from keeping their own vineyards'.[22] Yet Table 6.1 indicates that at least a quarter of those who began work as Congregational or Baptist ministers between 1810 and 1849 had some degree of active political life. This is no great surprise, since the ministers were the natural leaders of denominations in which notions of democracy and independence were deeply entrenched and whose adherents suffered from legally enshrined social and political discrimination. Furthermore, in a way, the very decision to enter the dissenting ministry at all was a political statement, a rejection of the very notion of a state Church. Then again, many public issues involved considerations of morality and justice to which ministers had perforce to be sensitive, although they were frequently equally anxious to avoid party politics. The only Independent comparable to Jay in the first half of the century was Thomas Binney and his view was clear: 'Politics are a branch of morals, and the Bible is the most political of books.'[23] In appealing for ministers to attend a special meeting of the Anti-Corn Law League in Manchester in 1843, the *Patriot* was at pains to assure potential participants that they would not be engaging in party matters by attending. In the event, over 600 ministers did turn up (including 182 Baptists and 274 Congregationalists) and there is evidence to suggest that more would have been present had communications or prior engagements permitted.[24] Guinness Rogers claimed later that this gathering was the start of ministerial involvement in public political life because for the first time in English history 'the voice of Nonconformist ministers was heard in such strength upon affairs which seemed to be

[22] G. Redford and J. A. James (eds.), *The Autobiography of the Rev William Jay* (1855), 113.
[23] Quoted in W. O'Neill, *Notes and Incidents of Home Missionary Life and Work* (1870), 13.
[24] See the letters of apology published in the *Patriot*, 19 and 26 Aug. 1843.

outside their proper province'.[25] He was right in the sense perhaps that this was the first major *collective* action, but Table 6.1 makes it clear that as individuals ministers were politically active long before 1843.

The several extensions of the parliamentary franchise, the application of the elective principle to the operation of the Poor Law, education, and local government, coupled with a growing awareness of widespread urban poverty made it increasingly difficult for ministers to avoid political and philanthropic issues as the century moved on. In its last two decades industrial unrest, social tension, and the publication of Andrew Mearns's pamphlet, *The Bitter Cry of Outcast London*, all served to encourage the formulation of the social gospel, a gospel which, it was hoped, would also enable the churches to reach the working classes more effectively. Perhaps because as a denomination Congregationalists were most readily abandoning the old Evangelical tenets, they also responded most enthusiastically to this fresh articulation of the Christian message.[26] True, a few individuals like Henry Stedwicke urged ministers to 'refrain from taking any active part in electoral contests of a purely party character' because, he alleged, great harm had been done by the 'fiercely partisan spirit with which not a few ministers entered into the elections of 1885 and 1886'.[27] Yet it was a Congregationalist, R. W. Dale, who was probably the social gospel's most able publicist, while another of the denomination's ministers, Charles Sylvester Horne, was its best known cynosure. The leisurely rhythms of Edwardian parliamentary life enabled him to combine his work as pastor with that of representing Ipswich in the House of Commons. Other contemporaries who had perhaps more successful political careers—Josiah Towyn Jones, a Congregational minister who became an MP in 1912 and ultimately a junior Treasury Lord, or a Baptist minister, Herbert Dunnico, who was Deputy Speaker between 1929 and 1931—abandoned their church careers for their politics.

[25] J. G. Rogers, *An Autobiography* (1903), 80.
[26] On this see D. Bebbington, 'The City, the Countryside and the Social Gospel in Victorian Nonconformity', *Studies in Church History*, 16 (1979).
[27] *Independent and Nonconformist*, 8 Jan. 1892.

The *Independent and Nonconformist*, a paper which owed its existence to the work of another former Congregational minister, Edward Miall, also lent its support to the social gospel cause, dismissing as 'superfine pietists' those ministers who regarded political activity as 'but slightly removed from the seven deadly sins'.[28] A similar line was followed in the *British Weekly*. Summing up the results of an essay competition on the merits and demerits of political involvement by ministers, the editor made his own stance very clear. Deployed against politics were the arguments that political life was too dishonest and would thus corrupt ministers, causing them to serve two very different masters, and risk splitting congregations. It was also argued that the properly conscientious pastor could not have time for an active political life, that his spirituality would suffer, and that he would forfeit his religious influence over those members of his congregation who did not share his own particular political standpoint. Much more space was devoted in the article, however, to the arguments in favour of such active involvement. They included an appeal to individuals' sense of civic responsibility much along the line pressed so consistently by Dale; the rather dubious assertion that ministers were entitled to offer political advice and leadership because they were better educated than their congregations; and the suggestions that the Kingdom of God depended for its establishment upon human agency, that moral questions required political answers, that sermons needed to be rooted in everyday issues, that party strife would be civilized by ministerial involvement (memory here was obviously short since no one apparently recalled the highly rancorous disputes which had rocked Methodism in the 1840s), and that a politically active minister would be able to widen the circle of his spiritual influence.[29] Yet neither the peculiar receptivity of Congregational ministers to the social gospel nor their high degree of political and social activism can be attributed simply to the influence of leading denominational journals and figures. Their social involvement also represented a reformulation of their understanding of the Christian faith, shorn now of

[28] Ibid. 29 Aug. 1895.
[29] *British Weekly*, 5 Nov. 1891.

much old Evangelical dogma to which many Congregationalists felt increasingly unable to subscribe.

Baptist response to the social gospel was rather more
varied. Some of those who did throw themselves into it with
considerable energy encountered rank and file opposition
from within their congregations. John Wilson, minister at
Woolwich after 1887, was an elected guardian, a school
board member, and also helped to found the Woolwich
Polytechnic, a record of achievement which antagonized
those members of his congregation who believed that the
cobbler should stick to his last.[30] Walter Hobbs, minister of
Gypsy Road Chapel in Lambeth, was also elected as a Poor
Law guardian but ran into difficulties when some of his
members objected on the grounds that they paid him to
minister in the Church, not the Poor Law Union. As a result,
he resigned the ministry altogether. Similarly, when A. Gra-
ham Barton appealed to Baptists to remember that the gospel had social implications he was much criticized. J. R.
Wood advised Baptist ministerial candidates in 1892 that
while it was acceptable to have views about social problems,
they should steer clear of party involvement. In his support
he quoted Robert Hall: 'When the devil saw a minister likely
to be useful in the church, his way of disposing of him was to
get on his back and ride him to death with engagements.'[31]
George Freeman summed up a fairly widespread Baptist
view when he attacked the establishment of the Nonconformist Socialist League in 1909: 'The ministry that departs
from the great mission of saving sinners and making souls is
a discredit in the world and a degradation to itself.'[32] President after president urged the Baptist Union's annual assembly delegates to carry back to their churches the message
that they should take care not to allow social work to side-
track them from the basic task of reconciling sinful man with
a forgiving God.[33] To some extent, perhaps, the tenacity of
the old Evangelical tradition among Baptists may be related

[30] F. S. Clayton, *John Wilson of Woolwich* (n.d.), 46.
[31] *Baptist Magazine*, 84 (1892), 551.
[32] *Anti-Socialist*, Sept. 1909, 90.
[33] See, for example, Macalpine's address in 1911 and Principal Edwards's comments
in similar vein in the same year.

to the disproportionate influence of Spurgeon's men, but
whatever its causes the adherence to the old surfaced again
after 1900. Baptist ministers were by far the most active of
any church ministers in the campaign of passive resistance
to the Balfour Education Act, a campaign rooted in anti-
Catholicism and also in the nonconformists' old, historic
sense of social exclusion.[34] Indeed, without this struggle it
seems likely that the downward trend of Baptist political
involvement, which became apparent with the generations
entering the ministry after 1850, would have been even
steeper.

Table 6.1 also suggests that Methodists generally were
not as politically involved as either of the two older dissenting traditions. Wesley himself had accepted that politics
were beyond his province, but if his stance was perhaps
more subtle than it sometimes appeared, it boiled down in
the end to supporting the status quo.[35] After his death the
contemporary social climate—the outworking of the French
Revolution, European war, social and industrial unrest at
home—was such that Methodist polity, with its overtones of
democracy and anti-establishmentarianism, was regarded
with some suspicion by the civil authority. To offset this the
Wesleyan hierarchy opted for a no-politics stance which in
practice served to reinforce the connexion's support for the
Establishment, since it entailed an emphasis on loyalty and
active discouragement of radical and political activity by
ministers and members alike. At the level of the local chapel
the no-politics rule (which was effectively a no-Whig-politics
rule) may often have been ignored as it was sometimes
incompatible with the personal interests of Wesleyan voters.
But the ministers, as Table 6.1 suggests, appear to have
preserved a relatively low political profile for most of the
nineteenth century. Thus Joseph Entwisle, later the first
governor of the Theological Institution, refused in 1792 to
preach a sermon on politics, arguing that 'the pulpit is

[34] The details are in J. E. B. Munson, 'A Study of Nonconformity in Edwardian
England as Revealed by the Passive Resistance Movement against the 1902 Education
Act', Oxford D.Phil. thesis, 1973, p. 288.
[35] The political views of Wesley are discussed very fully in D. Hempton, *Methodism
and Politics in British Society, 1750–1850* (1984), 43 ff.

sacred to better purposes'.[36] Although Jabez Bunting was not above threatening to use his considerable personal influence to bring down the government when it provided financial aid for the Catholic seminary at Maynooth, Wesleyan ministers generally were warned off party politics. Indeed, when the *Patriot* issued its appeal for a good attendance at the 1843 Manchester meeting of the Anti-Corn Law League, it more or less wrote off the Wesleyans, saying that they were much more interested in discovering who had written the *Wesleyan Takings* than with such considerable matters as the iniquities of the Corn Law.[37] Robert Newton expressed a common Wesleyan opinion in the first part of the nineteenth century when he argued that the solution to all social and political problems lay only in 'pure and undefiled religion'.[38] Here, perhaps, was a reflection of the Wesleyans' unique ecclesiastical and political position. They were full-blown supporters neither of the Establishment and conservatism, nor of nonconformity and liberalism. As is often the case with such hybrids, sterility was the result.

By the 1870s, however, it is possible to detect signs of the more concerned approach which accounts for the increase in political and philanthropic involvement apparent in Table 6.1. In his address to new ministers in 1875 the Conference President, Gervase Smith, was still warning his hearers against 'political confederations and party politics' but he went on to add that 'there are great Protestant and Evangelical subjects constantly rising up, with which you should be well acquainted'.[39] Four years later, the same theme was taken up in the Conference's 'Address to the Societies'. The main object of all outside work, it suggested, was to maintain the honour of Christ. 'So long as in this spirit you use your rights as citizens, there are objects which you may well endeavour to secure ...'[40] Temperance reform and the purification of the statute book were particularly recommended. By 1888 the Pastoral Address of Conference was calling attention to important public duties which Chris-

---

[36] J. Entwisle, *Memoir of the Rev Joseph Entwisle. By his Son* (Bristol, 1848), 91.
[37] *Patriot*, 12 Aug. 1843.
[38] T. Jackson, *The Life of Robert Newton* (1855), 96.
[39] A. O. Smith, *The Rev Gervase Smith DD* (1882), 241.
[40] Wesleyan Conference, *Minutes* (1879), 304.

tians ought to undertake. 'We want stalwart Christian
citizens at the polling booth, on Boards of Guardians, on
School Boards, in the Council Chamber, and in Parliament.'[41] Among ministers this was taken up most enthusiastically by Hugh Price Hughes, the foremost Wesleyan
exponent of the social gospel, a programme he pursued most
assiduously in the columns of the *Methodist Times*. It was,
however, the philanthropic rather than the directly political
to which ministers tended to gravitate. The Sigma Club, the
Wesleyan ministers' socialist society, had only sixty-five
members in 1909 and there was much substance in the
Christian World's comment that it was 'a well understood
thing among the more "safe" men in the Wesleyan ministry
that they had better abstain from any active participation in
Imperial politics'.[42] When Compton-Rickett invited nonconformist ministers to meet Campbell-Bannerman and Herbert
Gladstone in 1902 he invited mainly Congregationalists because they 'take a more prominent part in political work
than Methodists'.[43] It was apparently never more than a
minority of Wesleyans who responded positively to the new
emphasis. If Hughes represented the new, then the old survived, most significantly and vocally in the personage of
J. H. Rigg. At a lower level altogether, a similar division was
evident in the Guttery family, although it was more apparent than real. When the Revd T. Guttery wrote to tell his
ministerial son of his disquiet about the extent of his extra-
curricular activity, he received the following reply: 'I thank
you for your wise advice. You need not fear, however, that I
shall ever forget that my chief work is to preach the Gospel.
My most powerful motive for entering so largely into
Temperance and Political work is that it increases the audi-
ences and influence of my church.'[44] The son was as good as
his word, too, turning down several invitations to stand in
parliamentary election contests on the ground that 'the
ministry held his soul; the preaching of the Gospel was the
one thing he desired most to do'.[45]

[41] Ibid. (1888), 33.
[42] *Christian World*, 21 Jan. 1892.
[43] Quoted in Koss, p. 36
[44] J. G. Bowran, *The Life of Arthur Thomas Guttery DD* (1922), 46.
[45] Ibid. 107.

One by-product of the call to Wesleyans to take a more active part in public life was renewed debate about the appropriateness of their existing itinerant term. The *Patriot* had put the difficulty well as early as 1852: 'No man can ever hope to gain any great amount of local influence who is perpetually shifting.' It had gone on to point out that the Methodists were at a particular disadvantage in this respect since 'in many cases they come and go without ever being known beyond the narrow limits of their own denominational circle'.[46] Table 4.3 indicated how frequently Wesleyans were moved from one circuit to another, often remaining in one station for shorter periods than the notional maximum of three years, and it does seem possible that in this way the itinerant system contributed to the Wesleyans' low level of participation in political and charitable activity. As W. H. Lax pointed out, the short stays imposed by the system made it difficult for Wesleyan ministers to become embroiled in local politics; indeed, they often failed to acquire the residential qualifications necessary for the franchise.[47]

Certainly Lax himself became Mayor of Poplar only because he remained there long enough to build up a personal political following, but care should be taken not to exaggerate this negative aspect of the itinerancy. On average, the Primitive and United Methodist ministers served for shorter periods than did the Wesleyans, yet their political and philanthropic involvements were consistently greater. This suggests that the main explanation of the Wesleyans' relative lack of involvement lies mainly in the legacy of Wesley and Bunting, coupled with the connexion's unique ecclesiastical and political position. It is true that in the early part of the century the Primitive Consolidated Minutes barred preachers from speaking at political or parliamentary meetings but most of them seem to have interpreted this as a ban on speaking only in the Tory interest. Certainly as the century neared its end, they compared quite favourably with the Baptists in this respect if not reaching the same levels of involvement as the Congregationalists. Such activity was

[46] *Patriot*, 11 Mar. 1852.
[47] W. H. Lax, *Lax His Book* (1937), 196.

perhaps to be expected of a connexion which was generally acknowledged to have a special calling to the working classes. 'Of all denominations', commented the main connexional journal in 1874, 'these matters should interest and concern us. We have, emphatically, the poor with us, and we have them in larger numbers than any other community.'[48] It seems likely, too, that during years in which poverty was becoming a matter of growing public concern and when working-class political consciousness was rising, then lay influence, which was strongly entrenched in Primitive Methodism, would more or less compel ministers to take some part in the wider aspects of life. Certainly by the 1890s the *Primitive Methodist* was able to note with some approval that 'our ministers ... are taking more interest in public affairs than they used to'.[49] A similar lay impetus might also explain the growing levels of involvement evident among United Methodists, although given the circumstances of the connexion's origins it seems likely, and is confirmed by Table 6.1, that they had always had a relatively high (for Methodists) level of political awareness.

With the exception of Wesleyan and Baptist philanthropic activity, levels of involvement all began to turn down with those generations entering the ministry after 1890. It has been suggested that nonconformist political life began to fade somewhat after 1910 but the evidence of Table 6.1 might indicate that for ministers it had begun to diminish rather earlier, sustained perhaps only by the inspiration of the education issue.[50] One possible explanation for declining ministerial participation is that by the late nineteenth century the ministry itself was losing something of its importance as other channels of nonconformity came more to the fore. 'Some of the greatest spiritual forces of the age work from other centres than the pulpit', commented the *Christian World*.[51]

Another possibility is provided by the evidence in Table

---

[48] *Primitive Methodist*, 29 Jan. 1874.

[49] Ibid. 25 Jan. 1891.

[50] The suggestion is made by D. Bebbington, *The Nonconformist Conscience. Chapel and Politics 1870–1914* (1982), 104. It may be, of course, that obituaries of the post–1890 entrants were written during the retreat from politics after 1910, and thus omit as unimportant aspects of political activity which *had* been undertaken.

[51] *Christian World*, 11 Feb. 1892.

6.2, which plots the proportions of men involved in denominational administration of local or national dimensions. As the oldest of the centralized Methodist connexions, the Wesleyans always had quite a high percentage of men holding connexional office, and the figure increased steadily during the century, as it did, too, among the Primitives. The most startling increases, however, came among the Baptists and Congregationalists as their respective Unions acquired more powers of direction and spawned more organizational offshoots. It is tempting to posit some correlation between levels of public activity and administrative complexity since the highly organized Wesleyans had the lowest levels of public involvement. Yet this is too simple. There are, as we have seen, other explanations for the Wesleyans' passivity, while the correlation does not hold true for the Congregationalists. In their case, and indeed in other denominations, some of the most publicly active men, such as Dale and Clifford, were also among those most heavily involved in denominational administration. In many ways it was a mutually reinforcing process. A man who made a name either inside the denomination for administrative talent, or outside by public work, could expect to rise to high office which would involve him in more administration but to which there was also a public face. Nevertheless, there are some few hints that among the Methodists growing administrative burdens, both national and local, could divert men from more primary tasks, whether preaching or public activity. When Thomas Nightingale first became a Wesleyan circuit superintendent, he commented that 'I am in danger ... of thinking about old and new chapel deeds; who will be the best man for this and the other vacant office? Where can I get the new subscriber for this, that and the other fund ...?'[52] Obelkevich's study of Lincolnshire Methodism points in the same direction. In the long run, he concludes, 'energy was diverted from the spiritual ends to the proliferating bureaucratic means'.[53]

---

[52] T. Nightingale, *Some of the Reminiscences and Experiences of My Life* (1891), 141.

[53] J. Obelkevich, *Religion and Rural Society. South Lindsey, 1825–1875* (Oxford, 1976), 224. Identical comments are made about Primitive Methodists in G. M. Morris, 'Primitive Methodism in Nottinghamshire', Nottingham Ph.D. thesis, 1967, p. 113.

TABLE 6.2. Nonconformist Ministers' Administrative Involvement (%)

	Years of Entering Ministry							
	1830–59	1840–69	1850–79	1860–89	1870–99	1880–1909	1890–1919	1900–29
Wesleyan								
National Office	7.8	5.8	3.6	4.3	6.9	8.9	5.6	3.0
Other Office	6.9	12.5	11.1	16.4	16.4	24.3	26.3	22.9
Educational	0.9	1.6	2.2	2.5	3.7	4.4	3.2	1.5
Primitive								
National Office	4.8	4.3	4.5	4.5	7.4	10.1	8.8	5.8
Other Office	0.9	1.7	8.5	13.5	27.3	36.4	33.8	28.5
Educational	1.9	2.6	1.5	1.8	0.9	0.8	2.2	2.5
United								
National Office	All figures for this period are artificially inflated by the fact that three						11.0	
Other Office	separate connexional organizations are involved						41.8	
Educational							2.0	
Baptist								
National Office	3.0	4.6	6.6	7.3	6.9	6.8	7.4	8.5
Other Office	5.5	5.3	10.3	11.8	17.6	18.0	23.1	27.8
Educational	3.1	0.6	3.0	2.4	4.1	3.7	6.9	7.8
Congregational								
National Office	5.8	5.5	2.0	1.8	1.8	2.0	1.7	1.9
Other Office	6.6	6.2	4.6	6.3	6.8	10.7	14.2	17.3
Educational	3.6	3.7	3.1	3.8	3.4	3.0	4.0	4.0

Note: 'National Office' is defined as membership of central denominational committees, or central positions such as president, chairman, secretary, etc. 'Other Office' means circuit office in the case of Methodists, county or regional office in the case of Baptists and Congregationalists.

Some considerable space has been devoted to explaining changing shifts in the levels of ministerial participation in various aspects of Victorian public life, but this should not be allowed to obscure the most obvious and arguably the most significant conclusion to be drawn from Table 6.1. Throughout the years between 1810 and 1930 the total proportion of ministers who were active outside the immediate chapel community was almost always a minority, in some cases quite a small one. There were always at least 40 per cent, more usually 50 or 60 per cent, and sometimes as many as 80 per cent of men for whom no record of extra-curricular activity has been found. It must be reiterated that the table examines only a certain range of activities and can in no way measure the precise influence of particular individuals in particular locations.[54] Nevertheless, the general picture is surprisingly uniform over time and between denominations, fits in quite neatly with the more general interpretations of the pattern of nonconformist development, and is also what might be expected, given the rather restricted and confined domestic and educational experiences which, as Chapter 3 argues, were the lot of a good number of ministers. It is possible, therefore, that here as elsewhere both contemporaries and historians alike have been misled by the volubility and high profile of the famous, ignoring the more quiescent majority. Perhaps Alfred Cooke, a Baptist who remained totally remote from the public life of Luton where he ministered for almost half a century, is more representative than has hitherto been allowed. Perhaps W. H. Mills's *Grey Pastures* should be taken more seriously, for it is a work which reveals a particular texture of Victorian nonconformity and one somewhat obscured by the muscular jollity of some more general accounts.[55] Mills characterizes one of his ministers as 'a sensationally delicate man who seldom went out on Sundays except to risk his life at an important funeral'.[56] Finally, we should note the sentiments expressed

---

[54] The subtleties of such influences are well pursued in C. Binfield, *So Down to Prayers. Studies in English Nonconformity, 1780–1920* (1977), *passim*.

[55] Particularly that by K. Young, *Chapel: The Joyful Days and Prayerful Nights of the Nonconformists in Their Heyday c. 1850–1950* (1972).

[56] W. H. Mills, *Grey Pastures* (1924), 3.

by R. A. Vaughan, who, as Principal of Lancashire Independent College for twelve years, was presumably in a good position to assess ministerial character and motivation. How many men, he asked, went into the ministry 'to a large extent from their utter distaste for the coarse collision and vulgar brawl with which they would often be mixed up in other pursuits? What they covet in the Christian ministry, is its comparative quiet, and the sense of being useful without ever taking much part in the worldly contentions ever going on about them.'[57]

[57] R. Vaughan, *Memoir of Robert Alfred Vaughan* (1864), 27.

7

Postscript

In the course of the 1930s Edward Thompson wrote two
novels about the Arnison family. His quasi-autobiographical
accounts of the struggles of a young nonconformist to hold
on to faith and to find some sense of relevance and purpose
in a ministry which he had entered almost in spite of himself
were a cruel exposure of many contemporary nonconformist
delusions and were not well received.[1] Thompson suggested
that it was primarily the impact of the First World War
which 'took ... the heart out of the Nonconformist half of
our nation, and all its distinctiveness and vigour'.[2] Bishop
Wickham's later study of the religious history of Sheffield
placed a similar emphasis on the disruptive influence of the
war.[3] Both writers, however, did make reference to the difficulties of faith, organization, and role which were already
in evidence before the war, and it is generally accepted that
the seeds of nonconformity's dramatic collapse in the 1930s
were sown in the last decades of the nineteenth century.[4]
Some have argued that the seed was essentially an intellectual one, nonconformity declining as theological doubts dif-
fused through society to reach the ordinary rank and file
believer.[5] Others have advanced the theory of secularization,
according to which the churches were rendered irrelevant by
the development of alternative, specialized institutions, with

---

[1] E. Thompson, *Introducing the Arnisons* (1935); *John Arnison* (1939). In the preface
to his second novel, Thompson denied that his work was autobiographical but there is
little doubt that his stories were based on personal experience.

[2] Thompson, *John Arnison*, p. ix.

[3] E. R. Wickham, *Church and People in an Industrial City* (1957), 210 ff.

[4] For a good recent discussion of nonconformity's problems in the 1930s see
A. Hastings, *A History of English Christianity, 1920–1985* (1986), 262–72.

[5] A sophisticated form of this stratified diffusion theory appears in H. McLeod, *Class
and Religion in the Late Victorian City* (1974).

indifference and unbelief becoming the only tenable positions to hold in an increasingly pluralistic society.[6]

Whichever view is preferred, it is clear that one of the
concomitants of failing growth rates after 1880 was the
ministerial recruitment crisis which affected all three of the
leading nonconformist denominations in terms of numbers,
declining student quality, and inappropriate training programmes and organizations. As this study has suggested,
ministerial quality had perhaps never been all that high but
for most of the nineteenth century at least, a combination of
religious conviction, social and educational discrimination,
and expanding numbers had served to produce an adequate
supply in most denominations. By the end of Victoria's
reign, however, this was no longer the case. The expansion of
alternative employment opportunities meant that the ministry no longer represented the major vehicle of social
advancement for ambitious young nonconformists.[7] Furthermore, the development of both the press and education
challenged the uniquely influential position which the pulpit
had hitherto enjoyed.

By the end of the nineteenth century, therefore, the nonconformists were living largely off their accumulated ministerial fat, hence their failure to tackle at all radically or
urgently the ominous warning symptoms which were
appearing well before 1914—declining recruitment from a
narrowing social and occupational base; increased reliance
on the sons of ministers at a time when ministerial family
size was diminishing; a training whose relevance to contemporary society and thought was in doubt and which
was locked into an outmoded and inefficient institutional
structure; possibly much less public involvement than the
activities of a few prominent individuals might suggest; a
questioning of the very role and significance of the ministry;

---

[6] A good exposition of secularization theory applied to Britain is by A. Gilbert, *The Making of Post-Christian Britain: A History of the Secularization of Modern Society* (1980).

[7] Thus G. W. Conder had suggested in 1858 that entering the Independent ministry was for 'most men ... an elevation of ranks', *Memoir and Remains of the late Rev. J. Glyde* (1858), 22. Similarly George Eliot, *Essays and Leaves from a Notebook* (1884), 145, claimed that the ministry was the means by which an individual 'without the aid of birth or money ... may most easily attain power and reputation'.

poor morale induced by economic hardship and insecurity, one manifestation of which was the trend towards a more mobile ministry and, in some denominations, shorter pastorates. Such attention as the various churches did pay to these problems prior to 1914 was leisurely and dilatory. Things would probably have remained very much worse among the Baptists and Congregationalists had it not been for the prodigious efforts of J. H. Shakespeare and J. D. Jones respectively. Even so, the reduction in the drop-out rates from the ministry which became evident from the 1880s owed more to the declining number of applicants than to any improvements in material conditions for those already in service.

Once it became clear that the war against Germany was not going to be the brief affair which so many were expecting, the theological colleges emptied as existing and potential students alike volunteered for war service. By 1916 Cheshunt, for example, contained only 3 students and the college was occupied by Serbian troops. By 1916, of the students who had been at Headingley in the three previous years, 29 were in the army, 3 were working in the munitions industry, and 1 was an army chaplain. All of those in the forces, recorded the college Minutes, 'wrote confidently of having taken the right step in enlisting'.[8] Among the Baptists, a third of Bristol's students were engaged in war work by 1915, Midland had only 2 students by 1917, the year in which Rawdon closed completely for the duration. With the restoration of peace it became evident that it was not only bodies that lay dead and buried on the battlefields, but ideals and beliefs as well. Some of the men never resumed their interest in a ministerial career and before long almost every denomination was experiencing major problems of recruitment.[9] By 1921 there were only 245 men in the various Congregational colleges as against 347 when

---

[8] Headingley Management Committee Executive Minutes, 24 Mar. 1916, Headingley College Archives, B3/3/2, Wesley College, Bristol.

[9] In some cases, of course, war experience led men into the ministry although N. Goodall was exaggerating when he claimed in 1932 that 'there are many of us in the service of the Church who, as far as we can know, would never have been in the ministry but for the war', *Christian World*, 28 Apr. 1932.

the war began, a reduction of almost 30 per cent. Annual intake was down to less than 50 at a time when between 70 and 75 men were needed each year just to replace those retiring—and this ignored the heavy demand for British-trained ministers in the dominions.[10] The Baptists were in a similar position. By 1923 their five English colleges were turning out only 20 students a year—a marked drop on the 50 being produced annually in the 1890s.[11] As for the Methodists, only the Primitives appear to have had what they regarded as an adequate supply of men in the imme-diate post-war years, although even then the connexional authorities were concerned about the cumulative effects of high retirement rates.[12] The Wesleyan Conference had warned in 1917 that 'the future supply of the Ministry causes us anxiety' and if the revival of the 1920s, which saw the connexion recouping some of its earlier membership losses, perhaps served in the short term to avert the difficulty of numbers, the cost of maintaining the Theological Institute was a continual financial drain.[13] Declining applications for the United Methodist ministry were blamed squarely on the effects of the war.[14]

'The lack of candidates for the Christian ministry', wrote the editor of the *Christian World* in 1921, 'has become serious.'[15] In considering likely explanations for the decline he began by dismissing the suggestion, popular in some quarters, that it was due primarily to the availability of alternative and better paid jobs. The ministry, he asserted, had never been a mere job. In one sense, of course, he was right, because the ministry involved a sense of individual vocation and divine call. Yet in his book on the professions, which appeared in 1857, H. Byerley Thompson claimed that 'it is an assured fact that the true motives which practically

[10] Ibid. 13 Oct. 1921.
[11] *Baptist Times and Freeman*, 27 Apr. 1923. The 1890s figure is derived from the averages for 1890–1901 given in J. Munson, 'The Education of Baptist Ministers 1870–1914', *Baptist Quarterly*, 26 (1976), 325.
[12] *British Weekly*, 16 June 1921.
[13] Wesleyan Conference, *Minutes* (1917), 401. *Methodist Recorder*, 21 July 1927, claimed that the annual cost of the Theological Institution was £7,000 as against £4,000 before the war.
[14] *Christian World*, 21 July 1921.
[15] Ibid. 19 May 1921.

induce the youth of England to engage in the ministry of the
Establishment, are not one whit less time-serving, or selfish,
than those that create the lawyer'.[16] He may have been
writing about Anglicans but the evidence of this study certainly confirms that for some nonconformists, too, considerations of income, security, and working conditions were
equally as important, and that the sense of vocation was not
always as resistant to such pressures, or as certain, as is
sometimes assumed. When Mr Kirknas applied to Cheshunt
in 1894, for example, it was for no better reason than that he
wished 'to change his profession'.[17] By this time some ministers were adopting professional working habits, keeping
office hours and charging set fees for preaching, develop-
ments which, as one paper pointed out, implied that 'practically ... the ministry is a profession'.[18] Yet many of the
earlier grievances which ministers had expressed had
sprung from a belief that the financial rewards were inadequate to sustain that position in society which, it was
felt, the ministry warranted.[19] Certainly by the end of the
nineteenth century the most successful ministers in the larger denominations could afford a professional life style because they enjoyed an appropriate income. For the majority,
there was still a yawning gap between economic reality and
the status professionalism which contemporary society
afforded them.[20]

It was a gap which the war widened. Population movements undermined the financial security of many well-
established nonconformist communities. By 1916 the Con-

[16] H. B. Thompson, *The Choice of a Profession*, (1857), 69.
[17] Applications to Cheshunt, 1867–94, Cheshunt College Archives, C/9/9/5, Westminster College, Cambridge.
[18] *Independent and Nonconformist*, 28 Aug. 1891.
[19] Thus a writer in *Methodist Magazine*, 38 (1815), 779, claimed that the current level
of allowances for preachers' daughters was inadequate 'to enable her to preserve that
rank in society in which she was born'. Similarly Jonathan Crowther argued in 1817
that Wesleyan salaries did not permit preachers and their families to occupy the
'respectable station in society' which both the Church and society expected. Quoted in
W. R. Ward, *Religion and Society in England, 1790–1850* (1972), 102.
[20] For status professionalism, see P. Elliott, *The Sociology of the Professions* (1972);
H. J. Wilensky, 'The Professionalisation of Everyone', *American Journal of Sociology*, 70
(1964), 137 ff. Cf. C. Binfield, 'The Pastor as Professional: Some Preliminary Steps in a
Victorian Investigation', in W. Conze and J. Kocka (eds.), *Bildungsbürgertum im 19.
Jahrhundert, Part 1: Bildungssystem und Professionalisierung in Internationalen Verg-
leichen* (Stuttgart, 1985).

gregational Church Aid Committee was being compelled to
dip into special reserve funds in order to liquidate its
accumulated debts. By the end of the war it was still assist-
ing over 400 churches with nearly 300 ministers. The equivalent Baptist fund was helping 540 congregations by 1920,
600 by 1922, who could not afford to pay a full salary to
their ministers. In both denominations the steps taken immediately before the war to improve ministerial salaries and
pension arrangements were swamped by wartime inflation.
When M. E. Aubrey became secretary of the Baptist Union in
1925 almost his first task was to raise £300,000 for the super-
annuation fund. A minimum salary of £130 a year was
prescribed by the Baptist Union, later raised to £160. The
Congregationalists recommended minima of £220 a year for
men in rural pastorates and £250 for those serving in urban
situations. Such increases were necessary, ran the investigating commission's report, because 'a large number of
ministers are receiving stipends less than the wages now
being paid to manual workers, and the situation has become
acute. They can pay their way only by the severest economy
and even by forgoing what, to men in their positions, are
some of the necessaries of life.'[21] At national level, perhaps,
both churches succeeded in raising the necessary monies but
at local level the pressures were sometimes more damaging.
The Moderator for the Congregationalists' North Western
Province had a sorry tale to tell in 1931—dwindling congregations, declining influence, and critical financial
hardships.[22] On the other side of the Pennines, depression in
the woollen industry severely affected the funding of the
Congregational college in Bradford.[23] Nor were things much
better for the Methodists. Economic hardship and industrial
unrest on the coal fields caused some two dozen Primitive
circuits to ask in 1921 for a reduction in their full-time
staffing since they had insufficient resources to pay for their
full quota. Over half of the Wesleyan ministers interviewed

[21] 'Manifesto of the Laymens' Committee on Ministerial Stipends, 1920', DWL, Spicer Papers, 24/182/1.
[22] R. T. Jones, *Congregationalism in England, 1662–1962* (1962), 390.
[23] K. Wadsworth, *Yorkshire United Independent College* (1952), 176–7.

in the 1970s about careers which began in the 1920s believed that their salaries had been inadequate.[24]

Even if money could be raised, the effort involved was, in the eyes of some, a distraction from the Church's real mission. One Wesleyan had argued this as early as 1915, drawing attention to 'the financial pressure which is neutralising the spiritual energies in most circuits'.[25] 'Can anyone feel happy', asked H. E. Berry, 'about the disproportionate amount of time spent on finance due nearly always, directly or indirectly, to the necessity for raising ministers' stipends?'[26] Although he was addressing his question to fellow Congregationalists, it was pertinent to other nonconformist denominations as well. Indeed, in seeking explanations for declining recruitment the editor of the *Christian World* had in the end suggested that the churches had become too concerned with worldly matters such as salaries and pensions.[27] They could thus only produce men of like temper who were not likely to be attracted into the ministry. It is worth noting in this context the continued emphasis in post-war obituaries on financial skills, often at the expense of any spiritual gifts or virtues. Pecuniary considerations were by no means unimportant in the early nineteenth century but few nonconformists would have bracketed together the spiritual and the worldly in the way that Philip Bennett's obituarist did in 1932: 'He was a leader in the great revival which marked the years 1905 and 1906 in Britain when there were scores of conversions, many of them of a striking and permanent character. To this record should be added the timely repair of a dangerous roof at Hebron and the renovation of the church premises on an extensive scale.'[28] E. H. Whitham's reminiscences revealed a similar order of priorities among Wesleyans: 'I try to be fair all round in my ministry. I've raised quite a bit of money. I do

[24] C. Field, 'A Sociological Profile of English Methodism, 1900–1932', *Oral History*, 4 (1976), 82.

[25] J. Hardcastle in a letter to the *Methodist Recorder*, 17 June 1915.

[26] H. E. Berry, 'Concerning the Paid Ministry', *Congregational Quarterly*, 15 (1937), 181.

[27] *Christian World*, 19 May 1921.

[28] United Methodist Conference, *Minutes* (1932), 34.

my honest best at preaching. I reckon to be in touch with my folk . . .'[29]

One result of declining recruitment is seen in Table 7.1, which indicates that the nonconformists were increasingly reliant upon an ageing ministry. By 1931 over a quarter of the men serving the Baptist, United Methodist, and Congregational churches were over sixty-one. About 60 per cent were over fifty-one, almost an exact reversal of the balance prevailing in the mid-nineteenth century when the ministry had been a young man's calling.[30] The Wesleyans and Primitives were not quite so badly off in this respect, both enjoying a rather more even distribution of men over and below fifty-one, and also a slightly lower average age. But the trend was clear. In both connexions the average age of serving ministers had risen by ten years, since 1831 in the Wesleyan case, since 1871 among the Primitives. In most denominations the proportion of men over the age of seventy-one was higher in 1931 than at any time in the past. In part this was the natural outcome of longer life expectancies, which gave the ministry a higher age profile. But there is here some support for Dr Cox's contention that in the late nineteenth century it was among the children of Free Churchmen that commitment and conviction began to fade, the nonconformist cultural tradition making less sense to a generation wealthier and more socially integrated than its fathers had been.[31]

Another outcome of declining recruitment was the attempt made by some denominations to widen the potential pool of recruits by admitting women to the ministry. Thus women were deemed eligible for admission to Bristol Baptist College in 1919 but the first one did not enter the college until 1937. Mrs C. M. Coltman was the first woman in the Congregational ministry in 1917 but there was a lot of prejudice to overcome, not only within nonconformity itself but sometimes from within the families of aspiring female

[29] W. B. Brash and C. J. Wright, *Didsbury College Centenary, 1842–1942* (1942), 68.
[30] In the 1840s ministry in the Church of England had also been for young men. Over half the staff were under forty-five years old at that time, A. G. L. Haig, *The Victorian Clergy: An Ancient Profession under Strain* (1984), 4.
[31] J. Cox, *The English Churches in a Secular Society: Lambeth 1870–1930* (Oxford, 1982), 222 ff.

7. Postscript

TABLE 7.1. Age Profile of Serving Nonconformist Ministers: Main Sample (%)

	Date					
	1831	1851	1871	1891	1911	1931
Wesleyan n	120	148	165	180	215	195
Average Age	39.8	44.7	42.8	43.0	46.1	50.2
Under 30	21.6	13.5	24.8	17.7	15.3	6.1
31–40	28.3	33.1	16.3	27.7	22.3	13.8
41–50	31.6	21.6	21.8	28.3	25.1	33.8
51–60	16.6	21.6	21.8	17.7	20.0	24.1
61–70	1.6	12.1	10.9	7.7	15.8	18.9
71–80		1.3	1.8	1.1	1.3	3.5
Primitive n	18	77	137	148	161	163
Average Age			39.7	45.7	43.5	49.0
Under 30			27.0	13.5	14.9	6.1
31–40			32.1	22.9	34.2	15.9
41–50			16.8	26.4	19.9	30.0
51–60			17.5	25.7	18.6	32.5
61–70			6.6	8.8	11.8	14.1
71–80				2.7	0.6	1.2
United n	27	64	124	176	190	128
Average Age			40.0	41.8	46.2	51.6
Under 30			20.1	18.1	10.0	7.8
31–40			37.1	34.7	26.3	12.5
41–50			20.9	18.8	21.5	17.9
51–60			17.7	19.9	28.9	36.7
61–70			4.0	7.9	12.1	21.1
71–80				0.5	1.0	3.9
Baptist n	59	129	186	231	260	208
Average Age		44.5	47.2	44.5	46.9	54.2
Under 30		15.5	16.1	17.7	8.0	2.4
31–40		25.6	19.8	31.6	26.5	11.5
41–50		27.9	22.6	19.4	27.7	24.0
51–60		18.6	19.9	13.8	25.4	32.7
61–70		10.0	12.9	12.1	10.0	19.7
71–80		2.3	6.9	4.3	1.9	9.1
Congregational n	85	168	194	205	230	189
Average Age		46.9	44.4	45.6	47.9	52.7
Under 30		8.3	18.0	12.2	4.7	1.6
31–40		28.5	21.7	26.8	25.6	15.3
41–50		24.4	21.7	30.7	30.8	22.2
51–60		19.6	24.2	16.6	23.8	33.3
61–70		13.1	9.8	9.8	12.1	22.8
71–80		5.9	4.6	3.9	3.0	4.8

ministers. Eva Gibbons wrote in some despair to Dr Grieve at Lancashire, saying that she was 'meeting with considerable opposition at home.... My father has stated definitely that he will not give me one penny piece and that ... he will have nothing further to do with me. My mother is even more bitter and says she would refuse to allow me to come home during vacation.... They argue that, having gone so far with my music, it is not morally right of me to give it up and begin work which is *only suited to a man*.'[32]

More fruitfully, the churches turned to institutional reform and rationalization, a task undertaken now with considerably more vigour and urgency than had characterized pre-war efforts in the same direction; hardly surprising when one estimate reckoned that the cost of training a Congregational minister in 1921 was £1,000, double the pre-war figure.[33] Thus Ranmoor never reopened after the war, United Methodist training being concentrated at Victoria College. The students, however, lived in the nearby Primitive college and teaching was shared so effectively that by 1921 a real fusion had taken place.[34] The Wesleyans did not open Headingley until 1930 and then, like the rest of the connexional colleges, it was encouraged to establish close links with the adjacent university, in this case Leeds. The realization of the plan, first mooted just before the war, to open an establishment in Cambridge was further evidence of a substantial shift of attitude within the Wesleyan hierarchy towards the whole concept of university training. Baptists resisted calls to create one large, central college but did set up a college board in 1923 to oversee recruitment and training. College Sunday was also instituted in an attempt to remind chapel congregations of their responsibility to provide both men and money for the support of the ministry. Regent's Park took steps towards moving to Oxford, in the process rejecting a merger proposal with Cheshunt. Midland College closed down for good in 1920. In London, Hackney

[32] E. Lazenby (née Gibbons) to Dr Grieve, n.d., LIC, Register of Students, K–M, Northern College, Manchester. My italics.
[33] This was claimed by Professor Price of Yorkshire College at the Congregational Union's autumn assembly in 1921, *Christian World*, 13 Oct. 1921.
[34] *British Weekly*, 16 June 1921, gave details of the co-operation between the colleges.

and New Colleges pursued the closer relationship which had
begun in shared teaching before the war and in 1920 A. E.
Garvie was appointed principal of both institutions.

In terms of curriculum reform, efforts were made to meet
the charge—common before 1914—that the ministry was out
of touch with the realities of ordinary daily life. J. H. Ritson
pioneered new approaches among the Wesleyans, who held a
series of important conferences on the whole subject in the
mid-1920s. Yorkshire College introduced psychology to the
course in 1920 and later added a supplementary term to
enable students to cover, *inter alia*, pastoral theology and
social economics. At Bristol, a new principal, Arthur Dakin,
scrapped many of the old, irksome rules in an attempt to
introduce a more liberal climate. In Oxford, W. B. Selbie,
Principal of Mansfield College between 1909 and 1932, devoted himself to relating the Christian faith to the moral and
ethical issues of the twentieth century, rather than encouraging interest in more metaphysical matters. H. Wheeler
Robinson, who freely admitted that his own ministerial
shortcomings sprang from a lack of acquaintance with
ordinary people, tried to foster an interest among his Regent's Park students in Christian experience, thus effectively
sidestepping the contentious questions of biblical authority.
This, he hoped, would revitalize Christianity for modern
man. 'The great need today', he announced in his inaugural
lecture, 'is that ministers should understand more than they
do the experience and need of the general mass of men and
women.'[35] Others, of course, averred that the loss of personnel and vitality from the nonconformist churches had been
caused solely by the falling away from the old Evangelical
emphasis on judgement, hell, salvation, and redemption. 'I
miss', wrote G. Ruffell Laslett in 1933, 'the note of *urgency*,
the sense of men being in desperate need, utterly undone,
and altogether lost . . . Unable to make men new creatures
in Christ Jesus we build them new houses in the suburbs.'[36]

Yet in some ways it was too late. Ministers were recruited

---

[35] E. Payne, *Henry Wheeler Robinson: A Memoir* (1946), 145.
[36] G. H. Ruffell Laslett, 'Things I Miss in the Modern Pulpit', *Baptist Quarterly*, 6
(1932–3), 58–9.

from the body of the Church and, with the exception of some
short-lived Wesleyan recovery in the 1920s, that body was
shrinking and had been since 1880. 'A living Church', wrote
the editor of the *Christian World*, 'will produce a ministry, a
decaying Church or a worldly one will not get a ministry,
though it pays the top wage in the market and fills the
sky with pensions.'[37] It did not necessarily follow, of course,
that institutional atrophy, whether assessed financially or
numerically, implied theological sterility or social irrele-
vance. For many, nonconformity and its long established
institutional expressions continued to provide a necessary
pastoral, inspirational, and visionary dimension to life and
the supply of ministers did not dry up completely. Yet the
awfulness of war had simply added a further element to the
theological doubts and ministerial problems which had been
apparent long before 1914.

On the whole, British Christianity had reconciled itself
very quickly to war fever. Within a fortnight of hostilities
beginning, for example, leading Baptist opinion, hitherto
internationalist, anti-militaristic, and even pro-German,
had changed completely. Germany was accused of long-term
plotting towards war and the message of the cross was
turned into one of national self-preservation.[38] The problem,
the Principal of Bala-Bangor confided to a colleague, was
that those who 'had peace sentiments had no philosophy or
theology of peace, and sentiments gave way before a storm
of counter sentiment'.[39] The result—priests and ministers
blessing tanks and guns—was not, as A. J. P. Taylor has so
cuttingly remarked, a very good advertisement for the gospel of the Prince of Peace.[40] Small wonder that one despair-
ing minister should suggest in 1932 that they were dealing
only with the pre-war elders and some post-war children.
The generation which had survived the war, he claimed, had

[37] *Christian World*, 19 May 1921.
[38] K. Clements, 'Baptists and the Outbreak of the First World War', *Baptist Quarterly*, 24 (1975–6).
[39] T. Rees to M. Edwards, 14 May 1915, Brecon Memorial College, Correspondence, National Library of Wales.
[40] A. J. P. Taylor, *English History, 1914–1945* (Oxford, 1965), 169. For discussions of the theological gymnastics arising from the First World War see C. E. Playne, *Society at War* (1931), 185–219; G. S. Spinks, *Religion in Britain Since 1900* (1952), 65–70; Hastings, pp. 221–42.

turned its back on the Church for ever.[41] In such a climate
ministers were no longer able to ascend into the pulpit, as
the nineteenth-century princes had done, as on to a throne.
Rather now they had to approach it as a witness box from
which they had to defend and prove the axioms of Christianity, not expound their meaning and implications.[42]

'My job', wrote W. R. Jones in 1937, 'is to find the best I
can to tell them, to tell it in an interesting way, to tell it
within 25 minutes, and to tell it as a friend, not as a pulpit
Hitler.'[43] Even if, as this study has suggested, the reality of
working life for some ministers was neither as rosy nor as
publicly significant as it sometimes appears through the
lenses of personal memoirs, Jones's description of preaching
was not one which many of his predecessors in the pulpit
would have recognized. Yet it illustrates graphically the
change which had occurred in the approach, the role, and
the wider importance of the ministry in the course of a
century.[44] In their own, now much smaller world ministers
remained as important, as loved, and as abused as they had
always been. In the wider world, if still respected, they were
of marginal concern.[45] 'A life time's work—what is it?' asked
J. T. Goodacre when in 1952 he surveyed his fifty years in
the Methodist ministry:

Not much to those who have tried hard to serve. Not much for
what Christ did for us on The Cross. Not much in this busy, war-
torn, sinful world to help God to redeem it.

Really, we are like coral insects that live and die that the coral
reef might appear out of the water. Ours is the Gift of Self and our
little life that the Kingdom of Heaven may truly and surely come.
Soon are we forgotten.[46]

---

[41] N. Goodall in the *Christian World*, 28 Apr. 1932.

[42] This was the description employed by the assistant editor of the *Christian World*,
Harry Jeffs, in his *Princes of the Modern Pulpit* (1931), 3.

[43] W. R. Jones to M. Edwards, 28 Sept. 1937, Brecon Memorial College, Correspondence, National Library of Wales.

[44] For the replacement of ministerial functions by professional specialists see P.
Halmos, *The Faith of the Counsellors* (1966), *passim*.

[45] M. E. Aubrey, 'The Future of Our Ministry', *Baptist Quarterly*, 1 (1922–3), 172.
On the other hand an Independent Television survey in the early 1980s revealed that
34 per cent of people still rated the minister or priest as the person with the greatest
influence for good in the modern community: P. A. Welsby, *A History of the Church of
England, 1945–1980* (Oxford, 1984), 104.

[46] J. T. Goodacre, *My Golden Jubilee as a Methodist Minister* (1952), 29.

SELECT BIBLIOGRAPHY

1. ARCHIVES AND COLLEGE REPORTS

Baptist

Aberystwyth College *Reports*, Baptist Union Library (hereafter BUL).

Bristol College *Reports* and Register of Students.

COULING, S., MSS Biographical Dictionary of Baptist Ministers of Great Britain and Ireland Deceased from 1800 to the Close of 1875 (BUL).

Manchester College *Reports* (BUL).

Midland College Minutes and *Reports* (BUL).

North Wales College *Reports* (BUL).

Pontypool Baptist Institution *Reports* (BUL).

Rawdon College *Reports* (BUL).

Regent's Park College *Reports* (Regent's Park College, Oxford).

South Wales Baptist College *Reports* (BUL).

C. H. Spurgeon Correspondence (Spurgeon's College, London).

Spurgeon's College Archives and *Reports* (Spurgeon's College, London).

Stepney College *Reports* (BUL).

Congregationalist

Airedale Independent College *Reports*.

Axminster Academy, List of Students, 1804–1820, Dr Williams's Library (hereafter DWL).

Brecon Memorial College Correspondence (National Library of Wales).

Cheshunt College Archives and *Reports* (Westminster College, Cambridge).

Hackney College Archives and *Reports* (DWL).

Highbury College Archives and *Reports* (DWL).

Homerton Academy Archives and *Reports* (DWL).

Hoxton Academy Archives and *Reports* (DWL).

Lancashire Independent College Archives and *Reports* (Northern College, Manchester).

New College Archives and *Reports* (DWL).

Nineteenth Century Letters of Eminent Divines (DWL).
Rotherham College Archives (DWL).
Spicer Papers (DWL).
Wymondley Academy Archives (DWL).

Methodist

Cliff College Student Record Book, 1904–1925 (Cliff College, Sheffield).
Didsbury College Archives (Wesley College, Bristol).
Headingley College Archives (Wesley College, Bristol).
Miscellaneous Correspondence of Methodist Ministers, Methodist Archives, Rylands Library, University of Manchester (hereafter MAM).
MSS Journal of Timothy Moxon (MAM).
Joseph Preston's Journals and Notebooks (MAM).
Richmond College Archives and *Reports* (MAM).
Tyerman Collection of MSS Biographies (MAM).

2. NEWSPAPERS AND PERIODICALS

Aldersgate Magazine
Baptist
Baptist Magazine
Baptist Quarterly
Baptist Times and Freeman
Bible Christian Magazine
British Banner
British Weekly
Christian World
Congregationalist
Congregational Magazine
Congregational Quarterly
Evangelical Magazine
Free Church Chronicle
Freeman
Free Methodist
G. Dysgedydd
General Baptist Magazine
General Baptist Repository
Independent and Nonconformist
Methodist Church Record
Methodist Leader

Methodist Magazine
Methodist Monthly
Methodist New Connexion Magazine
Methodist Recorder
Methodist Times
Nonconformist
Patriot
Primitive Methodist
Primitive Methodist Leader
Primitive Methodist Magazine
Sword and Trowel
United Methodist
United Methodist Free Church Magazine
United Methodist Magazine
Watchman
Wesleyan Methodist Association Magazine
Wesleyan Methodist Church Record
Wesleyan Methodist Magazine
Wesleyan Times

3. CONFERENCE REPORTS AND MINUTES

Baptist Handbook
Baptist Manual
Bible Christian Conference, *Minutes*
Congregational Yearbook
Methodist New Connexion Conference, *Minutes*
Primitive Methodist Conference, *Minutes*
United Methodist Conference, *Minutes*
Wesleyan Methodist Conference, *Minutes*

4. REFERENCE WORKS (PLACE OF PUBLICATION IS LONDON UNLESS OTHERWISE STATED)

Baptist Who's Who (1933).
BECKERLEGGE, O. A., *United Methodist Ministers and Their Circuits, 1797–1932* (1968).
HALL, J., *Hall's Circuits and Ministers, 1765–1912* (1925).
HILL, W., *An Alphabetical Arrangement of All the Wesleyan Methodist Preachers etc., 1819–1932.*
——, *Ministers and Probationers of the Methodist Church* (1932 onwards).

JONES, E. P., *Oriel Coleg Caerfyrddin, 1796–1899* (Merthyr Tydfil, 1909).

LEARY, W., 'Primitive Methodist Ministers and Their Circuits' (MSS in MAM).

Methodist Who's Who (1911–15).

ROSE, E. A., 'Index to Methodist New Connexion Ministers and Their Circuits' (MSS in MAM).

SIBREE, J. (ed.), *Register of Missionaries, Deputations, etc., 1796–1923* (1923).

STEPHENS, T., *Album Aberhonddu, 1775–1880* (Merthyr Tydfil, 1898).

SURMAN, C. 'Index of Congregational Ministers' (DWL).

Who's Who in Congregationalism (1933).

Who's Who in Methodism (1933).

Who's Who in the Free Churches (1951).

WILLIAMS, D. J., *Hanes Coleg Bala-Bangor A'I Athrawn A'I Fyfyrwyr* (n.d.).

5. BIOGRAPHICAL COLLECTIONS

The biographies consulted in the course of writing this book are too numerous for individual listing, although many are mentioned in the footnotes. Below are listed only the most useful collections.

BARBER, B. A., *A Methodist Pageant* (1932).

BAXTER, M., *Memorials of the United Methodist Free Churches* (1865).

COOPER, W. H., *In Methodist Byways* (1904).

EAYRS, G., *Our Founders and Their Story* (1907).

FLEW, J., *Saints of Yesterday* (1914).

GORRIE, P. D., *The Lives of Eminent Methodist Ministers* (1852).

HEROD, G., *Historical and Biographical Sketches Forming a Compendium of the History of the Primitive Methodist Connexion to 1823* (1857).

JACKSON, T., *Lives of Early Methodist Preachers* (1865–6).

JONES, O., *Some of the Great Preachers of Wales* (1885).

KIRSOP, J., *Historic Sketches of Free Methodism* (n.d.).

MICHELL, W. J., *Brief Biographical Sketches of Bible Christian Ministers and Laymen*, 2 vols. (Jersey, 1905–6).

Ministerial Portrait Gallery of the United Methodist Free Churches (Manchester, 1860).

MITCHELL, T. and BROWNSON, W. J., *Heroic Men: The Death Roll of the Primitive Methodist Ministry, 1888–9* (1889).

MORGAN, J. V., *Welsh Religious Leaders in the Victorian Era* (1905).

PEEL, A., *The Congregational Two Hundred* (1948).

RFES, T. M., *Notable Welshmen, 1700–1900* (Carnarvon, 1908).

SLIM, C., *My Contemporaries of the Nineteenth Century: Brief Memorials of More than 400 Ministers* (n.d.).

SMITH, H., *Sketches of Eminent Methodist New Connexion Ministers* (1895).

SMITH, S., *Anecdotes and Biographical Sketches Connected with . . . the Primitive Methodist Connexion* (Isle of Man, 1872).

STEVENSON, G. J., *Methodist Worthies*, 6 vols. (1884–6).

VAUGHAN, J., *Life Stories of Remarkable Preachers* (1892).

WEST, R. A., *Sketches of Wesleyan Preachers* (1849).

WISE, D., *Heroic Methodists* (1882).

WITHROW, W. H., *Makers of Methodism* (1903).

6. COLLEGE HISTORIES

AVERY, W. J., 'The Late Midland College', *Baptist Quarterly*, 1 (1923).

BARRETT, J. O., *Rawdon College: A Short History* (1954).

BRASH, W. B., *The Story of Our Colleges, 1835–1935. A Centenary History of Ministerial Training in the Methodist Church* (1935).

——, and WRIGHT, C. J., *Didsbury College Centenary, 1842–1942* (1942).

BRETHERTON, F. F., 'The Sunderland Theological Institution', *Proceedings of the Wesley Historical Society*, 30 (1956).

CARTER, A. C., *A Popular Sketch, Historical and Biographical, of the Midland Baptist College* (1925).

COOPER, R. E., *From Stepney to St Giles, 1810–1960* (1960).

CRESSWELL, A., *The Story of Cliff* (Sheffield, 1965).

CUMBERS, F. H., (ed.), *Richmond College, 1843–1943* (1943).

DAVIES, W., *The Tewkesbury Academy* (n.d.).

DAVIES, W. T., *Mansfield College* (Oxford, 1947).

FIGURES, J. A., *The Formation of the Northern Congregational College* (1960).

GARLICK, K. B., 'The Wesleyan Theological Institution. Hoxton and Abney House, 1832–1842', *Proceedings of the Wesley Historical Society*, 39 (1973).

HAMILTON, A. G., 'Bristol Baptist College, 1674–1959' (Typescript in the college library).

HIMBURY, D. M., *The South Wales Baptist College, 1807–1957* (Cardiff, 1957).

HUMPHRIES, A. L., and BARKER, W., *The Story of the Hartley Primitive Methodist College, Manchester, 1881–1931* (1931).

JOHNSTONE, J. C., 'The Story of the Western College', *Transactions of the Congregational Historical Society*, 7 (1916–18).

LOWERY, R., 'The Wesleyan Theological Institution. Hoxton: a Further Study', *Proceedings of the Wesley Historical Society*, 39 (1973).

MOON, N. S., *Education for Ministry: Bristol Baptist College, 1679–1979* (Bristol, 1979).

MORRIS, A. D., *Hoxton Square and the Hoxton Academies* (1951).

PARKER, I., *The Dissenting Academies in England* (Cambridge, 1914).

PYKE, R., *Edgehill College, 1834–1934* (1934).

RIGNAL, C., *The Jubilee of the Manchester Baptist College, 1866–1916* (n.d.).

ROBERTS, H. P., 'Nonconformist Academies in Wales, 1662–1862' (Typescript in NLW).

SIMMS, T., *Homerton College, 1695–1978* (Cambridge, 1978).

THOMPSON, J., *Lancashire Independent College, 1843–1893* (Manchester, 1893).

TURNER, J. H., *Nonconformity in Idle with the History of Airedale College* (Bradford, 1876).

7. GENERAL BACKGROUND

BASSETT, T. M., *The Welsh Baptists* (Swansea, 1977).

BECKERLEGGE, O. A., *The United Methodist Free Churches: A Study in Freedom* (1957).

BINFIELD, C., *So Down to Prayers: Studies in English Nonconformity, 1780–1920* (1977).

BOWMER, J. C., *Pastor and People. A Study of Church and Ministry in Wesleyan Methodism from the Death of John Wesley to the Death of Jabez Bunting* (1975).

BRIGGS, J., and SELLARS, I., *Victorian Nonconformity* (1973).

CHADWICK, O., *The Victorian Church* (1966).

COX, J., *The English Churches in a Secular Society: Lambeth, 1870–1930* (Oxford, 1982).

CURRIE, R., *Methodism Divided* (1968).

——, GILBERT, A., and HORSLEY, L., *Churches and Churchgoers: Patterns of Church Growth in the British Isles since 1700* (Oxford, 1977).

DAVIES, R., GEORGE, A., and RUPP, G., (eds.), *A History of the Methodist Church in Great Britain*, 3 vols. (1965–83).

EAYRS, G., *Short History of the United Methodist Communion* (1914).

GAY, J. D., *The Geography of Religion in England* (1971).

GILBERT, A. D., *Religion and Society in Industrial England, 1740–1914* (1976).

GRANT, J. W., *Free Churchmanship in England, 1870–1940* (1955).

HAIG, A. G. L., *The Victorian Clergy: An Ancient Profession Under Strain* (1984).

HEMPTON, D., *Methodism and Politics in British Society, 1750–1850* (1984).

JONES, E. K., *The Baptists of Wales and Ministerial Education* (Wrexham, 1902).

JONES, R. T., *Congregationalism in England, 1662–1962* (1962).

KENDALL, H. B., *History of the Primitive Methodist Church* (1919).

KENT, J., *The Age of Disunity* (1966).

OBELKEVICH, J., *Religion and Rural Society: South Lindsey, 1825–1875* (Oxford, 1976).

PACKER, G., *A Centenary History of the Methodist New Connexion, 1797–1897* (1897).

PAYNE, E. A., *The Baptist Union: A Short History* (1959).

PYKE, R., *The Early Bible Christians* (1941).

RITSON, J., *The Romance of Primitive Methodism* (1909).

SHAW, T., *The Bible Christians, 1815–1907* (1965).

THOMPSON, D., *Nonconformity in the Nineteenth Century* (1972).

TOWNSEND, W., WORKMAN, H., and EAYRS, G., *A New History of Methodism*, 2 vols. (1909).

UNDERWOOD, A., *A History of English Baptists* (1947).

WARD, W. R., *Early Victorian Methodism: The Correspondence of Jabez Bunting, 1830–58* (Oxford, 1976).

___, *Religion and Society in England, 1790–1850* (1972).

WERNER, J. S., *The Primitive Methodist Connexion: Its Background and Early History* (Wisconsin, 1984).

WILLIAMS, A. H., *Welsh Wesleyan Methodism, 1800–1858* (Bangor, 1935).

YOUNG, D., *The Origin and History of Methodism in Wales and the Borders* (1893).

YOUNG, K., *Chapel: The Joyful Days and Prayerful Nights of the Nonconformists in Their Heyday c.1850–1950.* (1972).

INDEX